DEDICATION

This book is dedicated to our parents and students for everything they have taught us.

ACKNOWLEDGEMENTS

Conventional wisdom says, "You are only as good as the people who support your dreams."

This saying definitely applies to this book. The growth and development of this work has relied on a multitude of individuals whose knowledge, skills, and abilities have transformed this textbook over several editions and three titles. We would like to thank those individuals whose hard work and dedication have made the fourth edition of this textbook a reality:

Mark Kesson, Jeremy Klumpp, and all the individuals at Hayden-McNeil Publishing for their overwhelming support, commitment, and belief in publishing this book,

Dr. Laura Hamilton Brown, as the international scholar whose expertise improved the intercultural content in this edition,

Dr. Meghan Mahoney, for her expertise in social media and lending her insights for addressing social media in public speaking,

Ms. Rachel McMullen, as the librarian scholar whose knowledge and wisdom improved our discussion of online research in the book,

Dr. Kanan Sawyer, for her knowledge and direction in enhancing our discussion of PowerPoint as a presentational aid,

Our students for giving us a **reason** to write this book,

The reality of being a teacher/scholar for providing us the **incentive** to write this book.

Thank all of you for making this book a rewarding experience.

AUTHOR'S PAGE

Bruce G. Bryski is Associate Professor of Speech and Media Studies at Buffalo State College in Buffalo, New York. He has also taught as an adjunct Professor of Communication Studies at Canisius College and Medaille College in Buffalo, New York. A native of Buffalo, Dr. Bryski received his BA and MA degrees in speech communication from the University at Buffalo and an MA degree in rhetorical studies from the University of Iowa. He received his Ph.D. degree in speech communication from Pennsylvania State University in 1988. His dissertation was entitled, *The Rhetoric of Television News: "60 Minutes" as Media Persuasion*. Bryski teaches undergraduate and graduate courses in public speaking, group communication, media criticism, politics and media, communication for managers, and human communication theory. His current areas of research include American political cinema, group communication, television criticism, intergenerational communication, and political cartoons as a reflection of American culture. Bryski serves as a communication/image consultant with his seminars, workshops, and consultancies including businesses and the public service sector, as well as many media professionals and political candidates. He frequently serves as an analyst on several Buffalo radio and television stations, where he provides commentary on political and media issues. Professor Bryski is a much sought after speaker by local schools, community groups, and organizations in Buffalo and Western New York to discuss politics, media, and communication issues in society.

Dr. Bruce G. Bryski

Dr. Timothy J. Brown is Dean of the James L. Knight School of Communication and Professor of Media and Communication at Queens University of Charlotte. As Dean, he serves as the primary advocate and liaison for the School's faculty and staff in regards to curriculum, policy, program development, and resource allocation. Born and raised in Coatesville, PA, Dr. Brown received his B.A. and M.A. degrees in Communication Studies from West Chester University. He received his Ph.D. in Rhetoric and Public Address from the School of Communication Studies at Ohio University. He is a rhetorical scholar whose research, teaching, and consulting focus on the intersection of culture, communication, and identity. In addition, he has been a motivational speaker and workshop presenter on leadership skills for the Federal Government's Leadership Assessment Program at its Eastern Management Development Center.

His recent publications include: "Public Memory as Contested Site: The Struggle for Existence at the National Museum of African American History and Culture," published in Roger Aden's book, *U.S. Public Memory, Rhetoric, and the National Mall,* and "Listening to Speak and Speaking to be Heard: Empowering African American Parents Through the Oral Tradition" in the book *Social Justice and Parent Partnerships in Multicultural Education Contexts.* Moreover, he is the second author of the textbook: *Argumentation and Debate: A Public Speaking Approach.*

Dr. Timothy J. Brown

Dr. Brown has taught the undergraduate courses: Rhetorical Theory and Criticism, Public Speaking, African American Culture and Communication, and Communication Theory. On the graduate level, he has taught the courses: Culture, Media, and Representation, and Rhetoric and Leadership. Prior to his appointment at Queens University of Charlotte, Dr. Brown was a faculty member at West Chester University (WCU), where he served ten years as department chair, and before WCU, he was a faculty member at SUNY Buffalo State College.

PREFACE

The fifth edition of *Public Speaking for Success: Strategies for Diverse Audiences and Occasions* continues our endeavor of creating a textbook that instills confidence, direction, knowledge, and understanding for students learning how to make effective presentations. We believe the updated information and examples will further equip students to become effective public speakers.

The fifth edition is built upon the foundation of the first edition. It is a foundation that addresses the complexity of speaking in a culturally diverse society. We believe that our practical examples and knowledgeable advice will help beginning and advanced speakers create, develop, organize, and deliver effective presentations in diverse contexts.

PUBLIC SPEAKING FOR SUCCESS

"Because information can change society, and because the amount of information doubles every fifteen years, our culture, if it is to become enriched and improved by its information, needs to digest and assimilate this information and present it with clarity."

—*Otis Walter*

Table of Contents

THE NATURE OF COMMUNICATION 1

"What a man really says when he says that someone else can be persuaded by force, is that he himself is incapable of more rational means of communication."
—*Norman Cousins*

"Extremists think 'communication' means agreeing with them."
—*Leo Rosten*

"Good communication is as stimulating as black coffee, and just as hard to sleep after."
—*Anne Morrow Lindbergh*

This Chapter Examines:

+ the nature and process of communication

+ defining communication and identifying its characteristics

+ defining the transactional model of communication

+ the types of communication

+ the goals of communication

+ defining public speaking

+ the myths and misconceptions of public speaking

Perplexed about an argument he had with his brother, Carl, James reviewed in his mind what he said and how a simple discussion of who was going to take their ailing mother to her doctor's appointment could turn into a verbal disagreement. Maybe Carl misinterpreted James's sarcasm when James stated that Carl "does care about Mom," or maybe Carl was simply upset about his mother's condition and took his anger out on James. Regardless, James and Carl will have to work on restoring their relationship and improving their communication.

Communication is a simple, yet complex, phenomenon that takes into account not only what is said, but how it is said. Most of the time, we take communication for granted until there is a miscommunication or misinterpretation of a message, as illustrated by our opening example. Although we all communicate, we can all benefit from studying the principles, concepts, and theories of communication to become more confident, competent, and effective communicators. Therefore, our discussion of communication will begin by first focusing on the nature and process of communication.

THE NATURE AND PROCESS OF COMMUNICATION

We live in a world of rapid technological advancements where information is instantaneous and accessible like never before. Technology has transformed how we receive information, how we entertain ourselves, how we shop, how we learn, and even how we communicate. Despite the far-reaching influence of technology in our society, there is still a great need for individuals to communicate in a face-to-face context—whether it involves interpersonal, public, or group communication. However, in considering these contexts, do we ever consider what it takes to become a skilled and competent communicator? The first step in learning how to be an effective communicator is to understand the process of communication.

The process of communication is very complex because it involves individuals and groups who possess very different values, beliefs, and attitudes. People come from a variety of different backgrounds, environments, and cultures, while holding different opinions and perspectives on such issues as global warming, immigration, health care, and the war on terror. It is not surprising when communication problems arise between men and women, labor and management, children and adults, or between people of different cultures and religions. It is imperative that we understand these many complexities inherent in the process of human communication if we are to engage in effective communication transactions in a variety of contexts and situations.

The purpose of this chapter is to provide a better understanding and appreciation of the process of human communication in our everyday lives. Therefore, we provide a definition of communication and identify its characteristics. Also, we define the transactional model of communication, explain the different types of communication we engage in, and identify the goals of communication. In addition, we clarify the concept of public speaking by defining and explaining the myths and misconceptions of public speaking. From reading this chapter, you should have a better understanding of the communication process and the foundations of public speaking.

DEFINING COMMUNICATION AND IDENTIFYING ITS CHARACTERISTICS

We define communication as a *transactional process in which people create, send, and receive symbolic messages to construct and interpret meaning in a variety of situations and contexts*. What our definition illustrates is that communication is an ongoing and continuous process that is ever-evolving. Communication does not stop when we end a conversation. How we leave a conversation or situation will determine how we communicate with that same person the next time we meet. While our definition is broad and complex, there are a number of key terms that can be further explained to reveal the characteristics of the process we call communication.

Communication Is Symbolic

When we engage in communication, we use symbols to construct meaning. A **symbol** is an object that represents something abstract. In essence, we use symbols such as words, icons, images, tone of voice, and facial expressions to represent ideas or concepts. However, remember that when we use words, our words are not the actual idea. Instead, our words only *represent* our ideas. This is a very important concept of communication that we spend more time explaining in Chapter 11. For now, it is important to realize that miscommunication can occur between people because we forget that words only represent our ideas; they are not literally our ideas. A good example of how communication is symbolic is if you have ever been "stood up" by a friend to study. Although your friend said he would meet you at 8:00 p.m. in the library to study, he never did. In this case, his words only *represented* the idea that you would meet to study. This example illustrates that one person's symbolic construction can have a different meaning for another person.

Communication Is the Construction of Meaning

The idea of communication as a symbolic process leads into another characteristic of communication, that communication is the **construction of meaning**. We use symbols through verbal and nonverbal messages to construct meaning. This characteristic emphasizes how meaning is constructed through the sending and receiving of messages, ideas, and values through verbal and nonverbal communication.

The exchange of ideas occurs in a context, whether it is a lawyer in a courtroom attempting to sway a jury or a member of the clergy delivering a sermon in a place of worship. These are both examples of how communication is constructed for a specific context and audience. However, communication also takes place more implicitly. For example, film directors are also engaged in sending messages to vast and diverse audiences. A music video, television sitcom, television commercial, or newspaper editorial are also examples of how symbols are used to generate and construct meaning. These types of communication contain meaning that is generated by a source/speaker and sent to an audience in a particular context or situation. These examples illustrate that communication is much more than a speaker standing behind a podium addressing an audience. An artist, film director, or advertiser are all examples of sources generating and sending messages containing meaning for an intended (target) audience.

Communication Is Process Oriented

A third characteristic of communication is that it is **process oriented** in nature. The process-oriented nature of communication means communication is an ongoing and continuous process. One way to understand communication as process oriented is to conceptualize communication as an evolutionary process that develops and grows. For example, communication does not start and stop with each conversation. Instead, it evolves. How we end a previous conversation will influence how we begin the next conversation when we meet that same person.

4

When we talk about the process of communication, the element of feedback becomes a key ingredient in our understanding of how communication works. **Feedback** is any verbal or nonverbal response to a message. In other words, communication does not simply travel from "Source A" to "Destination B" and end there. It is the element of feedback that makes communication a process. Figure 1-1 illustrates the key elements in any communication transaction and demonstrates the element of feedback in the process of sending and receiving messages. This model of communication shows the dynamic nature of communication, indicating that communication is not a linear process, but a transactional process of continual action and reaction.

It is the verbal and nonverbal feedback we send and receive from interacting with others that makes human communication process oriented. For example, when professors lecture to a public speaking class and they observe half the class falling asleep, the audience is providing negative feedback. On the other hand, when professors are receiving positive feedback, the students are diligently taking notes and nodding affirmatively.

Another interesting trait of communication is that it is **irreversible** and **unrepeatable**. Inasmuch as communication is constantly changing and evolving, we can argue that it is irreversible; once it occurs, you can't take it back or "undo" communication. If you are engaged in an argument with your significant other and say something harsh or cruel, the damage is done! It is impossible to take it back no matter how much you apologize or say, "I didn't mean what I said." Similarly, in a courtroom, when the prosecuting attorney makes a statement about the defendant on trial and the defense attorney objects, the judge might then tell the court to "strike that last remark from the record." The problem, of course, is that everybody in the courtroom heard it, including the judge, the jury, and the media covering the trial, and the public observing the trial. This illustrates the irreversible nature of communication.

To say that communication is unrepeatable is a bit different than noting its irreversibility. There is an expression in the field of communication that states, "You can't step in the same river twice." This means you can never repeat the same message in the exact same way. If you see a movie, really enjoy it, and then see it for a second or third time, the movie (message) is different each additional time you see it. It is different for many reasons. Time has elapsed since you last saw the movie, or maybe you're seeing it with different people than you did before. More importantly, you are seeing the message from various perspectives and maybe even seeing different aspects of the movie every time you see it. Perhaps you are reading this chapter for a second time; we would argue that although you are reading the same words during your second reading, it is a different message because you have read it once previously. Imagine a group of professional actors who perform the same lines in the same play or musical over an extended period of time. Some of the original actors in *Cats* or *Phantom of the Opera* have delivered the same lines literally hundreds of times, yet each performance is different for these actors!

Communication Is Complex

Since communication involves human beings, it is necessarily **complex**. We all have different attitudes, beliefs, and values. People tend to communicate and perceive others based on those beliefs and values; this is where potential problems begin to emerge. When people discuss and debate major issues such as the death penalty, legalizing marijuana, or animal rights, their beliefs and values conflict with each other. Such variables as age, sex, race, and social status often affect our communication with others. That is why communication is so complex. For example, when it comes to issues such as how "enemy combatants" should be prosecuted or how illegal immigration should be addressed, public opinion often splits along cultural and ethnic backgrounds. It is also not uncommon for people of different generations to view issues and perceive reality differently from one another. Examples of communication being a complex process are evident every day in our democratic society.

Communication Is Situational and Contextual

Our fifth characteristic of communication states that this complex process is both **situational** and **contextual**. It just makes sense that the environment, setting, or context will affect our communication behavior. For example, the typical classroom setting invites a formal type of communication. Everything from seating arrangement to "role" or "status" plays a part in shaping the kind of communication that takes place. The situation or "context" dictates a different type of communication behavior than if the professor were to interact with a group of students at a social event or a football game. In these cases, the situation or setting dictates a more informal type of communication where status and roles, or "professor" and "student," are not as important as they would be in the classroom. Similarly, think about how people behave in elevators. The confined space and close physical proximity of people in a crowded elevator certainly does not invite much discussion or open communication behavior. It is even more awkward when only two people are alone on an elevator. Even eye contact is avoided to prevent communication from taking place. Unless the individuals know one another, the elevator ride will consist most likely of silence until an individual's floor is reached.

Communication Is Transactional

Finally, our communication model indicates that communication is also **transactional**. If two people are engaged in a heated debate or conversation, both verbal and nonverbal feedback might be exchanged. You might respond to a person with an angry remark or even profanity. On the other hand, your gestures and facial expression could communicate your feelings even more strongly. Have you ever found yourself expressing your feelings when another driver cuts you off in traffic by extending your middle finger or "flipping the bird" in a moment of anger? There is probably no need to roll down the car window to explain the meaning of the gesture. In this case, the nonverbal behavior says it all! It is the element of feedback that completes the process of communication by sending the feelings and responses of the audience back to the speaker or the source of the message.

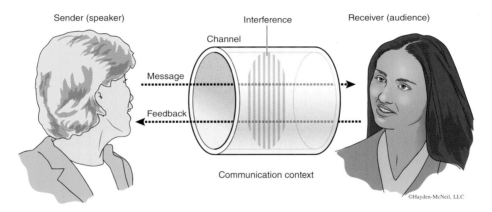

Figure 1-1.

DEFINING THE TRANSACTIONAL MODEL OF COMMUNICATION

Our transactional model of communication stresses the symbolic, constructed meaning, process-oriented, complex, and situational nature of communication. When we examine the transactional nature of communication, it becomes clear that communication is a dynamic process in which people are simultaneously sending and receiving verbal and nonverbal messages at the same time.

The distinct elements of the model provide a greater insight into how the process of communication works. However, it should be noted that while communication is taking place, all of these elements are working together in a symbolic relationship. We only separate them here to focus on each element individually.

Source

The place where the message originates is called the **source**. The purpose of the source or speaker (message creator) in any communication event will shape not only the message, but also the audience response. It is imperative that we take into account as many critical factors as possible in analyzing any communication transaction. The source is responding to a particular situation or context that contains a number of constraints and limitations, including the values and beliefs held by the audience. It is also important for the source to know the audience's purpose and create an appropriate message for them. We believe that taking this broader perspective of communication will give us a better understanding and appreciation for the pervasive nature of communication in our daily lives.

Message

The communication that is sent to the receiver is called the **message**. Our model also takes into account the three major types of communication messages created by a source. Generally, messages attempt to **inform**, **persuade**, or **entertain** an audience. Much of this book will explore the differences between communication designed to inform an audience (share knowledge and understanding with an audience) or to persuade (motivate, influence, and change) an audience member's attitude, belief, value, or behavior. It should also be stressed that all messages, whether they are verbal or nonverbal, contain meaning for an audience. When we exchange meaning through messages we are able to identify with each other through both language and nonverbal (body language) messages. While verbal messages are often reinforced by nonverbal behavior, they can also contradict each other. A person might say "I'm not angry," but their facial expression, tone of voice (paralanguage), and body language might say just the opposite!

Channel

The means of any communication or how the message is communicated is called the **channel**. The channel in the transactional model of communication allows the message to travel from the speaker/source to the audience/receiver. It provides the medium or "pathway" for the message and the meaning it contains to be disseminated. Radio, television, film, and the Internet all represent different channels in which an individual can receive a message. It should also be noted that the channel is instrumental in molding or shaping the message. For example, think about the difference of seeing the President of the United States give a speech in person, versus watching it on television. Marshall McLuhan once stated that the "medium is the message." The point McLuhan was making is that the channel through which we experience the message will affect our perception.

Receiver

The intended target of the source's message is the **receiver**. There is perhaps no element more important in the communication process than the audience or the receivers of communication. Whether the audience is an individual engaged in an intimate interpersonal relationship or a mass audience watching the Super Bowl, the audience has always been a central component in any communication transaction. An **audience-centered** focus on the communication process stresses the significance of shaping messages to affect the receivers of communication. This adds to the recognition that all communication is *purposeful* or *intentional* in nature. We communicate with others to inform, persuade, or entertain, and we must always be mindful of the composition, demographics, and characteristics of our intended audience. Most advertising and marketing research, as well as political polling, is based on this crucial principle of communication. The term "target audience" is used to refer to the primary or principal group of receivers the source is communicating with.

Feedback

As we previously mentioned, **feedback** is any verbal or nonverbal response to a message. The element of feedback in the transactional model of communication is what makes communication process oriented. Feedback (both verbal and non-verbal) literally completes the communication cycle and serves to complete the process of any communication event. Feedback proves that communication is a dynamic process and not linear or mechanical in nature. A simple nod of the head or an angry verbal reply during a heated conversation will attest to the importance of feedback in our communication model.

Noise

Sometimes miscommunication occurs between people due to the element of noise. Noise is any interference in the transactional process that affects the communication. Noise can be either physical or psychological. A **physical noise** is any external sound that hinders your ability to concentrate and listen to a message. For example, if you were outside trying to listen to your friend when an ambulance's siren suddenly blares, you probably would be the victim of physical noise. In this case, the ambulance siren prevented you from concentrating and listening to the message. On the other hand, **psychological noise** is any mental preoccupation that hinders your ability to concentrate and listen to a message. Consider the same example, but this time you are thinking about lunch instead of fully concentrating and listening to your friend's message. You would be the victim of psychological noise because you are preoccupied with your own thoughts, which prevent you from receiving the complete message.

Context

Finally, since communication does not take place in a vacuum, our transactional model would be incomplete without a reference to the element of context or situation. The **context** is the setting or environment in which the communication occurs. As we discussed earlier in this chapter, the setting or the environment in which communication events occur dictate the communication that takes place and the effect communication has on the audience. The context or situation of any communication transaction literally affects all of the elements found in the communication model and in our communication behavior.

THE TYPES OF COMMUNICATION

There are several distinct types of communication we engage in on a daily basis. These different levels of communication, while distinct from each other in some ways, also tend to overlap each other in some cases. They might also be distinguished by the role that the key element of feedback plays in each type of communication.

Intrapersonal Communication

Any communication that transpires within an individual is defined as **intrapersonal communication**. Intrapersonal communication is communication that occurs in our own minds. Intrapersonal communication is characterized by a lack of feedback from another individual and exists when a person interacts and responds to his or her environment only, with no communication or feedback from another individual. Examples of intrapersonal communication would include thinking, daydreaming, meditating, or even "talking to oneself" when engaging in an "internal conversation" with no other persons present.

Interpersonal Communication

Communication that occurs during a "face-to-face" conversation or interaction is called **interpersonal communication**. Interpersonal communication is characterized by immediate or direct feedback from another individual or group of people. While interpersonal communication is often a one-on-one interaction between two people, elements of interpersonal communication are also present during group interaction. When we are engaged in a conversation with another person, we are making continuous and constant eye contact. It is also common for us to provide feedback with facial expressions and even tone of voice, or paralanguage. The key to interpersonal communication is that the feedback is instantaneous and direct; when we ask somebody a question, that person might respond with either a verbal response (language) or even a nod of the head (nonverbal).

Group Communication

Communication that takes place between three or more persons in a group setting or context is called **group communication**. Often this type of communication is also referred to as small-group communication because each member in the group is able to communicate with one another face-to-face during each group meeting. Scholars often disagree as to the number of people required to constitute a group, but a group might be defined as at least three people engaged in some decision-making, problem-solving, or policy-recommendation situation.

Figure 1-2. Group Communication

Group communication also includes elements of interpersonal communication because of the close physical proximity of the members of the group. The rule of thumb for group communication is that the more individuals in any group, the *less personal* the feedback or communication. Think about a large introductory lecture course at a typical college or university. It is common for those classes to have between 100–300 students. The professor is at the bottom of a large lecture hall with a microphone, and students are stacked up in stadium-style seating. This is surely not very conducive for effective communication or feedback between the students and the professor. Compare this with a class of 20 students in a public speaking seminar. The communication is far more personal, and the feedback is direct and immediate. There is far greater opportunity in a smaller class for the professor to give individual attention to each student in the class.

Nonverbal Communication

Any communication that does not involve the written or spoken word is defined as nonverbal communication. We typically think about a person's body language when discussing this form of communication. Much of our communication is nonverbal in nature, which includes the use of gestures, facial expressions, eye contact, body type, dress/clothing, touch, paralanguage (tone of voice), territoriality (physical and social space), artifacts (objects that communicate, such as jewelry), and seating arrangement. We will discuss later in Chapter 10 how nonverbal communication and body language play a crucial role in the delivery and presentation of our speeches. Everything from tone of voice, gestures, eye contact, and body language affects our delivery in the presentation of speeches and panel discussions or public debates.

Mass Communication

In our contemporary, democratic society, **mass communication** plays a crucial role. Mass communication involves a person or organization that disseminates a message though mass media (such as television, radio, the Internet, or social media) to reach other individuals in the population at the same time. The development of the Internet and social media has changed the nature of mass communication from a one-way process (from a source to a public) to a dynamic process where everyone has the ability to create, distribute, and respond to information. The use of social media has made the dissemination of mediated messages more immediate and personalized. Individuals no longer have to wait for someone else to lead a cause, coordinate an effort, or raise public awareness. Social media has made these efforts easier and further demonstrates the democratic society we live in.

Intercultural Communication

Communication that examines human communication or behavior between people of different races, ethnic backgrounds, and cultures is called **intercultural communication** or **cross-cultural communication**. We cannot assume that all people share the same values, beliefs, and perspectives on issues, and this must be taken into account when persons with different ethnic backgrounds and cultures communicate. Effective speakers are able to understand and adapt messages to a multicultural audience (see Chapter 4). This is especially true when we take nonverbal communication into account. For example, certain gestures have different meanings in different cultures. While the smile (facial expression) might be one of the very few universal gestures, the "V" for victory sign does not necessarily translate across cultures or nations. In addition, certain aspects of communication, like touch, eye contact, or even acceptable physical space between two people during a conversation, can vary greatly between persons of different cultures.

THE GOALS OF COMMUNICATION (REASONS WHY PEOPLE COMMUNICATE)

1

Now that we've discussed the process, types, and characteristics of communication, it is imperative to look at the practical aspects of how communication serves as an important part of our daily interactions. Since communication is purposeful and always has an objective or motive, it is worthwhile examining just exactly why we communicate with others. There are three distinct reasons for engaging in communication behavior.

To Increase Our Personal Awareness

First, we communicate with others to **increase our personal awareness**. Communication is essential in our efforts to gain knowledge and understanding. Most people attend college to receive a general education, as well as specific, intensive knowledge about a specific discipline or field of study. Also, when we interact with others, especially those persons from other cultures, races, and backgrounds, we learn valuable information and lessons from these encounters.

To Improve Our Social and Professional Relationships

Another reason we communicate is to **improve our social and professional relationships**. That is, we communicate to make friends and acquaintances, and establish relationships that hopefully will last a lifetime. Communication is essential to our personal, social, and professional relationships with others. Whether we consider the interaction between a group of close friends, in our family, in a successful marriage, or between business associates, it becomes obvious that communication is the element required to make those relationships successful and fulfilling.

To Change Other People's Beliefs, Values, and Attitudes

Finally, we communicate **to change other people's beliefs, values, and attitudes**. Once again, we must stress the persuasive nature of communication as an attempt to influence others in a variety of personal, social, and professional contexts or situations. We might attempt to "empower" others by giving them knowledge, skills, or a particular area of expertise. Similarly, we might try to change someone's belief on an issue such as the death penalty or genetic engineering, or convince our boss to give us a pay raise. Whatever our goals and objectives might be, communication is the tool we use to influence others and move others to action.

DEFINING PUBLIC SPEAKING

The idea of communicating as a powerful tool to influence others to action is at the heart of public speaking. Unlike the other forms of communication that we have already discussed, public speaking can be defined as a *transactional process where a speaker creates and sends symbolic messages in the attempt to inform, persuade, and/ or entertain an audience in a variety of situations and contexts*. Like any form of communication, public speaking is an exchange of verbal and nonverbal messages between speaker(s) and audience. However, what makes public speaking unique is how speaker and audience are constantly and continuously exchanging messages that contain meaning, and are acting on and responding to the verbal and nonverbal feedback present in any speaking context. The accomplished speaker, in fact, is able to "read" the feedback of the audience while the speech is in progress and respond to that feedback during the speech. There is little doubt that this exchange of verbal and nonverbal messages makes public speaking a transactional process in which messages are delivered and received in a dynamic, symbolic relationship between the speaker and those receiving the messages.

We also emphasize that the dynamic, ongoing, and symbolic relationship between speaker and audience does not mean that speakers are "winging it" when making a presentation. To the contrary, effective speakers must plan and prepare their ideas that are adapted to a specific audience. Therefore, as we discuss the "how to" of public speaking, we are also mindful of the rhetorical strategy that is involved in planning, preparing, and adapting a message to an audience. Underlying our discussion of public speaking are the tenets of rhetorical theory. Scholars such as Lloyd Bitzer (the rhetorical situation), Kenneth Burke (identification), and classical rhetorical scholars such as Aristotle (the artistic proofs) along with Cicero and Quintilian (the canons of rhetoric) provide a theoretical basis to guide a speaker's approach to making an effective speech. It is the use of rhetorical theory that dispels many of the myths and misconceptions of public speaking that we discuss next.

THE MYTHS AND MISCONCEPTIONS OF PUBLIC SPEAKING

There exist several myths or misconceptions surrounding the art or craft of public speaking. We will address those myths here in order to provide a better understanding and appreciation for this transactional process of communication.

Myth One: Only Lawyers, Preachers, Teachers, and Politicians Engage in Public Speaking

Public speaking is not necessarily restricted to a speaker standing behind a podium delivering a formal speech to an audience in a court of law, a church service, a classroom, or on the floor of the United States Senate. Public speaking is something we all engage in, not just lawyers, preachers, teachers, and politicians. In fact, any time we hold and maintain the attention of an audience for an extended period of time, we are engaging in public speaking. Whether we are trying to convince a judge in traffic court that the light was yellow and not red, or running for election to some local political office, or speaking at a Parent-Teacher Association meeting, public speaking skills play a major role in our daily lives.

Myth Two: Good Public Speakers Are Born That Way

Nobody is born with an innate ability to speak in public. Public speaking is a skill that requires years of experience, trial and error, and many mistakes. While people often speak about a "natural born athlete" during an athletic contest, the same cannot be said about a public speaker.

Some of the greatest orators in history started their careers as average public speakers. President John F. Kennedy, for example, never demonstrated his prowess and ability as a speaker when he first entered the political arena. It took years of training, voice lessons, and experience facing real audiences to polish his skills, eventually making him one of our greatest orators ever. The same can be true for you. Experience is the key. As you begin to make presentations you will learn what your strengths and weaknesses are as a speaker. The goal is to improve your weaknesses one at a time.

Myth Three: Knowledge Alone Makes a Successful Speaker

There are many elements that go into effective public speaking. In order to become a "complete" speaker, several factors must be taken into consideration to be an effective public speaker. For example, knowledge alone does not guarantee speaking success. A speaker might possess a great deal of knowledge or expertise about any given topic. However, if the speaker has a weak delivery or an unorganized speech, all the knowledge and expertise in the world won't turn the speaker's knowledge into an effective speech.

Myth Four: Style Alone Makes a Good Speaker

Style in public speaking includes two very important components. First, style entails what we would call **speaker-topic involvement**, or enthusiasm on the speaker's behalf. While it is important to be relaxed and composed, a speaker who is too "laid back" or nonchalant is not very likely to motivate or keep an audience's attention. There is a myth, however, that if a speaker shows enthusiasm or concern toward the topic and audience, that this will make for a successful speaker. This is false, of course, because it takes much more than enthusiasm or effective style to have an effective speech.

In addition, style refers to the type of language a speaker utilizes in a speech or group presentation. Is the language appropriate for the type of speech and the audience's needs? The language for an informative message, for example, tends to be descriptive and denotative in nature. Conversely, the language found in a persuasive presentation is often more connotative, rhetorical, and argumentative than language suitable for the informative speech. The resulting myth, however, is that if the speaker incorporates effective and appropriate language, that this alone will make the speech successful. Once again, no one element could possibly achieve this.

Myth Five: Good Delivery Alone Makes a Speaker Effective

While delivery is an integral component in public speaking, as we discuss in Chapter 10, the presentation of the speech itself is of little value if the speech is not well structured and lacks evidence or support material. Delivery includes everything from eye contact to gestures to tone of voice, all major elements in making an effective speaker. However, superb delivery won't compensate for lack of knowledge, style, and organization in a speech.

Myth Six: A Speaker Is an Actor or an Entertainer

Many novice speakers believe all that is necessary to be an effective speaker is to make the audience laugh or to entertain them. While there is nothing wrong with using humor in a speech or panel presentation, it is imperative to understand that *a speaker is not an entertainer.* When late-night talk hosts or stand-up comedians deliver their monologues, they are not actually engaged in public speaking. However, most speakers have a far more serious and important purpose when delivering a speech, and it surely is not presenting a series of "one-liners" or jokes.

The myths and misconceptions discussed above illustrate that for a speaker to be effective, many factors must be taken into consideration. No single factor such as the speaker's knowledge or expertise, enthusiasm, style, or delivery can make a successful speaker. All of these elements must be included in any speech or group presentation to make a presentation effective, and to produce a "complete" speaker. As you continue to read the chapters in this book, we will tell you how to incorporate all these elements into your presentation to make an effective public speech.

This chapter has provided an overview of the communication process. The nature of communication has been defined and the characteristics of communication have been examined through the transactional model of communication. In addition, the distinct types of communication have been discussed in relationship to feedback. Then, we explained the goals of communication or reasons why people communicate. This was followed by defining the art of public speaking. From reading this chapter, you should have a better understanding of the communication process and the foundations of public speaking.

VOCABULARY

Channel — the means of any communication or how the message is communicated.

Communication — a transactional process in which people create, send, and receive messages to construct and interpret meaning in a variety of situations and contexts.

Context — the setting or environment in which the communication occurs; the situational aspects of communication.

Feedback — any verbal or nonverbal response to a message.

Group communication — any communication that takes place between two or more persons in a group setting or context.

Intercultural communication — human communication or behavior between people of different races, ethnic backgrounds, and cultures.

Interpersonal communication — communication that occurs during "face-to-face" conversations and interactions.

Intrapersonal communication — any communication that transpires within an individual. Examples include thinking, daydreaming, meditating, and "talking to yourself."

Mass communication (mass media) — involves a person or organization that disseminates a message through mass media (such as television, radio, the Internet, or social media) to reach other individuals in the population at the same time.

Message — the communication that is sent to the receiver.

Model (communication model) — a representation of the communication process and the elements comprising that process.

Myths of public speaking — popular misconceptions about the act and process of public speaking.

Noise — any interference in the transactional process that affects the communication. Noise can be either physical or psychological.

Nonverbal communication — any communication that does not involve the written or spoken word. Examples would include facial expression, gestures, physical appearance, spatial communication or territoriality, clothing, artifacts, paralanguage, and body language.

Physical noise — any external sound that hinders one's ability to concentrate and listen to a message.

Process oriented — the circular nature of communication and public speaking as a result of verbal and nonverbal feedback in any communication event or transaction.

Psychological noise — any mental preoccupation that hinders one's ability to concentrate and listen to a message.

Public speaking — a transactional process where a speaker creates and sends symbolic messages in an attempt to inform, persuade, and/or entertain an audience in a variety of situations and contexts.

Receiver — the intended target of the source's message; the audience.

Source — the place where the message originates.

Symbol — an object that represents something abstract.

The transactional model of communication — a model that represents the dynamic process of communication in which people are simultaneously sending and receiving verbal and nonverbal messages at the same time.

OVERCOMING SPEECH ANXIETY 2

"Bravery is being the only one who knows you're afraid."
—*Franklin P. Jones*

"Anxiety is a thin stream of fear trickling through the mind. If encouraged, it cuts a channel into which all other thoughts are drained."
—*Arthur Somers Roche*

"A day of worry is more exhausting than a day of work."
—*John Lubbock*

"To fear is one thing. To let fear grab you by the tail and swing you around is another."
—*Katherine Paterson*

This Chapter Examines:

+ the reasons for speech anxiety

+ how to manage speech anxiety

+ presentation tips for alleviating speech anxiety

+ additional suggestions

Gunner knew he would be nervous before his first presentation, but he did not expect his nervousness to be as intense when he walked to the front of the room—he felt his heart beating, his hands were sweaty, and his mouth was dry. He tried to make eye contact with the audience, but when he did, he forgot his speech. Therefore, he read from his note cards for the majority of his presentation. When he finished his speech, he knew he could have done better. If he could just manage his nervousness, he believed he could demonstrate a much better presentation.

When it comes to speech anxiety, Gunner is not alone. Every public speaker experiences nervousness before and during a presentation. However, what successful public speakers learn is to manage their anxiety in order to make an effective presentation. We will discuss in this chapter how speakers can manage speech anxiety.

THE REASONS FOR SPEECH ANXIETY

Many years ago a poll was taken. This poll asked Americans about their fears and anxieties. The poll revealed something very interesting. When asked what their number one fear was, a majority of Americans answered: public speaking. Death was number two![1]

Many people have a great deal of fear and anxiety about public speaking. One reason why people fear public speaking is due to the risk that is involved in speaking in front of an audience. We risk the chance of making a mistake and being laughed at and ridiculed or not being accepted by the audience. Since all communication involves some degree of risk-taking, public speaking is no different. We all want to be successful and accepted by others. The thought of failure haunts all of us.

Often, people fear public speaking and experience the anxiousness or those familiar "butterflies" in the stomach because they lack confidence. Most of us have had very little experience with public speaking or facing an audience. When we confront an audience and have very little faith in our ability to be effective, the result might be that we are overcome with speech anxiety. **Speech anxiety** is the fear of speaking in front of an audience, which causes the speaker to experience nervousness. For a speaker, speech anxiety creates a negative psychological state of extreme self-doubt ("I'm going to make a mistake, forget my speech, stumble over words, etc.") and/or an exaggerated fear of how the audience will respond ("They are going to laugh, no one will like what I have to say, etc.").[2]

In addition, speech anxiety can be the result of not being prepared. Whether speakers are experienced or not, they can become anxious or nervous because they are not prepared for their speeches and presentations. We will discuss the importance of preparation later in this chapter. In our opinion, preparation leads to confidence, and confidence goes a long way in overcoming speech anxiety or nervousness.

The increased flow of **adrenaline** throughout your body, perspiring palms, a dry "cotton" mouth, shaky knees, a "cracking" voice, and those ever-present "butterflies" in the pit of your stomach are some experiences to look forward to as you enter the world of public speaking! The good news is that all speakers experience some form of nervousness at some stage in their speaking careers. No one is immune from speech anxiety.

In fact, speech anxiety is often called **stage fright** because it is the same feeling an actor or actress experiences moments before going on stage. Professional athletes have similar anxious moments as they prepare for a big game or an important contest on the field of play. Regardless of what you might think about this now, the symptoms of speech anxiety or nervousness are actually positive signs. Your body is telling you it is prepared physically and psychologically to face your audience. Your body is telling you, "Let's go. I'm ready to confront my audience. I'm prepared and confident."

One of the best ways to manage your anxiety is to turn your anxiety and nervous energy into intensity, which provides focus for the speaker. This is what separates the good speaker from the average speaker. An effective speaker *is able to channel nervous energy or anxiety into a lively, animated, and intense presentation*. Remember that even the most experienced and "polished" speakers experience some degree of speech anxiety or nervousness. An effective speaker, however, is able to channel that energy toward the audience and the speech itself. Good speakers are able to overcome these speaking "jitters" by directing this nervous energy toward the audience in a positive and constructive manner.

Now that we know why we experience speech anxiety, and have become acquainted with the various symptoms of nervousness or stage fright, let's discuss ways in which we can alleviate our speech anxiety. The following considerations and specific behaviors should result in less anxiety and nervousness. However, it is important to realize that the only true way to alleviate your speech anxiety can be summed up in one word: *experience*! The more you speak, the easier it gets. The more confidence you acquire as a speaker, the less nervous you are likely to be.

2

HOW TO MANAGE SPEECH ANXIETY

Although speech anxiety is a common occurrence that most speakers experience, it does not mean that you always have to be affected by it. There are some practical strategies you can apply to your own presentations to help you manage and alleviate speech anxiety. The following information presents some helpful strategies to help abate speech anxiety.

Mental Preparation

Before you even step into the room to get ready for your presentation, you need to be mentally prepared for your speech. When you are mentally prepared you are focused on your task and you are concentrating on how you will present your information. Every speaker, no matter how great, must mentally prepare before the speech. Your mental preparation can occur almost anywhere such as the night before your speech or in an empty classroom or in the library. Even writing down your negative thoughts (before your presentation) and reviewing the likelihood of the negative thought happening in your speech can reduce speech anxiety.[3] Regardless of the place or the cognitive reflection that is involved, you should take the time to mentally prepare for your speech.

Remember that speech anxiety or nervousness is a normal physical and psychological phenomenon in public speaking. Although it might be hard to believe, speech anxiety, if handled properly, is actually a positive sign for any speaker. If you don't feel any nervousness at all, something is probably wrong! Any effective speaker must be on "edge" to some extent or what might result is a very lackadaisical delivery with little or no intensity. Your body is telling you that you are "psyched" to approach and confront an audience. Again, the effective speaker is then able to channel this nervous energy into a dynamic presentation with an energetic speaking style and animated delivery.

Also, mental preparation involves visualizing yourself giving a good, effective speech that is well received by your audience. This might be easier said than done, but it does point out that having a positive attitude in public speaking is very important. Try not to dwell on any negative aspects or anticipate making mistakes during your speech. Don't carry on an internal conversation where you are constantly thinking, "What if I mess up or make a mistake?" Think positive!

We all make mistakes, but approach your speech with an upbeat attitude, and this will surely add to your confidence as a speaker.

Prepare Yourself Thoroughly

Even the most accomplished speakers tend to feel a bit anxious or nervous when they know their speech lacks preparation. Once you have selected an interesting topic in which you are confident, the most obvious way to control speech anxiety is thorough preparation. The more prepared you are as a speaker, the less nervous you will be when you present your information.[4]

The speaker who is in command of the topic, enhances the speech with ample evidence and support material, and knows the material well enough to demonstrate an **extemporaneous** delivery. An extemporaneous delivery is when a speaker plans and prepares a speech ahead of time and delivers the actual speech from an outline or notes (see Chapter 10). When you are able to demonstrate an extemporaneous delivery, you will begin to develop a sense of confidence from your preparation and research. In order to demonstrate an extemporaneous delivery, speakers have to know their information to convey their ideas smoothly and coherently to the audience.

If you cannot record your speech (for self-evaluation), have a friend, roommate, or colleague watch your speech. He or she will be sure to comment on all aspects of your speech that might be lacking or need improvement. Are you talking too fast? Do you keep repeating the same words or phrases over and over? How about the so-called **verbal fillers** or linguistic crutches like "um," "er," and "you know," sprinkled throughout the speech? How is your eye contact? What about your gestures? When a speaker is thoroughly prepared it builds speaker confidence, an essential ingredient in our recipe for public speaking.

Familiarize Yourself with the Speaking Environment

Never underestimate the importance of familiarizing yourself with your speaking environment. The more you know about the arrangement of the room and the equipment you have access to, the more you will be able to concentrate on the speech itself. Nobody likes surprises when it comes to public speaking. It is strongly recommended, therefore, that speakers become acquainted with as many elements of the speaking situation as possible *before* the speech.

If possible, it is ideal for the speaker to visit the location of the speech. Check the room size, acoustics, location of the podium, outlets for equipment, and even the seating arrangement. Is it a large or small room? Will you be speaking on a stage? Are there pillars in the middle of the room? Will you need a microphone to make your voice "carry" to your audience? Is there a podium or lectern? Are the chairs and/or tables stationary? Will you be seated at a table with other speakers? Visualize how you will set up any necessary charts, diagrams, or tables for demonstrations. If nothing else, visiting your speaking location might serve to put you at ease and allow time for any last minute changes you might have to incorporate. This is just another aspect of planning that might help alleviate some of your nervousness by making the unknown, such as the room arrangement and equipment considerations, known.

Practicing the Speech

A simple but overlooked aspect of reducing anxiety is practicing your speech. The more you practice your speech, the better the actual speech will be. As we mentioned earlier, being unprepared for a speech is one of the main causes of speech anxiety. You can avoid this problem by simply giving yourself time to practice your speech before your actual presentation. We will now discuss a few guidelines you should keep in mind as you practice your speech.

Do Not Read or Memorize Your Speech

The confident speaker never attempts to "read" the speech word for word in manuscript style; reading is *not speaking*. In addition, it is "speaker suicide" for the speaker to attempt to "memorize" an entire speech. Use your outline, index cards, and research material to your advantage, but know your topic well enough so you can communicate your information with a dynamic and animated delivery. Songwriter and poet Bob Dylan once wrote that you need to "know your song and sing it well." The same can be said of your speech. If you can literally "look your audience in the eye," this will give you a sense of command and control; this will increase your confidence and help alleviate your speech anxiety.

Devote Extra Time to Your Introduction

For many novice speakers, the hardest part is beginning the speech in a confident manner. However, most experienced speakers will say, "I'm OK, once I get going." In keeping with this philosophy, it is advised that speakers devote extra time and attention to the introduction of the speech. The introduction of any speech gains the audience's attention, establishes the topic for the audience, and previews the major areas to be covered during the speech. More importantly, the introduction of the speech "points the way" by "navigating" the speaker and the audience through the body of the speech. As in so many other areas of life, when a speaker can start a speech well, it builds confidence and momentum for an effective speech.

Try Deep-Breathing Exercises to Relieve Tension

Many speakers take a cue from professional athletes and engage in deep-breathing and muscle-relaxing exercises to relieve tension in their bodies. Deep-breathing exercises help the speaker to relax the muscles of the face, arms, legs, and neck.

Take a few deep breaths, hold it, and then release it. Many people find this to be extremely relaxing. Also, before your speech, tense up the muscles of your body, then release. Many speakers feel this loosens them up and reduces stress before a major speech. Our advice is simple. Do whatever it takes, and try anything you find useful, to feel more relaxed and to lessen your speech anxiety.

Act Poised

Alright, we know this sounds like common sense and is probably easier said than done, but it is important to demonstrate a sense of confidence, command, and control in front of your audience. Body language or your nonverbal delivery is a very powerful indicator of a speaker's composure and confidence. You need to convey a sense of control and this, in turn, will make you more relaxed, confident, and less anxious. Your movements and posture should also convey a sense of preparedness and a grasp of the topic.

PRESENTATION TIPS FOR ALLEVIATING SPEECH ANXIETY

We have discussed several ways speakers can manage speech anxiety as they are preparing for their speech. We add that speakers should not overlook some approaches that can be implemented in the speech itself to alleviate speech anxiety. The benefit of adding these presentational techniques into your speech is that it takes some of the pressure off of you as a speaker. These techniques are discussed next.

Incorporate Audience Participation

One of the easiest ways to "break the ice" with your listeners is to include some form of audience participation or feedback during the speech. Asking for a simple show of hands, posing a rhetorical question, or even asking for a volunteer from the audience allows the speaker to gain the upper hand by receiving some sort of reinforcement or response. Not only does this benefit the speaker, but it also puts the audience at ease and gives them a sense of participation during your presentation. Although audience participation is a great way to introduce a speech, it does not have to be limited to the beginning of the speech. Effective speakers use audience participation strategically during any part of the presentation.

2

Use Presentational Aids during Your Speech

For many speakers, the use of **presentational aids** (such as PowerPoint, media clips, and handouts) serves to diminish or alleviate the speaker's nervousness. As we discuss in Chapter 14, presentational aids function to enhance, clarify, and reinforce the verbal message. In addition to making your message more vivid, they literally act as a secondary form of evidence or support material. They are also helpful in alleviating speech anxiety by shifting the focus off the speaker by adding dynamism to the speech. For example, when a speaker presents a PowerPoint slide, media clip, or even a simple handout, the audience pays attention to these presentational aids and is not constantly "glued" to the speaker. It might be psychological, but many experts believe that presentational aids function to take pressure off of the speaker.

Use Nonverbal Communication to Dissipate Your Speech Anxiety and Nervous Energy

In Chapter 10 we will discuss the role of nonverbal communication and how it relates to delivery in public speaking. However, it should be noted that nonverbal elements such as appearance, breathing, eye contact, tone of voice (**paralanguage**), gestures, and body movement can all be used to alleviate speech anxiety and lessen the audience's perception of speaker nervousness. We believe that a speaker needs to be "loose" and animated rather than stiff or rigid. Use gestures to enhance your verbal message. Rather than holding on to the podium until your fingertips turn white, nervously "tapping" your pen, playing with your hair, or rubbing your hands and fingers together, use your gestures and body language to create a more dynamic speaking style that will enhance your overall delivery.

Figure 2-1. Nonverbal Communication

Establish and Maintain Direct Eye Contact with Your Audience as Often as Possible

Have you ever heard the expression, "He couldn't look me in the eye"? In our culture, direct eye contact is a sign of control and confidence. A speaker who won't look in the eyes of the audience might be perceived as reticent, unprepared, or having something to hide. Conversely, the speaker who incorporates effective eye contact during a speech psychologically takes command and control of the speaking situation. More importantly, direct eye contact throughout the speech allows the speaker to constantly read the feedback of the listeners and interact with the audience verbally and nonverbally.

ADDITIONAL SUGGESTIONS

Finally, we offer some additional advice for managing speech anxiety. When you can follow these suggestions they will help take the "pressure" off of yourself and help you concentrate on your speech. Speakers should keep these ideas in mind when making a presentation.

Don't Expect or Demand Perfection of Yourself

While it is always important to try your best in any endeavor you undertake in life, you should never expect to deliver a perfect speech. Everybody slips once in a while and mistakes happen. Don't let these "slips" bother you or affect your concentration; just keep on moving through the speech. Your audience would never expect the speaker to be perfect because we are all human and everyone on occasion makes mistakes. If you should "mess up" during the speech, don't dwell on it or apologize for the error. Instead, maintain your focus and continue presenting your information.

Don't Concentrate or Dwell on Your Nervousness

Although it might not be easy to do, try not to think about your speech anxiety or nervousness. Instead, you should be concentrating on your speech, your delivery, and the feedback from the audience. When you can focus on the speech itself, you will be able to concentrate on the content and organization of the message and how the audience is receiving the speech. After a while, you will rarely think about your nervousness.

Don't Call Attention to Your Nervousness or Apologize for It

Everybody experiences some nervousness or anxiousness before a speech or a panel presentation. There is no need to apologize for it; like the famous sneaker commercial says, "Just do it!" Concentrate on the introduction of the speech, and use it as your springboard to get off to a strong start in the speech. *Remember, unless you actually tell your audience you are nervous, few, if any, of your symptoms of nervousness, are ever even detected by the audience.*

It is quite surprising how many speakers will begin a speech by telling their audience how nervous they are. What purpose does that serve? It is almost like admitting defeat before you begin battle. Don't plant any seeds in the minds of the audience about your psychological preparedness or fear of the audience. Instead, let your audience know that you are pleased to be with them and look forward to interacting with them. This should be accomplished both verbally and nonverbally. It's your speech, and you need to take control.

Don't Let Your Audience Upset You

Since your authors will be stressing what is known as **extemporaneous delivery** throughout this book, which includes constant and consistent eye contact with your audience, there will be times when you receive "negative" feedback from your listeners. People in the audience might be whispering or talking to each other. They might appear bored or angry. Some of them might even fall asleep! How would you react if someone was reading a newspaper or working on an assignment from another class during your speech? Try not to let these distractions or discourteous actions affect your concentration. You need to understand that much of this bothersome audience behavior might not even be intended, and from the speaker's perspective at least, the behavior looks worse than it actually is. Oftentimes, the listener is not even aware of such behavior, distracting as it might be.

Don't Be Afraid to Make Mistakes

Finally, just remember that no speaker is perfect and even the very best make occasional mistakes. The art of speaking is based on experience as well as trial and error. If you do make a mistake, keep right on going. Your audience will respect you even more if you can recover from such missteps rather than getting flustered and losing your concentration. The very best speakers are even able to joke about an error or misstatement during a speech, making them look even more comfortable and confident in the eyes of the audience.

In this chapter, we have discussed speech anxiety in public speaking. In order to manage speech anxiety, we first defined it and reviewed the reasons for speech anxiety. Then, we explained several approaches for managing speech anxiety and we discussed presentation tips that can be incorporated into a speech to alleviate speech anxiety. Finally, we provided additional tips for speakers to combat speech anxiety. From reading this chapter, speakers should be more equipped to address and manage speech anxiety in preparing for their presentations.

VOCABULARY

Adrenaline — a hormone secreted by adrenal glands that stimulates circulation and muscular activity.

Extemporaneous delivery — when a speaker plans and prepares a speech ahead of time and delivers the actual speech from an outline or notes.

Feedback — when a receiver responds verbally and nonverbally to a source's message.

Paralanguage — the tone of voice.

Presentational aid — any physical device or material that speakers use in a speech to enhance, clarify, and/or reinforce the verbal message.

Speech anxiety — the fear of speaking in front of an audience, which causes the speaker to experience nervousness.

Stage fright — another term for speech anxiety.

Verbal fillers — making utterances such as *ah* and *um*.

REFERENCES

[1] Bodie, G. D. (2010). A racing heart, rattling knees, and ruminative thoughts: Defining, explaining, and treating public speaking anxiety. *Communication Education, 59(1)*, 70–105.

[2] DiBartolo, P. M., & Molina, K. (2010). A brief self-directed written cognitive exercise to reduce public speaking anxiety in college courses. *Communication Teacher, 24(3)*, 160–164.

[3] DiBartolo and Molina, 161.

[4] Daly, J. A., Vangelisti, A. L., & Weber, D. J. (1995). Speech anxiety affects how people prepare speeches: a protocol analysis of the preparation process of speakers. *Communication Monographs, 62(4)*, 383–395.

2

THE LISTENING PROCESS 3

"No man would listen to you talk if he didn't know it was his turn next."
—*Samuel Johnson (1709–1784)*

"Beware of the man who goes to cocktail parties not to drink but to listen."
—*Pierre Daninos*

"It takes a great man to make a great listener."
—*Sir Arthur Helps (1813–1875)*

This Chapter Examines:

+ a definition of listening

+ characteristics of the listening process

+ the components of the listening process

+ ways to improve your listening skills and habits

It was the most important day of the business meeting because after all the presentations, discussions, and modifications, Keiko's team was ready to make their offer. However, in the last meeting Keiko had with her supervisor before the business trip, she was distracted and missed some of the important "talking points" her supervisor said were crucial for her to mention when making the final offer. Was Keiko supposed to start with praise, then thank the hosts for their hospitality, before making the offer? Maybe she was supposed to thank the hosts for their hospitality first, then give praise, followed by the offer. On second thought, was she supposed to only engage in polite conversation and not discuss the offer at all? If she would have paid attention to what her supervisor was saying, she would feel more confident about how she was supposed to respond.

Although we might not have experienced a high stakes business meeting like Keiko's, we all can identify with the problem of not listening to a message. We are all guilty of missing part of a message, which at the very least can lead to a misunderstanding, but at its worst can lead to conflict, hurt feelings, and misperceptions. Listening is such a vital aspect in the process of communication that without it, the construction of meaning (between speaker and listener) fails to take place. Since listening is a key component in the process of communication, we will discuss in this chapter the listening process. More specifically, we will provide a definition of listening, followed by an identification of the characteristics of the listening process. We will also explain the components of the listening process and suggest ways for individuals to improve their listening skills and habits.

A DEFINITION OF LISTENING

Listening might be one of the most important communication skills humans engage in. Unfortunately, it is also one of the most neglected and misunderstood skills because we tend to take our listening habits for granted. Perhaps the most common myth about communication is that humans spend most of their time speaking or writing; in other words, sending communication to others. The truth is, however, that we spend over half of our communication behavior *receiving* messages or "taking communication in." Listening is the process through which we accomplish receiving a message so we can interpret and understand the source's message.

Listening is defined as the process by which human beings deliberately and psychologically focus on and interpret selective stimuli aurally. There are three types of **aural stimuli** that we commonly receive: verbal, vocal (paralanguage), and noise (other kinds of sounds). As an important component in the communication process, listening is a process-oriented activity that we engage in on a daily basis. When we listen to others, we are actually listening to verbal messages (language, words, jargon), vocal messages (paralanguage, voice inflection, articulation), and noise (other kinds of sounds such as background noise or psychological distractions that can hinder listening effectiveness).[1]

Whether we engage in a conversation with a group of close friends, listen to a professor's lecture in a public speaking class, or participate in a campus rally to protest funding cuts to higher education, we listen to the three major types of stimuli presented above. The words or language we listen to obviously constitute verbal stimuli. However, there is much more to effective listening than simply understanding and interpreting a speaker's language.

Experienced and skilled listening must go beyond language and include what we have previously called **paralanguage** or tone of voice. Paralanguage and vocal stimuli, in fact, might often communicate far more than the verbal elements of language. We can often sense anger, depression, or optimism just by listening to *how* a person says something. In fact, paralanguage or tone of voice might often communicate more accurately than language alone. If a close friend says, "I'm not angry," but the paralinguistic cues make the person *sound* as if they actually are angry or upset, we are much more likely to believe the vocal cues or tone of voice. We can often sense people's mood based on their paralanguage or vocal cues.

Effective listening is often impeded or hindered by what is commonly called "**noise**" in the listening process. Noise, or other kinds of sounds, might negatively affect our listening effectiveness. If we are listening to a speaker on a warm summer day and construction workers are using a jackhammer outside the building, or if an air conditioner is making it difficult to hear what the speaker is saying, the audience's ability to listen effectively can be affected. Even such factors as a very warm room, the listener being ill, or the speaker talking too softly will hinder our listening effectiveness. We will discuss ways to overcome noise in the listening process later in this chapter.

CHARACTERISTICS OF THE LISTENING PROCESS

Listening is much more than simply *hearing* what a speaker is saying. Listening goes far beyond the simple process of receiving verbal messages and aural stimuli. The following characteristics of listening will further distinguish listening from hearing and illustrate the complexity of the listening process.

Figure 3-1. Listening

Listening Is a Psychological Process

Another myth most people believe is that listening and hearing are the same process. However, they are not the same. **Hearing** is a *physical process* based upon the reception of stimuli that involves sound waves being received by the hearing mechanism (eardrum). After the stimuli are received, it is interpreted by the brain for understanding. Provided the physical apparatus for hearing is functioning correctly, we hear a multitude of stimuli. On the other hand, **listening** is a *deliberate* and *psychological process* based upon focusing on and interpreting selective stimuli aurally.

Most of us engage in **selective listening**; we tend to listen to and comprehend those messages that we find interesting and with which we agree, those messages that reinforce our perceptions, beliefs, and values. One major problem with selective listening is the role of bias and prejudice. We will discuss this aspect of the listening process later in the chapter because of its prevalence and significance. Overall, it is crucial for the listener to reserve all judgement and set aside stereotypes before engaging in the listening process.

Listening Is an Interpretive or Proactive Process

During the listening process, we are constantly interpreting messages we receive. The verbal and vocal data we listen to must be categorized and interpreted. It is this interpretive aspect of listening that makes the process much more than simply hearing what a speaker is saying. Since we have so much "spare time" during the listening process, it is crucial to constantly interpret and make sense of what we are listening to. Listening needs to be a proactive process where the listener is continuously interpreting and evaluating messages.

As a proactive process, listening is crucial for all types of communication. Whether we are engaged in a group setting (group communication), an intimate relationship with a loved one (interpersonal), responding to our environment (intrapersonal), participating in an environmental protest (public communication), or enjoying an evening at the movies (mass communication), listening is an essential process for effective communication.

Listening Is a Critical Process

In addition to being a proactive process, listening is a critical process, which is much more than simply hearing. When we listen to others, we critically analyze the verbal and vocal data we receive. The effective listener must evaluate and judge the evidence and content of the speech, as well as the paralanguage and other nonverbal communication of the speaker. While our perception of the speaker might affect our listening and critical judgement of those messages we receive, it is precisely this critical perspective or approach that distinguishes listening from the physical act of hearing.

Listening Is an Art, Skill, and Craft that Can Be Strengthened and Improved with Experience and Practice

Listening is a skill very important in public speaking. Studies indicate that after only 10 minutes, listeners are operating at only 25% of their listening capacity. Imagine the listener's plight after an hour lecture, meeting, or church service. More significantly, the average person has the ability to listen to approximately 400 words per minute, while the average person can only speak at 100 words per minute. This 300 word per minute gap is what causes us to be such poor listeners. Our minds tend to "wander" during the listening process, and we lose our concentration very easily. To become better listeners, we must learn to narrow this gap. The only way to narrow this gap is through practice and experience.

THE COMPONENTS OF THE LISTENING PROCESS

There are two very important similarities between listening and public speaking. Both are process oriented because of the element of feedback and the dynamic nature of communication in general. Even more significant, however, is the fact that both listening and speaking are skills that must be developed by a communicator through experience and practice. The remainder of the chapter will explore the importance of listening as part of the communication process and discuss a variety of habits and behaviors you can engage in to improve your listening effectiveness.

Since listening is arguably the most neglected communication skill we engage in, it is imperative that we not take it for granted. More importantly, to become an effective listener requires practicing positive listening habits. Since listening occurs at all levels of communication, it is possible to improve our listening ability every time we engage in a communication act. Whether we attentively listen to a professor's lecture in communication class, attend a sermon on Sunday morning, or participate in a community debate at a town meeting, daily opportunities arise for us to practice good listening habits.

Joseph DeVito, in his excellent book on human communication, discusses a five-step model for effective listening. He believes that all effective listeners must *receive*, *understand*, *remember*, *evaluate*, and *respond* as they engage in the listening process.[2]

Receiving

+ focus your attention on the speaker's verbal and nonverbal messages

+ avoid distractions in the environment

+ focus your attention on the speaker, not on what you will say next

+ maintain your role as a listener; avoid interrupting the speaker until he or she is finished

Understanding

+ relate the speaker's new information to what you already know

+ see the speaker's message from the speaker's perspective or point of view

+ ask questions for clarification

+ rephrase (paraphrase) the speaker's ideas

Remembering

+ identify the central ideas and the major areas of support or evidence presented

+ summarize the message in an easier to retain form, but don't ignore crucial details

+ repeat names and key concepts to yourself, or if appropriate, out loud

+ if this is a formal talk with a recognizable organizational structure, identify this pattern and use it (see it in your mind) to organize what the speaker is saying

Evaluating

+ resist evaluation until you fully understand the speaker's point of view

+ assume the speaker is a person of goodwill and give the speaker the benefit of the doubt by asking for clarification on issues you object to

+ distinguish facts from inferences, opinions, and personal interpretations

+ identify any biases, self-interests, or prejudices that may lead the speaker to unfairly slant information presented

Responding

+ be supportive of the speaker throughout the talk by using varied "back-channeling" cues; using only one—for example, saying "uh-huh" throughout—will make it appear that you are not listening but are merely on automatic pilot

+ express support for the speaker in your final responses

+ own your own responses; state your thoughts and feelings as your own

WAYS TO IMPROVE YOUR LISTENING SKILLS AND HABITS

We have previously discussed the fact that we spend more than half of our communication behavior engaged in the listening process. However, research tells us that most people are very poor listeners. We operate at only 25% of our listening capacity after only 10 minutes of listening. In addition, we now know there is a large "gap" between our ability to listen effectively (400 words per minute) and the average person's rate of speaking (100 words per minute). This presents a problem because we have so much "free time" as we participate in the listening process. Our minds tend to wander, and we might even "daydream" or lose our concentration while we listen to others.

The following skills and habits represent ways in which we can improve our listening effectiveness. They are presented as a means of narrowing the 300 word per minute gap that exists because of our tremendous capacity to listen to and comprehend verbal and nonverbal messages. The following are specific communication behaviors we can engage in during the listening process.[3]

How to Approach the Listening Situation

Before you begin the process of active listening, you want to mentally prepare yourself for the public speaking situation. As we mentioned earlier, we can be mentally distracted by our thoughts, which will prevent us from practicing effective listening. We will discuss three ways you can mentally prepare yourself for the public speaking situation.

Be Aware of Your Biases, Prejudices, and Stereotypes as a Listener

It is often difficult to prevent our preconceived images from affecting our communication, including our listening habits. Since listening is selective in nature, it is imperative that we be aware of any biases, prejudices, and stereotypes we have. An effective listener will not allow any "baggage" to cloud the speaker's message. It is equally important that the listener does not prejudge the speaker before hearing the message. Sometimes, political affiliation, culture, ethnicity, and sexual orientation can impact a listener's ability to focus on the speaker's message and hinder the listening process. If listeners use these prejudices to prejudge the speaker, the listening process will not be successful or fruitful.

Figure 3-2. Listening

Avoid Perceiving the Speaker or the Speech as Unimportant, Uninteresting, or Overly Difficult

If you approach any listening situation expecting the speaker to be boring or the presentation to be unimportant, your listening effectiveness is bound to be hindered. Your purpose as a listener is not always to be entertained by a speaker, and it is important to realize that some speakers are more dynamic and interesting than others. However, entering a listening situation or attending a speech with the attitude that it will be either boring or unimportant is self-defeating and will certainly hinder your listening effectiveness. An upbeat approach in which you see new possibilities and a chance to gain knowledge and information from the speech will greatly enhance the listening situation for you. Finally, many listeners will "tune out" difficult or complicated messages by rationalizing that the material is boring or irrelevant and in effect cut off all channels of communication.

Determine Your Purpose or Goals as a Listener

Just as it is important to try to determine the purpose or motive of the speaker in any listening situation, the effective listener must also enter the listening process with a definite set of goals and objectives. Even during a class lecture or business meeting, make sure you know what your objectives are as a listener. Are you listening for general concepts, main ideas, or the "big picture"? Or, are you listening for specific information or details in the presentation? Defining goals for each listening situation will greatly enhance your chances of listening successfully.

How to Retain Information

One reason why we listen is to receive information. Although we "listen" all the time, rarely do we listen well. Since we listen so poorly it is a wonder how we can communicate at all! Here are some listening strategies to help you retain information more effectively.

Listen for General Concepts and Major Ideas

Have you ever seen a student in a classroom or a business executive at a meeting feverishly taking notes, trying to record every single word uttered by a speaker? Many experts believe you will be a far more effective listener if you listen for broader, more general ideas and concepts, rather than specific details and mundane facts. Don't become preoccupied with taking notes verbatim; simply outline the major areas and some supporting facts and examples. Attempt to maintain eye contact with the speaker periodically as opposed to taking excessive notes with your head buried in your notebook, report, or portfolio.

3

While you are engaged in the act of listening, it is imperative to constantly consider what the speaker is saying. Is the speaker's message logical and does it make sense? Is it appropriate for the audience and the occasion? Since we have a capacity to listen to and understand far more information than a speaker can possibly disseminate in any given period of time, there is plenty of time to evaluate and judge the message by the speaker. Take time to listen for the "big picture" being presented by the speaker.

Make Periodic Reviews and Mental Summaries while Listening

Just as it is helpful to listen to general concepts and major ideas, it is equally useful to make periodic reviews or "mini" summaries throughout the speech or presentation. These reviews will allow the listener to continue to evaluate and retain the content of the message, as well as the structural flow and organization of the presentation. In addition, they allow the listener to analyze the consistency and continuity of the message and look for any possible contradictions in the speech.

How to Be a Critical Listener

Many times when we are engaged in listening, we are attempting to evaluate a persuasive message. We are constantly the target of persuasive messages from advertisers, friends, and family. It is important to listen critically to these messages in order to evaluate and make a judgment on the persuasive message you received. We will discuss five strategies that will help you be a more critical listener.

Attempt to Determine the Motive or Purpose of the Speaker

An effective listener should attempt to guess the motive or purpose of the speaker during any speech or presentation. What is it that the speaker is attempting to elicit from the audience? What are the goals and motives of the speaker? How will this affect the listeners? An effective listener must always determine what the speaker is trying to achieve. Is the speaker attempting to simply share information with the listener, motivate the audience, or persuade the listeners to take definite action?

Continuously Evaluate the Evidence and Content of the Message

The effective listener is always evaluating and weighing the content of any speech or message. The texts of evidence can be applied to any speech or presentation to determine whether the evidence, research, and source material used by the speaker is valid, legitimate, and recent. In examining the evidence presented by any speaker, the listener is able to determine whether the speaker is using legitimate and accurate information. Do the statistics used by the speaker sound logical? What source did they come from? Who is this person being cited as "expert testimony" and what are their qualifications? Just exactly who conducted the scientific "studies" referred to? What site on the Internet did the speaker use as research?

Listen "between the Lines" by Watching the Nonverbal Communication of the Speaker

We've already discussed how important paralanguage or tone of voice is during the listening process. The effective listener needs to be aware of several other elements of the speaker's nonverbal delivery (which is further discussed in Chapter 10). In addition to listening to the verbal and vocal messages being sent by the speaker, it is also important to be attentive to the eye contact, facial expressions, gestures, body movement, and general "body language" of the speaker. Does the speaker's nonverbal communication and body language reinforce or contradict what is being said verbally? Is the speaker's vocal delivery and nonverbal behavior expressing a particular mood or attitude? Does the speaker appear relaxed or nervous?

Think Ahead of the Speaker, Trying to Anticipate What Will Come Next

To be an effective, proactive listener, it is important to look ahead and anticipate what the speaker might say next. Listeners should closely follow the logic (logos) of the arguments and the structure and organization of the message being presented by the speaker. Is the speaker making a logical argument? Does the message make sense and flow smoothly? What is the main conclusion the speaker is leading up to? Is the argument being presented persuasively? What outcome or conclusion is the speaker's message leading to?

Try to Determine if You Share Common Meanings and Definitions for Concepts and Ideas with the Speaker (Operational Definition)

As you participate in the listening process, you will find it useful to incorporate the concept of the operational definition. When you hear the words "poverty," "conservative," or "democracy" used by a speaker, what exactly do these terms and concepts mean? As an active listener, attempt to understand these value-oriented terms and concepts from the speaker's perspective. Such terms as "affirmative action," "sexual harassment," or "middle age" can mean different things to different people, and the proactive listener needs to determine just exactly how the speaker is using those terms.

Additional Suggestions

Finally, we have compiled some additional suggestions that will help you to become an active listener. While our suggestions might seem like simple advice, they are actually very sound advice because these ideas target familiar poor listening habits that hinder our ability to listen effectively.

Don't Be Easily Distracted

There can be many distractions during the listening process and this "noise" tends to affect our concentration from time to time. Avoid letting minor disturbances affect your listening; concentrate on both the speaker and the message, not the lawnmower cutting the grass outside the window, or a noisy furnace in the room. Also, don't let any strange mannerisms by the speaker distract you. Have you ever found yourself watching a speaker pace back and forth, play with his or her hair or jewelry, or perhaps even tap a pen on the podium? We can become so preoccupied with this behavior that we tend to lose our focus, which should ideally be on the speaker and the message itself. It often takes years of listening experience before the listener can overcome these distractions.

Don't Fake Attention or Interest as a Listener

As any college student will tell you, it's not easy pretending to pay attention during a long lecture on a warm spring day! That takes a great deal of concentration. However, your authors would argue that listening attentively and concentrating on the speaker during the listening process would be a better way to expend your energy. Many people tend to fake interest and attention while listening to a speaker. They might smile and nod their heads in agreement, but in reality, they are not really listening to the speaker or making any attempt to understand the speaker's message. Quite frankly, listeners engaging in this kind of behavior are only really hurting themselves because they are not taking advantage of the listening process or working on their listening skills and habits.

We recommend that to avoid this pitfall, the listener should come to the listening situation well rested, with a positive frame of mind. Making continuous eye contact with the speaker and responding to the speaker's body language will also allow you to get more involved in the listening process. In addition, asking questions or making comments during the speech will also help you get more involved and force you to be a "contender," not a "pretender."

Don't Get Emotionally Involved as a Listener

It is often difficult to stay neutral and objective while listening to some speakers, especially when the content of the speech is controversial, emotional, or upsetting. However, it is very important to avoid reacting emotionally to a particular speaker or topic. Try not to let certain words or language anger or upset you. If you are listening to a speaker who takes an opposing view on abortion or gun control, you need to remain detached, calm, and rational, not allowing your emotions to color your perceptions of the speaker or speech content. Even responding to certain words or phrases like "welfare," "left-wing," "right-wing," "politician," "pro-life," "pro-choice," "liberal," "conservative," and countless others, will make you a less effective listener.

In this chapter we have discussed the listening process and we have explained several strategies for becoming a more effective listener. Similar to most other aspects in life, practice and experience are necessary when perfecting any skill or talent; listening is no different. Take advantage of those listening opportunities during class lectures, business and community meetings, or even during an intimate encounter with a loved one, to practice your listening skills and develop positive habits.

While you might not become a proficient listener overnight, continue to work on the behaviors and skills discussed above to improve and strengthen your abilities as a critical listener. This is yet another way to become a more "complete" communicator. While listening might be one of the most neglected communication skills today, those people who do not take the listening process for granted, and work to improve their own personal listening skills, will become more efficient listeners and more adept communicators in today's society.

VOCABULARY

Aural stimuli — stimuli such as verbal, vocal (paralanguage), and noise (other kinds of sounds) that we hear with our ears.

Hearing — a physical process based upon the reception of stimuli that involves sound waves being received by the hearing mechanism (eardrum).

Listening — the process by which human beings deliberately and psychologically focus on and interpret selective stimuli aurally.

Noise — any interference in the transactional process that affects the communication. Noise can be either physical or psychological.

Paralanguage — tone of voice.

Selective listening — the process of deliberately and psychologically focusing on and interpreting those messages that we find interesting and with which we agree, those messages which reinforce our perceptions, beliefs, and values.

REFERENCES

[1] Carl Weaver, *Human Listening: Processes and Behavior*, (Indianapolis and New York: The Bobbs-Merrill Company, Inc., 1972), 5–7.

[2] Joseph A. DeVito, *Essentials of Human Communication*, 8th edition (Boston: Pearson, 2013), 51–54.

[3] Ronald L. Applbaum and Karl W. E. Anatol, *Effective Oral Communication for Business and the Professions*, (Chicago: Science Research Associates, 1982), 50–56.

AUDIENCE ANALYSIS 4

"Make sure you have finished speaking before your audience has finished listening."
–Dorothy Sarnoff

"My audience was my life. What I did and how I did it, was all for my audience."
–Cab Calloway

"The easiest type of relationship with me is with ten thousand people. The hardest is with one."
–Joan Baez

This Chapter Examines:

+ the rhetorical situation

+ the nature of a multicultural audience

+ analyzing the multicultural audience

+ methods of audience analysis

+ the concept of "identification" in public speaking

+ building identification with the multicultural audience

It was only eight years ago that Robert was in the same situation as his audience: unemployed, homeless, and addicted to drugs. At the request of the director of the transition center that helped transform his life eight years ago, Robert has returned to address an audience of men who have only known life as desperation and destitution. It is a life Robert knew intimately, and he was prepared to discuss his own struggles, setbacks, and triumphs in his journey to get off the streets and back into "real" life. Since Robert knew the circumstances of the audience well, he planned on speaking to them from their perspective. "All I used to know," he began, "was lying, hustling, and cheating. I would do anything to anyone to get by. I didn't know any other way. I didn't know how to go another way! However, I'm here to tell you that if you are finally sick and tired of being sick and tired, then today is the first day of your transformation."

The powerful words spoken by Robert illustrate the importance of audience analysis when making a presentation. In this example, Robert was familiar with the audience since he had directly experienced their issues of unemployment, homelessness, and drug addiction. Therefore, he was able to appeal to the audience through examples and reasoning that the audience could understand. When speakers are able to establish a connection or "common bond" on an issue, it is called **identification**. How speakers establish identification is through the process of audience analysis. Given the multicultural nature of our society, it is critical for speakers to analyze their audience in order to present an effective speech.

Therefore, the importance of audience analysis and identification is the focus of this chapter. All effective speakers analyze their audience in order to adapt their speech topic to the audience's interests. We will begin our discussion of audience analysis with an explanation of the context for all presentations, which is the rhetorical situation.

THE RHETORICAL SITUATION

One of scholar Lloyd Bitzer's major contributions to the study of rhetoric is the concept of the rhetorical situation.[1] Bitzer explained that when someone is speaking it is always in response to a situation. How well a speaker can address the circumstances in the situation will determine the effectiveness of the speech. Bitzer declared that rhetoric (speaking) is the primary mode for altering reality with the audience being the mediators for change. Therefore, a rhetorical situation is a complex context involving persons, events, and motivations that create a need to speak. Any rhetorical situation involves three concepts: exigency—the urgency or motivation for the individual to speak; constraints—any obstacle that inhibits decisions and/or actions that are needed to modify the exigency; and audience—the individuals who are impacted by or have an interest in the exigency, who can be influenced by rhetoric, and who can be the mediators for change.

4

It is the concept of the rhetorical situation that compels speakers to conduct an audience analysis in order to create an effective speech. As Bitzer argued, an effective speech requires a fitting response to the situation. If a speaker understands the characteristics and motivations of the audience, the more effective the speaker will be in adapting a message to the audience. We will expand upon the importance of audience in the rhetorical situation and how understanding the audience provides the means for identification.

The **audience** is an integral component in the rhetorical situation. The audience influences the construction of a speech and the evaluation of its effectiveness. In fact, public speaking is often referred to as an **audience-centered process** because all preparation and research must be directed towards the audience if the speaker is to be effective. From topic selection to the type of evidence to the mode of delivery, the audience must be the central concern of any speaker. Speakers need to make a concerted effort to find out who the audience is demographically, what cultural beliefs they might hold, what their motivations and desires are, and how to best adapt the message to their needs.

The speaker must constantly consider how the audience will respond to the speech topic, the evidence presented, and the perspective taken by the speaker. The speaker should ask, "What do my listeners know about my topic?" "How will they react to the topic and the opinions I express?" "How can the demographics, cultural beliefs, and needs of my audience guide my approach to the topic?" "What will my audience find informative and important (informative speech) or convincing and motivational (persuasive speech)?" Finally, "What does my audience analysis, as well as the topic, tell me about preparing and presenting an effective speech?"

Another reason public speaking is referred to as an audience-centered process is due to the element of feedback. An effective speaker must continuously "monitor" the **verbal** and **nonverbal feedback** of the listeners during any presentation. The audience will constantly keep the speaker apprised about how they feel, whether they nod approvingly, appear bored and tired, or disagree through nonverbal expressions with what the speaker is saying. Effective speakers respond to the verbal and nonverbal feedback of the audience to adapt and modify the speech to maintain the audience's interest and attention. Whatever the reaction of the audience might be, they are a central ingredient in the public speaking process. As a speaker, developing an awareness and sensitivity to audience feedback is critical to making an effective presentation. The ability to adapt messages is ever more critical as audiences become more diverse.

THE NATURE OF THE MULTICULTURAL AUDIENCE

American society in the new millennium is undergoing a rapid transformation of its population. Aided by the influx of immigrants from South and Central America, the Caribbean, Southeast and East Asia, and from increasing population rates of co-cultures within the United States, American society is composed of a multicultural mosaic of ethnicities, nationalities, religions, and languages. As researchers Chen and Starosta explain, diversity will become the norm and not the exception.[2] As people of color continue to make strides in all aspects of public life from the workforce to educational institutions, our society will become even more diverse, which will place a greater importance on intercultural communication competence.

From a public speaking perspective, speakers have to be aware of and knowledgeable of the multitude of values, beliefs, and norms that are held by individuals from different cultures that comprise diverse audiences. An understanding of cultural differences begins with a brief discussion of culture.

Culture

Culture can be understood as the traditions, customs, beliefs, values, norms, and perspectives that are learned through shared behavioral patterns and cultural practices that are passed down from generation to generation. Culture is learned subtly and implicitly, but it greatly impacts our *perception* and how we make sense of reality. In fact, culture provides the foundation for the meanings we *attribute* to our perceptions and influences how we describe events.[3] Culture can be thought of as a pair of eyeglasses—culture is a lens that helps us perceive and interpret reality. Through the repetition of attributing meaning to what we perceive, culture constructs norms and values that become "common sense" for those who belong to a particular culture. Therefore, people from different cultures can perceive and interpret behaviors and meanings in different ways. An example is the controversial immigration law that was passed in Arizona. Under the "show me your papers" provision of the law, police officers have the power to detain anyone who is suspected to be an illegal alien. If a person in Arizona is detained and does not have documentation that he/she is a U.S. citizen or does not have immigration papers, the person will be arrested and deported. Opponents of the new law argue that since Mexicans comprise the majority of illegal aliens, only Hispanics (whether they are citizens or not) will be targeted by law enforcement. Not surprisingly, non-Hispanics tend to favor the law, while Hispanics do not.[4]

Figure 4-1. Culture

Cultures can occur on a variety of levels. For example, the United States is comprised of a number of cultures. Those everyday norms and practices held by the majority of Americans are referred to as the **dominant culture**. American culture has many values that guide our behavior, shape our perception, and how we attribute meaning. One cultural value stressed in American society is individuality—individuals are raised to reach individual goals and achievements even at the expense of group goals and achievements. In addition to the cultural values held by a majority of Americans, there are additional cultures that exist within the larger dominant culture, which are referred to as co-cultures. A **co-culture** can be defined by one's nationality, ethnicity, or religion, such as Japanese culture, African American culture, or Jewish culture. Furthermore, cultures are created by organizations, groups, and major corporations such as Wal-Mart or even by athletes at your college or university. All cultures have norms and perspectives that are followed and practiced by those in the group. **Values** are deeply ingrained social morals that are shaped by culture. **Beliefs** are what we accept to be true even if these beliefs are not scientifically accurate. For example it was once a widely held belief that the earth was flat. This inaccurate belief nonetheless influenced the behaviors of people and societies centuries ago. When certain values and beliefs are held by most individuals in a culture, they are referred to as **cultural values** and **cultural beliefs**.

Culture provides different values and beliefs, which influence perception, interpretation, and the attribution of meaning for the individuals who are a part of that culture. For example, the value of talk versus silence in a conversation varies greatly depending on the culture. Native Americans in the United States place a different cultural value on silence than European Americans.[5] Being reserved and quiet is generally considered by Native Americans as the acceptable way for communicating with other individuals, especially other Native Americans. Remaining silent and not initiating conversation demonstrates respect and politeness in Native American culture. Whether it is the classroom, work team, or academic department, if someone is not familiar with this cultural value, he or she might attribute the silence to ignorance or being unconfident, when it is simply a sign of politeness.

High- and Low-Context Cultures

Intercultural scholar Edward T. Hall[6] created the concepts of high- and low-context cultures to explain the amount of information that is either implied or directly stated in a communication message. In a **high-context culture**, the meanings of a communication message are imbedded in the situation, the relationship of the individuals, and the implicit norms, beliefs, and values of the culture. For example, Eastern Cultures, such as Japanese culture, are high-context cultures where the interpretation of meaning in a communication message is found in the context of the message rather than in the direct and explicit expression of the message. In Japan, the concept of face is an implicit value that influences the communication between individuals. **Face** is the public self-image that a person wants to maintain in a specific social context.[7] Since the Japanese culture places high value on maintaining positive interpersonal relationships, individuals are concerned about the feelings of others. Maintaining face is to avoid looking foolish or making a social error that could lead to guilt or embarrassment. For this reason, there are seven different ways a Japanese person can say "no" without actually saying "no." A specific example would be if a person offers another person something to eat. The correct response would not be, "No, I'm not hungry," but instead an indirect or ambiguous response such as, "It looks too good to eat," which would allow the other person to save face. The key is understanding that most of the meaning of the message comes not from the actual message but from the context in which the message takes place. Meanwhile, in low-context cultures, the meanings of a communication message are directly communicated and less reliant on the situation. In a **low-context culture**, the meanings of a communication message are directly communicated by individuals through verbal expressions of intention, opinion, and thought. An example of low-context culture is the dominant culture in the United States.

The following chart provided by Chen and Starosta[8] further clarifies the differences between high- and low-context cultures as they relate to public speaking:

LOW-CONTEXT CULTURE	HIGH-CONTEXT CULTURE
1. Overly displays meanings through direct communication forms	1. Implicitly embeds meanings at different levels of the sociocultural context
2. Values individualism	2. Values collectivism
3. Emphasizes linear logic	3. Emphasizes spiral logic
4. Values direct verbal interaction and is less able to read nonverbal expressions	4. Values indirect verbal interaction and is more able to read nonverbal expressions
5. Tends to use "logic" to present ideas	5. Tends to use more "feeling" in expression
6. Tends to emphasize highly structured messages, give details, and place great stress on words and technical signs	6. Tends to give simple, ambiguous, non-contexting messages

A speaker needs to determine whether another culture or co-culture is a high- or low-context culture because this can influence whether a message is effectively received by an audience. A high- or low-context orientation influences the content of the message and how the message is presented. It also affects how we think about logic and the way a message is organized (see Chapter 8). Therefore, the challenge for any speaker is how to adapt a message to a diverse audience. Adapting a message is dependent on audience analysis. Audience analysis helps speakers to understand the demographics, culture, and desires of an audience to create a message that meets the audience's needs.

ANALYZING THE MULTICULTURAL AUDIENCE

The great Roman orator Cicero (106–43 BC) once stated that the "proper concern of the orator (speaker) is language of power and elegance accommodated to the feelings and understandings of mankind." Even in ancient Rome, speakers knew the importance of analyzing and adapting to an audience.[9]

Today, the role of audience remains a central and crucial variable in the process of public speaking in the rhetorical situation. For any presentation to be successful, the speaker must conduct an audience analysis, which includes discovering the demographics (which suggests certain attitudes, beliefs, and values) of the audience. The purpose of an **audience analysis** is to discover as much as possible about an audience so the speaker can adapt an appropriate message that meets the needs of the audience and provides a "fitting response" to the situation. When you can understand the characteristics and the needs of your audience, then you have successfully completed an audience analysis. We will discuss the primary variables or demographics that comprise an audience; we will identify some methods of audience analysis; and we will highlight some situational factors that can affect how the message is adapted.

Demographics

Any speaker who attempts to inform or persuade an audience should know as much as possible about who the audience is, what they know, how their needs and wants can be addressed, and what biases they might have toward the speaker or topic. Effective speakers also identify the level of knowledge the listeners already possess about the topic, what the audience might want to know more about, and what their attitudes and beliefs are regarding the topic. All these factors can be better understood when the speaker uses research (using the various methods of audience analysis) to discover the demographics of the audience. **Demographics** are simply the characteristics of the audience.

Understanding the demographics of an audience provides the speaker with clues about the audience's attitudes, beliefs, needs, and wants. When the speaker has an idea of these demographics, the speaker can relate the topic to the audience's needs. While there are many demographics, we will mention only a few key demographics that are important to be aware of when adapting a message to the audience.

Culture

A critical place to start in understanding the multicultural audience is identifying the cultural composition of the audience. Understanding the cultural composition of the audience is important because culture serves as a lens through which we understand, perceive, and make sense of the world. There are many co-cultures that comprise American society and knowing the nuances of these co-cultures will help the speaker adapt an effective message to these co-cultures.

For example, consider a salesperson selling educational investment funds. American culture is based on the value of **individualism**, which means the individual is more important than the group. In selling the product to European Americans, the salesperson would explain that the fund would help the child achieve financial independence to afford higher education. However, other co-cultures such as Chinese Americans or Japanese Americans value **collectivism**, which means the group is more important than the individual. In this instance, the salesperson would probably stress how the fund benefits everyone in the family rather than simply benefiting the future college student. The salesperson could explain how the attainment of a college degree could bring financial prosperity to the entire family. In this case, the salesperson understands the collective nature of the culture and uses this knowledge to adapt her message to the potential customer. The example also illustrates how knowing the norms and values of a culture can make the difference between an effective and ineffective message.

Ethnicity

Closely related to the demographic of culture is ethnicity. **Ethnicity** refers to those individuals who have a heritage that is based upon a common orientation to the past, ancestry, nationality, language, and religion. An individual's ethnicity is determined by family heritage, by self-identification, and by societal definition. Culture can be understood as what is practiced and ethnicity as what has been inherited and self-identified. For example, a man who was born to Cuban parents in the United States could label his ethnicity as Cuban or Cuban-American, but his culture would be determined by what traditions and customs he and his family practice (which means his culture could be American, Cuban, or Cuban-American).

In addition, we prefer using the label ethnicity instead of race when describing a particular group of people because ethnicity comprises what is inherited and most importantly how the person self-identifies. **Race** is simply a social construction that is based upon arbitrary and ill-defined classifications that are unscientific and illogical.[10] Historically, the U.S. Census Bureau has used a variety of racial categories to classify people and different definitions have been applied depending on the social climate of the times. Examples include the **one-drop rule**, which designated a person Black if the person had a single drop of "Black blood" in the person's ancestry, or the **eyeball test**, where laypersons (such as the hospital staff or census takers) determined a person's racial classification based upon their own perceptions of race-based physical characteristics. These examples briefly illustrate how the classification of race is problematic and, more importantly, nonspecific in understanding groups who have a shared heritage and who self-identify with a particular group.

When receiving information about the ethnic composition of your audience, it is important to remember that some people have a stronger connection to their ethnicity than others do. As a speaker, be aware of variations in how individuals self-identify with ethnicity and how ethnicity is an additional variable that can shape perception and the interpretation of meaning. The audience's ethnicity can affect how the speaker prepares for a speech, especially the type of evidence and examples that are used. There is also the challenge of creating a common bond with a multiethnic audience. These are all factors a speaker must keep in mind when preparing for a presentation.

Public speakers must attempt to present their information in a manner that does not offend or ridicule another person's ethnicity (or culture). Sometimes speakers do not even realize that they are expressing a biased, stereotypical, or inappropriate viewpoint until their message is coolly received by a diverse audience. To avoid this situation, speakers should share their ideas with people from various co-cultures and ethnic groups during their practice sessions to "test" the information and manner of presentation. People from different co-cultures can point out ideas or remarks that might be insensitive, open to misinterpretation, or offensive, and they can offer suggestions for how to present the speech in a more acceptable manner. Also, students can check with their instructors, who can give them ideas for how to present their ideas in a non-offensive manner. A further discussion of how to avoid offensive language is provided in Chapter 11.

Gender

The multicultural audience we refer to not only relates to the culture and ethnicity of the audience but to gender as well. Gender is a social construction that can influence how individuals perceive and interpret meaning. Men and women's perceptions are not only shaped by how they are socialized into their gender roles, but also through their experiences as men and women in our society.[11] The gender composition of the audience is important for some issues that tend to be perceived and interpreted differently by men and women. Issues such as health care, national security, and education spending are often perceived differently by men and women. In addition, types of evidence tend to appeal to men and women differently. In general, men are more moved by facts and women are influenced more significantly by personal stories. Effective speakers should be aware of the "gender gap" pertinent to particular issues and should be prepared to adapt their message so that it appeals to both genders.

Speakers can keep the following questions in mind when preparing for a speech: "Are you discussing a topic that might be viewed differently by men and women?" "Does gender matter when considering background, experience, and knowledge about the topic?" Gender can become an important variable in planning and preparing for a presentation. For example, a speech that discusses hormone replacement therapy can be perceived as a gender-specific topic. Therefore, the speaker must present information and reasoning for why, in this case, men would want to listen to the topic. Gender is a social construct that serves as one lens that individuals use to interpret, perceive, and make sense of the world. Effective speakers are aware of gender and take it into account when adapting the topic, the type of support material, and the goal of the speech.

Age

The age of the audience is also an important variable to discover when constructing a speech. Knowing the age range, the median age, and the majority age of the audience provides important clues to interests and needs. Issues affect individuals differently based upon what they have been able to experience and have experienced. For example, a speech about refinancing a home probably would be of little interest to college students—the majority of whom live on campus or in apartments and do not own homes. However, a speech about how to create a budget when living in an apartment would probably be of greater interest. Likewise, a speech about how to plan for retirement would be best suited for a more mature audience.

Be aware of age when adapting a message. In relation to your topic, does the age of the listeners make a difference in how you approach and prepare for the topic? Do you need to modify your examples or evidence in any way based on the age of your audience? Are there specific examples, language, or popular culture references that should be used in your speech to demonstrate your credibility with a particular audience? These are all ideas to consider when identifying the demographic of age.

Education

Most people who read this textbook are college students who often overlook the educational level of the audience when considering audience analysis. Since students are surrounded by other students, seldom is education considered to be an important demographic. However, one's educational level provides clues to one's ability to absorb information, being open to different points of view, and having knowledge on a variety of information and perspectives. In addition, colleges are composed of on-campus students, commuting students, nontraditional students, evening-only students, full-time students, and part-time students who bring their own unique experiences to higher education.

The education level is important in adapting a message to an audience. Educational level is especially pertinent if there is a large discrepancy between the speaker's educational level and the audience's level of education. In general, the educational level of an audience can affect how to plan and present the information, what ideas to refer to, and the choice of evidence and reasoning. Educational level is often but not always directly correlated to economic status.

Economic Status

One of the least discussed issues in American society is one's economic status. We live in a society that values "self-made" individuals who can rise above obstacles to make something of themselves. As a result, individuals pursue careers and jobs to earn a particular income and with it social status. (Interestingly, one reason credit card debt is so rampant in our society is because through acquiring and displaying material items, one can feign a particular social status regardless of one's actual income.)

The economic status of an audience is a key characteristic to keep in mind when preparing a speech. For example, a working class family that has limited disposable income might be more concerned with issues such as health care, education, and retirement and/or education funds than an upper class family. Audiences can become alienated and distant from speakers who they perceive as not understanding their concerns. Income provides for certain lifestyles and also creates certain needs and concerns for those who share the same economic status.

Religion

Religion is an important variable that provides guidance and perspective for how individuals live their lives. Since the United States proclaims freedom of religion, there are many religions that are practiced in this country. Therefore, individuals follow different religions, which provide different perspectives, guidelines, and morals for people to adhere to. These variations are important not just between different religions such as Christianity and Islam but between different denominations and sects within religions such as Christians who consider themselves Catholic, Presbyterian, or Pentecostal—all of which can be fundamental or liberal. Individuals also have varying associations with religion from those who follow and practice their religion faithfully to those who are of a certain faith but do not practice it, to those who are atheist. Some feel it's fine to discuss religion while others want to evangelize to those who feel religion has no place in the public sphere.

One reason religion is a volatile issue is because religion involves discussing deeply held beliefs or values that guide individual behavior. Religion is also problematic due to centuries-old conflicts and historical tensions associated with the dissemination of religion. Examples include conflicts in Northern Ireland between Catholics and Protestants, in the Middle East between Jews and Muslims, and even the recent war with Iraq where many in the Arabic world saw the war not as a search for weapons of mass destruction or for the liberation of the Iraqi people but as a conflict between Christianity and Islam.[12] Therefore, speakers need to be extremely careful when referring to or making references to religion. Speakers should know the religions represented in the audience and how strongly audience members identify with them. In addition, speakers should always be mindful to refer to religion in an intelligent and respectful way.

Political Identification

Another emotional characteristic is political identification. **Political identification** refers to the policies one supports that determine how people in a given society should be governed. While Democrats and Republicans represent the two major parties in this country, there are many smaller parties such as the Reform party, the Libertarian party, and the Green party, which espouse a particular political platform. While smaller parties have distinct ideologies, so do the major parties. The ideology (conservative, moderate, liberal) of the party is sometimes more important in defining political platforms and issues than the actual party. Regardless of whether individuals identify with a party, they have ideological views on issues from affirmative action to abortion to capital punishment.

When a speaker knows the political identification and the ideological breakdown of the audience, this provides a better understanding of various opinions held by the audience. For example, addressing a primarily conservative audience on the topic of capital punishment leads to the inference that the audience is more interested in the enforcement of laws and sentencing than in rehabilitation. Depending on the goal of the speaker, this inference can help plan the evidence and reasoning used in the speech. Similar to religion, politics can be a very emotional issue, as illustrated by the various political talk shows that showcase commentators debating issues along strict party lines.

4

Region

An often overlooked audience characteristic is the geographical region represented by the audience. Sometimes individuals from particular regions have local needs or concerns that are different from another region. For example, coal-mining communities of West Virginia and Kentucky have economic, environmental, and educational concerns that are different from the central Florida communities that surround Disney World. Different regions have particular norms and politics that influence how individuals interpret and perceive information. Effective speakers are able to identify the local issues that are a concern to individuals and understand the impact of these issues on the region.

Other Factors

Depending on your topic, you might need to consider additional factors or variables concerning audience demographics when you are preparing a speech. Demographics such as marital status, disabilities (see Chapter 5), sexual orientation, occupation, and knowledge/access to technology might be important for you to consider as you adapt your information to your audience. When preparing your speech, it is always wise to contemplate whether there are special concerns or needs of your specific audience that you should consider.

METHODS OF AUDIENCE ANALYSIS

We have listed and discussed various demographics that speakers should be aware of when adapting a speech to an audience. While we provided examples of how these demographics can influence the preparation of a speech, how can speakers identify these characteristics in their actual audience? The answer lies in using one of several methods of audience analysis. Professional marketers, advertisers, and public relation specialists use comprehensive research instruments to collect information about audiences in order to develop well-crafted messages.[13] However, we discuss five informal ways to perform an audience analysis: observation, personal contact, interview, questionnaire, and social media.

Audience Analysis

One of the most useful means of audience analysis is through direct observation of the audience. **Observation** is simply perceiving firsthand the characteristics of the audience. If you are invited to speak at an event or occasion, most likely you will have the opportunity to observe the audience before your presentation.

Demographics you can often observe in an audience include cultural and ethnic backgrounds, gender, age, and economic status. In the classroom, you will become familiar with your classmates through class exercises, and from their speeches where you can learn more about them and what they believe. Observation is a helpful way of adapting a message to an audience.

Another method of audience analysis is being informed through a personal contact. A **personal contact** is someone from the group or organization who invited you to speak and who knows the audience very well. Personal contacts are good sources for providing information quickly. For example, a personal contact can tell you why you were chosen to speak, the topics the group or organization would like you to address, and the setting or occasion of the event. Personal contacts should also be able to tell you how long you should speak, the number of people who will attend, and the demographics of the audience. These are all key questions that when answered help you as a speaker-construct an appropriate message for the audience.

Figure 4-2. Audience Analysis

If it is not possible to acquire information from a personal contact, then it might be necessary for you to conduct interviews with one or two people associated with the group/organization you are addressing. **Interviews** are transactional processes between at least two people in which one person conducts an oral examination of the other, while other people speak and listen from time to time. More specifically, this type of interview is referred to as the **research/survey interview** because you are obtaining knowledge from experts and authorities in some particular organization, field, or discipline.

For the purpose of audience analysis, interviews can be conducted by a variety of means, such as in person, by phone, or by e-mail. The importance is to gather as much feedback as you can from knowledgeable people in the group or organization in order to construct an appropriate message for the audience. You want to ask the same questions that were mentioned under personal contact.

In the classroom, online course management systems such as Blackboard and D2L enable students to post questions and receive feedback from their classmates in order to adapt a relevant message to the audience. The benefit of posting questions on course management systems is it allows students to gain specific insights into the needs of their specific audience. It is a quick and effective way to gain feedback for classroom presentations.

Another method of audience analysis is questionnaires. A **questionnaire** is a document (ranging from one page to several pages) that lists a series of questions for individuals to answer in order to receive specific information about the audience. Constructing a questionnaire takes time because your questions are determined by what information you want to know about the audience. Thus the questions must be constructed clearly and unambiguously. A key principle for questionnaires is to keep the questions brief (people tend not to respond to long questionnaires).

Questionnaires ask a variety of questions in order to gain information such as close-ended questions, degree questions, and open-ended questions. **Close-ended questions** are direct and restrictive questions that seek specific information and can often be answered with a simple "yes" or "no." **Degree questions** enable individuals to answer a question based upon a continuum or scale. **Open-ended questions** are general, broad, and far-reaching questions that allow for in-depth and detailed responses. Examples of each type of question follow.

HOMELAND SECURITY QUESTIONNAIRE

(Close-ended questions)

1. Gender: _____ 2. Age: _____ 3. Ethnicity: _____

4. City/town: _____

5. I know what to do if there is a biological/chemical attack in my city/town.

   Yes ____ No ____

(Degree question)

6. I think my city/town is prepared for a biological/chemical attack.

   strongly agree   agree   no opinion   disagree   strongly disagree

(Open-ended question)

7. What information or procedures concerning homeland security do you believe your city/town needs to convey to the general public?

Social media and social networking provide additional methods for gathering information on an audience. **Social media** are Internet-based tools that enable individuals to deliver a message. Meanwhile, **social networking** is the act of using one or more social media to meet new individuals and/or maintain relationships with individuals. Both social media and social networking can make the process of identification transactional as individuals (speaker or audience) can respond and interact to further communicate on ideas. Furthermore, social networking enables individuals to build relationships with others who share similar interests and experiences. When speakers can use social media and social networking to adapt a speech to an audience, it is a further means for providing a fitting response to the situation.

Situational Analysis

In addition to conducting an audience analysis, it is also important to be mindful of the situational factors that comprise any rhetorical situation. Situational factors have great influence on the planning of your presentation. We briefly discuss size, occasion, significance, and time.

The **size** of the audience will influence how you present your information. For example, a large audience limits the amount of interaction a speaker can have with the audience, so the presentation will be more formal. Moreover, larger audiences might require the use of a microphone, podium, or presentational slides. In contrast, smaller audiences enable the speaker to be more informal, invite interaction, and demonstrate impromptu speaking. With smaller audiences, the speaker can be more flexible and personal. Regardless of the size of the audience, speakers should be prepared to adapt their presentation based upon the number of people in attendance.

The **occasion** of the speech can impact the content presented. As we discuss in Chapter 15, special occasion speeches, such as ceremonial speeches, are governed by implicit norms and rules that speakers must be aware of in order to present an effective message. For example, the information presented in a toast to the bride and groom is different from the information presented during a "pep talk" with a team before a game. Effective speakers understand the implicit norms that govern the situation and speech and construct their message accordingly.

Another situational factor speakers should be aware of is the **significance** of the occasion. The more important the event, the more formal and more prepared you should be as a speaker. As we discuss in Chapter 15, the importance of the speech can be dictated by the importance of the event. In these cases, you want your speech to match the level of expectation for the event. In general, the more important the event, the more planning, preparation, and practice will be necessary for the presentation to be successful.

4

A final situational factor that speakers need to be mindful of is the aspect of **time**. Time can refer to the amount of time given to speak, the time of day when the speech is given, and/or the timing of the speech in relation to other speeches or other events taking place. Again, each speaking opportunity is unique and whether the time allowed is dictated by norms or from audience analysis, the speaker should not exceed the time allotted.

Now that we have discussed audience demographics, methods of audience analysis, and situational factors that influence a presentation, it is important to address the concept of identification in adapting a message to an audience. How well speakers can adapt their message will determine the effectiveness of the presentation. For this reason, we will now discuss identification.

THE CONCEPT OF "IDENTIFICATION" IN PUBLIC SPEAKING

We began this chapter with the example of Robert, who was able to adapt a specific message to his audience because he knew their demographics. Robert's example also demonstrates how it is imperative for any speaker in the rhetorical situation to establish a "common bond" with the audience. The term most closely associated with this strategy in public speaking is called identification. **Identification** is any attempt by the speaker to establish some sort of common ground on an issue or problem. The concept of identification is a part of audience analysis and public speaking. We believe that you will never inform or persuade your listeners until you first identify or become *consubstantial* with them. The person most often identified with the concept of identification is Kenneth Burke. In his book, *Rhetoric of Motives*, Burke states that, "You persuade a man only insofar as you can talk his language by speech, gesture, tonality, order, image, attitude, idea, identifying your ways with his."[14]

The concept of identification is interesting, but how does identification work in public speaking? In political campaigns, candidates often want to demonstrate on the campaign trail and in television advertisements that they are "common" Americans who understand the everyday problems of hardworking, middle-class families. The idea behind these "plain folks" images is to have potential voters perceive the candidate as "one of us" and not just another politician vying for votes.

The concept of identification also occurs in persuasive social movements. Think about a speech or testimonial given by a breast cancer survivor during Breast Cancer Awareness Month (BCAM). If the speaker talks about overcoming breast cancer and is speaking to a group of listeners who have also survived breast cancer, the audience can immediately identify with what the speaker is saying. Burke called this common bond with the audience consubstantiality. **Consubstantiality** is any attempt by the speaker to "become one" with the audience and to establish some sort of common ground on an issue or problem.[15]

A historical example of consubstantiality can be found in Abraham Lincoln's "Gettysburg Address." Lincoln, who is widely considered one of the great American presidents, commemorated the sacrifice made at Gettysburg by reaffirming American ideals that bind all Americans:

> *But, in a larger sense, we cannot dedicate—we cannot consecrate—we cannot hallow—this ground. The brave men, living and dead, who struggled here, have consecrated it, far above our poor power to add or detract. The world will little note, nor long remember what we say here, but it can never forget what they did here. It is for us the living, rather, to be dedicated here to the unfinished work which they who fought here have thus far so nobly advanced. It is rather for us to be here dedicated to the great task remaining before us—that from these honored dead we take increased devotion to that cause for which they gave the last full measure of devotion—that we here highly resolve that these dead shall not have died in vain—that this nation, under God, shall have a new birth of freedom—and that government of the people, by the people, for the people shall not perish from the earth.*

Rhetorically, Lincoln created identification with all Americans through the sacrifice that was made by soldiers on both sides of the battle. Note how Lincoln did not fault find or endorse a political ideology; instead, he emphasized the common bond of American values and ideals that were shared by all Americans. The use of repetition is another rhetorical strategy that created identification with the audience. Notice how Lincoln employed repetition through phrases such as "of the people" to reinforce the ideals shared by the audience. His use of the pronouns "us" and "we" also demonstrates how identification is used to unify and establish **common ground** with multiple audiences. He is also saying throughout this passage that all Americans (including himself) have an obligation to honor the dead by living out the ideals of the founding fathers. This brief example shows how Abraham Lincoln became consubstantial with his listeners. Effective speakers use identification to influence an audience through a common bond—in this case the ideals, values, experiences, and perspectives of a democratic society.

Finally, a speaker can use the strategy of identification by making simple statements about unity with the audience or by attacking a "common enemy or foe." For example, two previous enemy "superpower" nations like the United States and Russia have created new common bonds to attack the problem of international terrorism or to condemn other nations from developing nuclear weapons.

4

Thonnssen, Baird, and Braden, in their classic book, *Speech Criticism*, summarize the importance of identification and audience analysis when they state:

> *Identification, it should be noted, if it fulfills the concept of close correspondence, and fairly complete communication, calls for the speaker's self-analysis with respect to his own intellectual, social, and moral equipment. He must both understand himself and his audience.*[16]

BUILDING IDENTIFICATION WITH THE MULTICULTURAL AUDIENCE

We have discussed the importance of understanding the multicultural audience, identified audience demographics, provided some methods of audience analysis, and discussed the importance of identification. Once a speaker completes an audience analysis, how does the speaker use it effectively to adapt a message to an audience that holds different values and often conflicting needs? We believe the challenge for all speakers in the rhetorical situation is to adapt messages that transcend cultural, ethnic, and religious differences in order to appeal to more universal values. The key is to acknowledge and adjust to cultural differences but build upon commonality.[17]

This means speakers must be intimately familiar with not only different cultural values, but how these values shape perception, interpretation, and the attribution of meaning. A speaker cannot simply make a presentation built on the theme of "we are all alike" until the speaker can acknowledge and understand how cultural differences shape individual and group consciousness. When speakers are able to mutually accommodate cultural differences, they are actually third-culture building.[18] In the public speaking context, **third-culture building** involves a speaker identifying common universal values that help the speaker and the multicultural audience create a new culture that draws from and extends the norms and values from the independent cultures. It is a challenging task, but a worthy challenge in attempting to identify with (and not exclude) other cultures and co-cultures in the public sphere.

While it might be impossible to please each audience member, appealing to more universal values enables speakers to identify with individuals across cultures to build unity with a diverse audience. We believe that identification with a diverse audience is achieved when speakers are able to acknowledge and adapt messages to cultural differences, followed by appealing to universal values that transcend cultural differences. Speakers can appeal to diverse audiences by appealing to universal values such as cultural values, cultural beliefs, and motivations.

Cultural Values

As we mentioned earlier in the chapter, values are deeply ingrained social morals. When values are held by most individuals in a culture they are referred to as **cultural values**. Cultural values reflect the foundation of citizenship and the rights expected for those individuals in a particular society. Cultural values are highly held ideals that most people, regardless of culture, ethnicity, gender, or religion have come to value in this country. Some examples of American cultural values include liberty, freedom, and equality.

The idea of **liberty** is the concept of having the right to live as one pleases (as long as it does not infringe on another person's rights). Liberty is a founding idea of this country, and it continues to be one of the basic rights of citizenship. Speeches that appeal to liberty appeal to a basic right that is held and enjoyed by all Americans, such as life, liberty, and the pursuit of happiness.

Closely related to liberty is **freedom**. The Constitution defines our basic freedoms, such as the freedom of speech, freedom of the press, freedom of assembly, and freedom of religion. Speeches that appeal to the ideas of freedom highlight the value of living in an open society. These are ideas that set America apart from other nations.

Equality is the idea of treating people fairly in order to enjoy all the inalienable rights of citizenship. Equality continues to be one of the ideals that the country is continuing to achieve as emphasized by political and social battles surrounding issues from affirmative action to the death penalty. However, equality is a powerful value that any individual can identify with and be motivated to achieve.

Cultural values when used correctly can appeal to a diverse audience. Regardless of the demographic, cultural values are highly regarded. They are also abstract ideals that people are continuously trying to achieve. Since cultural values are abstract ideas, they can never be totally described or experienced. For this reason, speakers can always appeal to these cultural values.

Cultural Beliefs

Related to cultural values are cultural beliefs. **Cultural beliefs** are what a majority of individuals in a culture believe to be true. All cultures hold particular cultural beliefs that influence perception, the interpretation of reality, and the attribution of meaning.[19] Cultural beliefs make powerful persuasive appeals, because the speaker is eliciting deeply held ideas that the audience believes to be true. Some examples of cultural values include the possibility of success, the value of challenge, the value of humbleness, and the eternal return.[20]

The possibility of success is the belief that hard work will lead to success. Researcher Charles Larson mentions how this cultural belief is foundational to our culture, and it has always appealed to immigrants, the poor, and the outcasts of society searching to improve their life in the United States. It is an appealing belief because it is individualistic and internally motivating; if you demonstrate the values of hard work, sincerity, honesty, responsibility, and dependability, you will be able to be a self-made man or woman in the United States.

The value of challenge is the belief that wisdom is gained only through great challenge and testing. It assumes that a person gains invaluable experience and knowledge through testing. This belief can be thought of as a rite of passage because when the person is tested (and responds successfully to the test), knowledge, strength, and power are achieved. From a cultural perspective, Americans like individuals in leadership positions to have been tested. It's one thing to have theoretical knowledge, book knowledge, or to be born with a silver spoon in one's mouth, but unless the individual has been "through some things" and has overcome them successfully, it is difficult to motivate others to action.

The value of humbleness is the belief in individuals who express knowledge but are modest and unassuming about their level of expertise. According to this belief a person can demonstrate superior intelligence and possess important information, but if the person is not humble, the individual can not be persuasive. American society does not like "know-it-alls." Rather, being humble and using "common logic" is the best way to influence others. American culture is full of folktales about individuals such as Abraham Lincoln who possessed ability and humbleness and became great leaders because of it.

The eternal return is the belief that the culture must return to a time in the past where things were perfect and harmonious. This belief emphasizes the need for stability in a society of rapid change. In addition, this belief is further strengthened by media reports that bombard individuals with messages of how imperfect the current society is. As a result, the eternal return appeals to those who long for a more simplistic time in the past when society was more harmonious.

Cultural beliefs are powerful appeals that can build identification with a diverse audience. As with cultural values, cultural beliefs are abstract ideals that individuals are continuously trying to achieve. Since individuals are continuously trying to achieve these ideas, speakers can always appeal to these cultural beliefs.

Maslow's Hierarchy of Needs

Another way for speakers to establish identification with a multicultural audience is to appeal to the motivations of the audience. A **motivation** is an internal drive that explains why people behave and act (or react) in a certain way when engaged in human communication.

Understanding an audience's motivation can be accomplished by discovering the needs of the audience. **Needs** are physical and psychological desires and wants. While everyone has different individual needs, researchers contend that our needs resemble one another's enough that our needs can be classified into distinct common categories.[21] The classification of motives and human needs is most often attributed to Abraham H. Maslow and what is called Maslow's hierarchy of needs. Maslow has categorized the following needs and wants which dictate human behavior.

The need for food, water, air, and sleep represent our physiological needs. **Physiological needs** are our basic needs essential for survival and basic bodily functions. According to Maslow, these basic needs are the strongest needs we have because until these needs are met, we cannot concern ourselves with other, higher needs.

The second level of motivation we have is the need for safety. **Safety needs** are our needs for a sense of well-being, safety, security, protection, and stability. Our safety needs also include the need for law and order, predictability, and the freedom from fear and chaos. Since we live in a world of rapid change and technological advances, people have a need for safety. The need for safety gives people a sense of stability in a world that appears to be rapidly changing.

Belonging and love needs represent our need for acceptance or approval from others. The need for belonging and love is a very powerful need because everyone has the need to be loved by others, especially family and friends. In addition, we have the need to feel a part of the community or a social group. In fact, one reason why people join groups is to fulfill the need for belonging and love.

The fourth level of motivation is esteem needs. **Esteem needs** are the needs for self-esteem based on the achievement, competence, freedom, and independence. Once we have satisfied our belonging and love needs, we have a desire and the need for self-esteem in order to enhance our reputation and status, along with achieving prestige and recognition.

According to Maslow, self-actualization is our highest level of needs. The need for **self-actualization** is the desire for self-fulfillment and the need to live up to your potential. Most people have the desire to be successful and to actualize their wants and dreams.

The audience's needs are a very important factor in communication and in audience analysis. Needs help explain why people behave the way they do. When we apply needs to public speaking, speakers can inform or persuade based upon how well the speech fulfills certain needs held by the audience. After all, in the persuasive speech, the purpose of the speaker is to make the audience aware of a need and then show them a way to fulfill or satisfy that need. However, speakers also appeal to needs in speeches that inform. Your audience will listen to and be interested in

4

your topic if you can show them *why* the topic is important and *how* it might affect them. This is what we will later call the *rationale* in public speaking.

This chapter has examined the importance of audience analysis in public speaking. In the act of public speaking, audience analysis is crucial. Speakers must learn as much as possible about the audience through careful research and preparation in order to adapt their message to the audience. All effective speakers attempt to adapt their messages to the demographics, culture, and motivations of their listeners.

VOCABULARY

Attribution — how we interpret the meaning of another person's behavior based upon our own past experience or history.

Audience — the people who gather in a public setting to receive a message from a speaker.

Audience analysis — to discover as much as possible about an audience so the speaker can adapt an appropriate message that meets the needs of the audience. Audience analysis includes discovering the demographics, cultural values, cultural beliefs, and motivations of the audience.

Audience-centered process — the idea that a speaker must direct all preparation and research toward the audience in order to make an effective presentation.

Beliefs — what we accept to be true.

Belonging and love needs — our need for acceptance or approval from others.

Close-ended questions — direct and restrictive questions that seek specific information and can often be answered with a simple "yes" or "no."

Co-culture — cultural values held by a group of individuals who exist within a larger dominant culture, which are referred to as co-cultures. A co-culture can be defined by one's nationality, ethnicity, or religion, such as Japanese culture, African American culture, or Jewish culture.

Collectivism — cultural value that emphasizes the importance of the group instead of the individual.

Common ground — when the speaker explains to the audience how a topic relates to the audience to establish a common interest between speaker and audience (similar to the concept of consubstantiality).

Consubstantiality — it is any attempt by the speaker to "become one" with the audience and establish some sort of common bond on an issue or problem (similar to the concept of common ground).

Cultural beliefs — what a majority of individuals in a culture believe to be true.

Culture — the traditions, customs, beliefs, values, norms, and perspectives that are learned through shared behavioral patterns and cultural practices that are passed down from generation to generation.

Cultural values — when values are held by most individuals in a culture.

Degree questions — enables individuals to answer a question based upon a continuum or scale.

Demographics — the characteristics of the audience, such as culture, ethnicity, and gender.

Dominant culture — those everyday norms and practices held by the majority of Americans.

Equality — a cultural value based upon the idea of treating people fairly in order to enjoy all the inalienable rights of citizenship.

Esteem needs — are the needs for self-esteem based on achievement, competence, freedom, and independence.

The eternal return — the cultural belief that the culture must return to a time in the past where things were perfect and harmonious.

Ethnicity — those individuals who have inherited a heritage that is based upon a common orientation to the past, ancestry, nationality, language, and religion.

The eyeball test — an arbitrary and confusing means of classifying a person's identity that was determined by laypersons (such as the hospital staff, census taker) who based their classification upon their own perceptions of race-based physical characteristics.

Face — the public self-image that a person wants to present in a specific social context.

Freedom — a cultural value based upon the constitutional right to basic freedoms such as the freedom of speech, freedom of the press, freedom of assembly, and freedom of religion.

High-context culture — the meanings of a communication message are imbedded in the situation, the relationship of the individuals, and the implicit norms, beliefs, and values of the culture.

Identification — is any attempt by the speaker to establish some sort of common ground on an issue or problem.

Individualism — cultural value that emphasizes the importance of the individual more than the group.

Liberty — a cultural value that emphasizes one's ability to live as one pleases (as long as it does not infringe on another person's right).

Low-context culture — the meanings of a communication message are directly communicated by individuals through the verbal expression of intentions, opinions, and thoughts.

Maslow's hierarchy of needs — a classification of motives and wants, attributed to Abraham H. Maslow, which dictate human behavior. The classification includes physiological needs, safety needs, belonging and love needs, esteem needs, and self-actualization needs.

Motivation — an internal drive that explains why people behave and act (or react) in a certain way when engaged in human communication.

Needs — are physical and psychological desires and wants.

Nonverbal feedback — any nonverbal response (such as facial expression, hand raise, or head nod) to a speaker's message.

Observation — one means of audience analysis that involves simply perceiving firsthand the characteristics of the audience.

One-drop rule — an arbitrary and confusing means of classifying a person's identity by determining that a single drop of Black blood in a person's ancestry makes a person Black.

Open-ended questions — general, broad, and far-reaching questions that allow for in-depth and detailed responses.

Perception — the way an individual uses the senses to interpret meaning.

Personal contact — one means of audience analysis where someone from the group or organization who invited a speaker to make a presentation, informs the speaker to the demographics, needs, and situational factors of the presentation.

Physiological needs — are our basic needs essential for survival and basic bodily functions.

Political identification — affiliation with a party and/or ideology that has specific ideas for how individuals in a given society should be governed.

The possibility of the success — the cultural belief that hard work will lead to success.

Questionnaire — a document (ranging from one page to several pages) that lists a series of questions for individuals to answer in order to receive specific information about the audience.

Race — a social construction that is based upon arbitrary and confusing classifications (such as the one-drop rule and the eyeball test) that are unscientific and illogical.

Rationale — the benefits and significance of the topic to the audience.

Safety needs — are our needs for a sense of well-being, safety, security, protection, and stability.

Self-actualization needs — is the desire for self-fulfillment and the need to live up to one's potential.

Social media – Internet-based tools that enable individuals to deliver a message.

Social networking – the act of using one or more social media to meet new individuals and/or maintain relationships with individuals.

Third-culture building — involves a speaker identifying common universal values that help the speaker and the multicultural audience create a new culture that draws from and extends the norms and values from the independent cultures.

The value of challenge — the cultural belief that wisdom is gained only through great challenge and testing.

The value of humbleness — the cultural belief in individuals who possess knowledge but are modest and unassuming.

Values — deeply ingrained social morals that are shaped by culture.

Verbal feedback — any verbal response (such as a question) to a speaker's message.

REFERENCES

[1] Lloyd Bitzer, "The Rhetorical Situation," *Philosophy and Rhetoric 1* (1968): 1–14.

[2] Guo-Ming Chen and William J. Starosta, *Foundations of Intercultural Communication* (Lanham, MD: University Press of America, 2005), 7.

[3] Chen and Starosta, 35.

[4] Jerry Seper, "Hispanics take political aim at Arizona's law." *The Washington Times*, (17 May 2010), A4.

[5] Everett M. Rogers and Thomas M. Steinfatt, *Intercultural Communication* (Prospect Heights, IL: Waveland Press, 1999), 150.

[6] Edward T. Hall, *Beyond Culture* (Garden City, NY: Anchor Press, 1976).

[7] Rogers and Steinfatt, 154–155.

[8] Chen and Starosta, 51.

[9] Lester Thonnssen, A. Craig Baird, and Waldo W. Braden, *Speech Criticism*, 2nd edition, (New York: The Ronald Press Company, 1970), 433.

[10] Mark P. Orbe and Tina M. Harris, *Interracial Communication* (USA: Wadsworth, 2001), 41–42.

[11] Lea Stewart, Pamela Cooper, Alan Stewart, and Sheryl Friedley, *Communication and Gender*, 3rd ed. (Boston: Allyn and Bacon, 1998), 7–8.

[12] Mitch Potter, "Iraqi Protest Turns Tragic." *Toronto Star* (4 March 2003), A14.

[13] Ralph R. Behnke, Dan O'Hair, and Audrey Hardman, "Audience Analysis Systems in Advertising and Marketing," *Applied Communication Theory and Research*, eds. Dan O'Hair and Gary L. Kreps (Hillsdale, NJ: Lawrence Erlbaum Associates, 1990), 203–21.

[14] Kenneth Burke, *A Rhetoric of Motives* (Berkeley: University of California Press, 1969), 19–23. First edition published by Prentice-Hall Inc., 1950.

[15] Burke, 20–21.

[16] Thonnssen, Baird, and Braden, 90.

[17] Chen and Starosta, 7.

[18] Orbe and Harris, 135.

[19] Timothy J. Brown, "Deconstructing the Dialectical Tensions in The Horse Whisperer: How Myths Represent Competing Cultural Values," *Journal of Popular Culture* 38.2 (2004): 274–295.

[20] Charles Larson, *Persuasion: Reception and Responsibility*, 12th edition (Boston: Wadsworth, 2010), 235–241.

[21] Abraham H. Maslow, *Motivation and Personality* (New York: Harper & Row, 1954).

DISABILITIES AND PUBLIC SPEAKING 5

"Don't give up. Don't lose hope. Don't sell out."
–Christopher Reeve

"Conquering any difficulty always gives one a secret joy, for it means pushing back a boundary-ne and adding to one's liberty."
–Henri Frederic Amiel

"When I hear somebody sigh, 'Life is hard,' I am always tempted to ask, 'Compared to what?'"
–Sidney Harris

This Chapter Examines:

+ defining disability

+ building community

+ building identification with persons with disabilities

+ strategies for persons with disabilities

For Blair Hornstine, a Moorestown (N.J.) High School senior, being named vale-dictorian was a great honor. During her high school career, the aspiring lawyer earned 23 grades of A+ in achieving a 4.68 grade point average. Furthermore, she scored 1570 out of 1600 on her SAT. Despite her achievements, however, school officials attempted to change the criteria for valedictorian because some believed Hornstine had an unfair advantage—due to an immune deficiency disorder, she was able to take some classes at home. Hornstine decided to fight the proposal and filed a lawsuit to prevent the school from allowing co-valedictorians. After hearing the case, the judge agreed with Hornstine and said, "If forced to share the award, the stigma would likely be unshakeable. She would be seen as 'the dis-abled valedictorian,' not the 'valedictorian.' "[1]

The highly publicized case of Blair Hornstine, in addition to emphasizing the ever-present problem of discrimination in today's society, highlights a significant portion of the population who are often overlooked—persons with disabilities. This is especially true in the area of public speaking. Many textbooks discuss audience analysis, but few address the demographic of persons with disabilities in a substantial manner. Omitting persons with disabilities is surprising considering that 20% of the U.S. population (or 45 million people) and nearly 9% of students who enter post-secondary education have a disability.[2]

Although persons with disabilities continue to overcome societal barriers, the passage of the Americans with Disabilities Act has helped persons with disabilities to participate more fully in society. The **Americans with Disabilities Act** is a federal law that prohibits discrimination on the basis of disability in employment, state and local government programs, transportation, public accommodations, and telecommunications. The act was revolutionary because it covered any public institution—whether it received federal financial assistance or not. The act mandates that public services, programs, and activities must be readily accessible and usable by persons with disabilities. This means that institutions of higher education must provide accommodations for students with disabilities that allow for their full participation in services, programs, and activities. This issue of accommodations was what the Hornstine case was centered upon. The school district attempted to penalize Hornstine for the accommodations it created and which are required by law.[3]

Given our focus on multicultural audiences and the lack of attention persons with disabilities are given, we continue our discussion of *audience analysis* by focusing on disabilities and public speaking. Speakers need to be knowledgeable of and skillful in adapting messages to multicultural audiences that include persons with disabilities. Therefore, in this chapter, we discuss what disabilities are and how to create a supportive and inclusive environment for persons with disabilities. We also consulted a few distinguished individuals with disabilities to gain personal insight into how to build *identification* with persons with disabilities and to provide public speaking strategies for persons with disabilities.

DEFINING DISABILITY

A **person with a disability** is defined as "someone with a physical or mental impairment that substantially limits one or more major life activities."[4] The Americans with Disabilities Act further clarifies that a person is considered to have a disability when the disability is directly observable, when the person has a record of the disability, and/or when the person is considered to have a disability (as determined through testing). Although we refer to people with disabilities as a homogenous group, the type of disability creates various lived experiences (which need different types of accommodations). For example, a person with a mobility impairment will obviously have different needs than a person with a visual impairment.

What are the different types of disabilities? Disabilities vary depending on how the disability is defined, but some of the most common disabilities include: learning disabilities, attention deficit disorder, mobility impairments, visual impairments, and hearing impairments. **Learning disabilities** are characterized as difficulties in demonstrating effective listening, speaking, reading, writing, reasoning, and/or mathematical skills. Interestingly, individuals with learning disabilities comprise the largest number of disabilities in higher education. **Attention deficit disorder** includes a multitude of difficulties with concentration and paying attention. Often, attention deficit disorder is manifested by impulsiveness and hyperactivity. **Mobility impairments** include a wide range of causes such as cerebral palsy, muscular dystrophy, and multiple sclerosis. Mobility impairments can also be caused by accidents that cause traumatic brain injury. Regardless of the cause, mobility impairments affect people's ability to walk, write, and/or talk. **Visual impairments** affect a person's ability to see or prevents him/her from seeing at all, while **hearing impairments** prevent individuals from hearing effectively or from hearing at all.

5

Although there are a variety of disabilities, speakers should be prepared to adapt a message to persons with disabilities. One way for speakers to be prepared is to build community for a public presentation. This idea is discussed next.

BUILDING COMMUNITY

In Chapter 4 we discussed the importance of establishing identification with a multicultural audience. **Identification** is any attempt by the speaker to establish a common bond with the audience. Effective public speakers create identification with persons with disabilities by factoring these disabilities into their audience analysis. **Audience analysis** is the process of discovering as much as possible about an audience so the speaker can adapt an appropriate message that meets the needs of the audience. We believe that before identification can be achieved, speakers must build community by creating a supportive and inclusive environment. **Inclusive** means there is a general acceptance and understanding of cultural differences and the recognition that differences are unique and valuable.

Building community starts in the classroom. It can be facilitated by the instructor, but it is the responsibility of everyone to create a supportive environment.[5] A teaching principle that helps build a supportive and inclusive environment is called universal instruction design. **Universal instruction design** (UID) is the designing of instructional materials and activities that allow learning goals to be achieved by individuals with wide differences in abilities, regardless of a person's disability. The aim of UID is to eliminate the barriers between classroom instruction and a student's learning style, ability, and/or disability.[6] UID is a teaching method that requires instructors to rethink how they teach a course and revise the course where appropriate in order to accommodate unique learning styles and disabilities. For example, if an instructor has a hearing impaired student in class, the instructor should have lecture notes available through an online course management system such as Blackboard or D2L for the student to access and review.

The key to UID is to have multiple means of representation, engagement, and expression in the classroom. Representation means instructors should have essential class materials such as syllabi, handouts, assignments, readings, and study guides available in hard copy and in electronic form. With UID offering multiple means of engagement means providing a variety of ways to convey information, such as through small group discussion, critical thinking exercises, and group projects. Meanwhile, multiple forms of expression means evaluating students in a variety of ways, such as through papers, short writing assignments, examinations, participation, homework assignments, and group projects. Similarly, examinations should be comprised of different components such as objective, essay, and short-answer questions.

We have deliberately discussed how UID is used to build a supportive and inclusive environment in the classroom because UID is an important principle that speakers can follow in order to establish identification with persons with disabilities. When speakers make a presentation that is adapted to different learning styles and disabilities it enables persons with disabilities to be fully engaged in the presentation. These strategies will be further discussed in the next section.

BUILDING IDENTIFICATION WITH PERSONS WITH DISABILITIES

We interviewed some prominent persons with disabilities who engage in public speaking to gain their insights into how a speaker can build identification with multicultural audiences that include persons with disabilities.[7] The key is being aware of difference and using that awareness to adapt a message appropriately. From our interviews we have summarized the following themes that explain how speakers can build identification with people with disabilities.

Be Mindful of Disabilities when Conducting Your Audience Analysis

Often speakers overlook disabilities when analyzing the audience. In order to establish identification with persons with disabilities, the speaker must plan ahead. Although as a speaker, you might not be responsible for where the presentation will take place or the quality of the sound system, these are questions you should ask when planning the presentation. Don't assume the room (or the building) is accessible for people with disabilities or that it is wired for a multimedia presentation. If a person with a disability is not able to fully participate in (or attend) your presentation due to accessibility difficulties, you as a speaker have missed a great opportunity to make the presentation inclusive.

Have Materials Prepared in Multiple Formats

As we mentioned, UID is an excellent way to build a supportive and inclusive environment for persons with disabilities. When preparing your presentation, think of multiple ways information/materials can be conveyed and/or accessed. For example, speakers can have information accessible online. Also, speakers can have the presentation recorded. If a media clip is used during the presentation, it should have closed captioning to accommodate hearing-impaired individuals.

Explain Presentational Aids

We live in a visual age where we like to see information being presented. Therefore, multimedia presentations that use PowerPoint are able to convey words, images, and video to an audience, which saves the speaker from discussing everything. When this is done, however, it prevents individuals with visual impairments from fully engaging in the presentation. When using any type of presentational aid that is visual, the speaker should also state the main points that are on the presentational slide or handout. Images and media clips should be explained in detail in order to accommodate individuals who are visually impaired (see Chapter 14 for a full discussion of presentational aids).

Address the Person and Not the Interpreter

Sometimes there are questions and answers as part of a presentation. These are excellent ways for speakers to interact with and adapt to audiences. If you are in a situation where you are receiving a question from someone who is hearing impaired through an interpreter, it is important to address the person and not the interpreter. When speakers only look at the interpreter, the hearing-impaired person might be offended, because the speaker is not addressing or looking at them. Instead, the speaker should look at the person when responding and include frequent pauses (if it is a long answer) to allow the interpreter to follow and sign what the speaker is saying. This is a simple but important way to include the person in the conversation.

Acknowledge Nonverbals

Another way to be inclusive and sensitive to the needs of persons with disabilities (if the group is small enough) is to acknowledge their nonverbals. This is especially true for individuals who are sight impaired. Since the sight-impaired person might not know if they are called upon or if they are responding at the right time, the speaker needs to acknowledge their nonverbals to indicate when they can respond. For example, if it is during a question and answer session, the speaker can simply acknowledge the person by saying, "Ma'am, I see your hand, and I will respond to you next."

Ask How to Be Inclusive

Sometimes persons with disabilities who are in a wheelchair are ignored as audience members because they are positioned in front of the first row (this is especially true of large auditoriums, where the speaker on stage is looking out towards the audience and not down at the space in front of the first row). Therefore, the speaker is not in position to make direct eye contact with the person with the disability. This can result in the person with the disability feeling isolated from the rest of the audience. According to our consultant, "If a person looks out of place then he/she probably is." It is a good idea for the speaker to approach the individual (before the presentation and not over the microphone) to ask him/her if his/her spot is a good place to be positioned for the presentation. If the position is not in a good place, ask if something can be done for the person to move to a more appropriate place.

Facilitate Interaction

Incorporating audience interaction is an effective way for speakers to maintain audience attention and interest in a presentation. Speakers, however, should be aware that a person with a disability might need a little help being placed into a group. For example, a person with a wheelchair might be isolated if a speaker asks for individuals to break into small groups. In theater auditoriums where the person with the disability is up front, it is difficult for the person to get down a side aisle towards everyone in the front. In this case the speaker should organize a group of individuals to meet down front. This would help eliminate some awkwardness.

Avoid Offensive Language

In Chapter 11, we discuss how to avoid offensive language by eliminating *stereotypes*, *sexist language*, and *marking language* (see Chapter 11 for a full discussion of these concepts). Speakers also need to be mindful of their language when addressing a multicultural audience. Whether what was said was intentional or not, multicultural audiences can be unforgiving towards a speaker who is perceived to be offensive, insensitive, or ignorant. Therefore, the label "persons with disabilities" is preferable to the label "handicapped." The choice of labels is important because the meaning associated with the phrase "handicapped" signifies that the person is defined by his or her disability, whereas the phrase "persons with disabilities" acknowledges the disability without making the disability the sum and total of who that person is. Finally, eliminate flippant remarks that might seem harmless but can be offensive such as saying someone is "blind as a bat" or that a comment left you "crippled."

When speakers are able to incorporate these strategies into their preparations, they not only are making their presentation more inclusive, but they are implementing the principles of UID. UID is also a means for speakers to achieve third-culture building to establish identification with the audience. **Third-culture**

building involves a speaker identifying common universal values that help the speaker and the multicultural audience create a new culture that draws from and extends the norms and values from the independent cultures.

STRATEGIES FOR PERSONS WITH DISABILITIES

Our chapter on disabilities and public speaking would not be complete without providing some presentation strategies for individuals with disabilities who are engaged in public speaking. Again, we rely on the insights of our consultants who emphasized many of the principles of public speaking that apply to any public speaker, such as organization, clarity, gaining the audience's attention, logic, and appealing to the audience's emotions. However, they mentioned additional strategies that are relevant for persons with disabilities, which are discussed below.

Managing Disability

One of the most challenging issues for public speakers with disabilities is how the audience perceives them. For individuals who are affected by a learning disability this might not be as important as for individuals whose disability is observable to the audience.

How the person with the disability manages this issue is an individual and personal matter as our consultants differed in regards to managing their disability in front of an audience. One consultant explained that when making a presentation his job is to present information and not to inform the audience about his disability. The consultant explained that an audience does not need to know the cause of his disability in order to learn, be informed, or persuaded even when discussing disability issues. This consultant only uses personal experience when discussing a disability issue if it is relevant and provides greater understanding for the audience.

Meanwhile, another consultant takes the opposite perspective. The consultant believes that persons with disabilities should be mindful of their disability because audiences tend to be focused on the disability anyway. This consultant believes that the speaker can turn the disability into an asset by talking about it in order to put the audience at ease (which eliminates the barrier between speaker and audience). Moreover, addressing the disability enables the consultant to become more personable with the audience. Another consultant explained that when you acknowledge the disability right away, it disarms any doubts or negative thoughts the audience might have. This consultant equated the disability to an "elephant" in the room that must be addressed. The consultant discussed that as much as a speaker wants to avoid the elephant, if the elephant is not addressed, it will haunt the speaker for the rest of the presentation. Furthermore, the consultant explained that you don't have to have a "pity party"; just explain to the audience the nature of the disability and how you have feelings and experiences that are similar with everyone else. Addressing the disability helps create **empathy** and identification with the audience.

Again, these are two different perspectives that are based upon individual choices for how to manage disability in a presentation. Each person with a disability will have to decide for him- or herself how to address the issue. Most of the time experience, context, and personality will influence how speakers manage their disability.

Preparation

Preparation is a strategy that is helpful for all speakers regardless if they have a disability or not. We emphasize preparation for persons with disabilities because it was a theme that was expressed by all our consultants. Leave no detail to chance. Speakers should check the room and facilities where the presentation will take place to identify any problems ahead of time. For example, the speaker should check access to the building and the stage, the location of the lights, and the sound system. If the speaker needs the podium or microphone repositioned or help with the lights, these issues can be addressed and taken care of ahead of time. Furthermore, audience analysis, organization of ideas, planning of materials, and practicing the speech all need to be accomplished in order to make an effective presentation. Most of this textbook deals with how to prepare for a presentation, and reading Chapters 4, 6, 7, 8, 9, 10, 11, 12, 13, and 14 will provide speakers with a comprehensive understanding of how to prepare for a presentation.

Establishing Authority (Ethos)

When speakers are thoroughly prepared it helps to establish the speakers' authority or ethos for the presentation. **Ethos**, also known as credibility, is the audience's perception of the speaker's integrity, honesty, knowledge, and competence (see Chapters 12 and 13). The consultants discussed how a person's demeanor is just as important as the content. If the speaker appears to be confident, then that is how the audience will perceive the speaker. In fact, one consultant explained that persons with disabilities have to have more credibility because audiences tend to make judgments based on what they see. According to one consultant, credibility for the speaker with a disability is not automatic. Therefore, the speaker needs to establish it up front with the audience. In addition, the consultants stressed that persons with disabilities should remember they are in charge during the presentation and they are the experts on the topic. The confidence the speaker demonstrates in the presentation will dispel any doubts or limitations the audience might have placed on the speaker before the presentation.

Monitoring the Audience

Depending on the type of disability, the speaker might have to incorporate ways to monitor the feedback of the audience. For example, visually impaired speakers might want to "check in" periodically with questions to maintain audience attention and interest. With experience, the visually impaired speaker will also be able to get a sense of audience feedback through nonverbal feedback such as laughter, gasps, or unnecessary chatter.

This chapter provides a unique and long overdue discussion of disabilities and public speaking. We believe this chapter begins an important discussion that needs to be investigated and studied in more detail in order to teach speakers how to create supportive and inclusive environments for persons with disabilities who are part of a multicultural audience. In addition, this chapter has initiated the discussion of how to build identification with persons with disabilities and identified public speaking strategies for the speaker with a disability.

VOCABULARY

Americans with Disabilities Act — a federal law that prohibits discrimination on the basis of disability in employment, state and local government programs, transportation, public accommodations, and telecommunications.

Attention deficit disorder — a disability that includes a multitude of difficulties with concentration and paying attention.

Audience analysis — is the process of discovering as much as possible about an audience so the speaker can adapt an appropriate message that meets the needs of the audience (see Chapter 4).

Empathy — involves demonstrating respect and understanding for another by projecting yourself into the other person's position.

Ethos — also known as credibility, it is the audience's perception of the speaker's integrity, honesty, knowledge, and competence (see Chapters 12 and 13).

Hearing impairments — a disability that prevents individuals from hearing effectively or at all.

Identification — is any attempt by the speaker to establish a common bond with the audience (see Chapter 4).

Inclusive — means there is a general acceptance and understanding of cultural differences and the recognition that differences are unique and valuable.

Learning disabilities — a disability that is characterized as difficulties in demonstrating effective listening, speaking, reading, writing, reasoning, and/or mathematical skills.

Mobility impairments — a disability that includes a wide range of causes such as cerebral palsy, muscular dystrophy, multiple sclerosis, and/or accidents that cause traumatic brain injury.

Person with disabilities — is defined as "someone with a physical or mental impairment that substantially limits one or more major life activities."

Third-culture building — involves a speaker identifying common universal values that help the speaker and the multicultural audience create a new culture that draws from and extends the norms and values from the independent cultures (see Chapters 4 and 11).

Universal instruction design (UID) — the designing of instructional materials and activities that allow learning goals to be achieved by individuals with wide differences in learning styles, abilities, and/or disability.

Visual impairments — a disability that affects a person's ability to see or prevents them from seeing at all.

5

REFERENCES

[1] Qtd. in John Shiffman and Toni Callas, "Disabled S. Jersey Senior is Ruled Sole Valedictorian" *Philadelphia Inquirer* (9 May 2003), A1.

[2] Office of Services for Students with Disabilities. *Handbook on Disabilities.* (West Chester, PA: West Chester University Press, 2001), 10.

[3] Shiffman and Callas, A12.

[4] *Handbook on Disabilities*, 12.

[5] Mark P. Orbe and Tina M. Harris, *Interracial Communication* (USA: Wadsworth, 2001). 17–20.

[6] Martin Patwell, Coordinator Services for Students with Disabilities, West Chester University, personal interview (24 April 2003).

[7] Paul Longmore, Professor of History, San Francisco State University, phone interview (22 May 2003), John W. Smith, Associate Professor of Rhetoric, Ohio University, phone interview (29 April 2003), Lori Holm, Ph.D. candidate in Broadcast Journalism, Ohio University, phone interview (30 May 2003); Paul Longmore is a Professor of History at San Francisco State University. In addition to teaching early American history courses, Dr. Longmore is a frequent presenter on disability rights. Among his publications, Dr. Longmore is the author of *Why I Burned My Book*, which provides a detailed analysis of disability issues from historical, social, and cultural perspectives. Also, he is the co-editor of the book *The New Disabilities History*. John W. Smith is an Associate Professor of Rhetoric at Ohio University. Dr. Smith is also President of the National Chapter of the Blind of Southeastern Ohio. As president, Dr. Smith has worked with businesses and public institutions in the Midwest to implement accommodations for people with visual impairments (such has having Braille menus available at restaurants). In addition, Dr. Smith is a presenter on African American issues and disabilities, and he performs as a gospel singer. Lori Holm is a Ph.D. candidate in Broadcast Journalism at Ohio University. Professor Holm is an instructor of public speaking and one of her research interests focuses upon disabilities and communication.

TOPIC SELECTION AND RESEARCH 6

"Try to know everything of something, and something of everything."
–Henry Peter

"We can invent only with memory."
–Alphonse Karr

"We do not know one millionth of one percent about anything."
–Thomas Alva Edison

This Chapter Examines:

+ developing topic ideas

+ refining your topic

+ information literacy

+ researching your topic: online research

+ examples of references

As her first speech drew nearer, Sally struggled to choose a topic. She thought about giving a speech on CPR (Cardio-Pulmonary Resuscitation), but she could not decide what information to talk about or where to begin with a topic as broad as CPR. She also thought about speaking about the topic of origami (the art of paper folding), but she did not think her audience would be interested in that topic. It seemed every topic she considered was not good enough for a speech topic. However, she would have to decide on a topic quickly, because her speech was less than a week away.

Choosing a topic does not have to be as difficult as Sally and most other speakers perceive it to be. Almost any topic that falls within ethical, moral, and social standards can be an appropriate speech topic. Selecting an appropriate topic is dependent on how developed and refined the topic is, how much new information is presented, and how well the topic is adapted to the audience. It is also important to select a topic as early as possible to give yourself enough time to research, prepare, and practice your speech. In Sally's case, she is discovering ideas, but she is not systematically developing ideas that will lead to a more focused topic. Plus, she is not giving herself enough time to properly research, organize, and practice the speech. You do not want to increase your speech anxiety by waiting until the last minute to select a topic. Find a topic early so you can begin researching your topic. In this chapter, we will discuss strategies for selecting a topic and for researching a topic.

DEVELOPING TOPIC IDEAS

When searching for a speech topic, try to generate as many ideas as possible. It is important to generate many ideas for a speech because the more ideas you generate, the more topic options you will have. An efficient way to generate topic ideas is to be systematic in your topic selection. When you use a systematic method for topic selection, you follow a logical thought pattern in generating topic ideas.

Usually, for any speech you have a wide range of topics that can be considered. Therefore, do not limit yourself when attempting to generate ideas. We will look at five systematic ways you can generate speech topics.

Consider Personal Experience and Knowledge

One of the best places to begin your topic search is to consider your own personal experience and knowledge. People usually overlook their personal experiences, but they can be a great place to begin your topic search. When you consider your personal experiences such as traveling, occupations, educational experiences, special occasions, activities, or hobbies, you can develop these experiences into a speech topic. For example, one student who had vacationed in England and visited Stonehenge decided to give an informative speech on Stonehenge. Since the student was already familiar with the topic, she had an idea of what information she wanted to talk about. All she had to do was find some additional information to fill in the gaps. All of us have developed knowledge in certain areas because we all have different interests, hobbies, and goals. Any one of these personal interests could be probed to generate possible topics.

Consider Brainstorming

Sometimes people have difficulty seeing anything relevant from their own personal experience and knowledge. In this case, it might be more helpful for the person to brainstorm ideas. Brainstorming is when you generate as many speech topic ideas as possible to produce a quantity of ideas rather than quality. Do not be concerned with the quality of ideas early in the process, because later you can refine your ideas. Once a speaker has listed as many ideas as possible, then the speaker can decide which topics might be appropriate speech topics. Sometimes brainstorming is difficult for a person to do, because this freestyle approach is too broad and too unstructured. In these instances, the person might want to try more structured forms of brainstorming. The person can try brainstorming by category, by narrowing down, and by clustering.

Figure 6-1. Brainstorming

Brainstorming by Category

When a speaker lists several topics on a piece of paper and then fills in related subjects underneath each topic, this is called **brainstorming by category**. For example, the speaker can list personal categories such as *Interests, Hobbies, Experiences,* and *Activities* or general categories such as *Persons, Events, Occasions, Current Topics,* and *Entertainment*. As you can see, there is really no limit in how a person can set up categories. Again, the speaker should try to fill in as many topics as possible for each category.

Brainstorming by Narrowing

When a speaker starts with a general topic and then makes each general topic more specific, this is called **brainstorming by narrowing**. Often after brainstorming, a speaker is left with broad topics that need to be made more specific in order to be an appropriate speech topic. A speaker can start with a general category such as *Entertainment* and narrow it down until it becomes a more specific topic. Take the following example:

1) Entertainment → 2) Amusement Parks → 3) Disney World → 4) New Rides at Disney World

In this example, the speaker started with the general topic of *Entertainment* and narrowed the topic to *New Rides at Disney World*. When speakers do this for each topic, they will have a lot of possibilities for a speech topic.

Brainstorming by Clustering

Brainstorming by clustering is when you start with an idea and then form associations that radiate out from the original idea. For example:

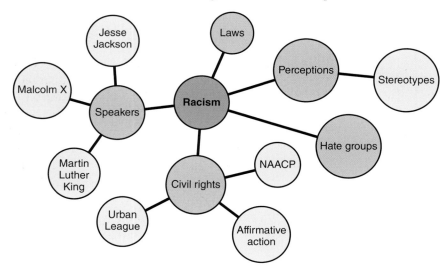

When you start with one idea and then branch out to other ideas, you will have generated plenty of options for speech topics. In the example above, the original idea was *Racism*. The speaker developed a series of associations from this idea that generated many possible topics. Some of the topics need to be more specific, but all of the topics have the potential to be developed into speech topics.

Consider Current Topics

Another way to generate speech topics is by considering current topics. There are always new topics waiting to be explored and discussed in class. Sometimes you can find new and interesting topics by keeping abreast of current events and by listening to what people are talking about. Some examples of current topics that have been developed into speech topics include: Political Correctness, Airport Security, Bioterrorism, LASIK Vision Correction, Human Growth Hormone, Bilingual Education, and Consumer Debt. An advantage of using current topics is that your information will be new and refreshing for your audience.

Consider Researching Topics That Interest You

Most of us have interests that for one reason or another we have never had the opportunity to explore. Giving a speech on topics that interest us but we don't know a lot about allows us to investigate those interests. What have you always been curious about or wanted to know more about? For example, maybe you have always wanted to visit Cancun, Mexico, or you have a desire to go mountain climbing, or you have always wanted to open your own business, but you have never explored any of these interests. Any one of these interests could easily be developed into a speech topic.

Consider Browsing Topics

For individuals who might have difficultly identifying a topic by the strategies we have already mentioned, it might be helpful to browse topics on the Internet or inquire about topics through social media (which can be another means for locating a current topic). Later on in the chapter we do stress the importance of using credible sources for locating sources for a speech whether it is a specialized research database such as EBSCOhost or free search engines such as Google Scholar. However, the Internet and social media can be useful in generating ideas for a speech topic (and in learning more about the interests of specific audiences). The key is using your browsing and/or the use of social media as a starting point— let the Internet and/or social media assist you in identifying a topic. Then, you can research your topic using credible research databases to locate sources for your speech.

Consider Reference Materials

Another strategy for generating topic ideas that can be combined with browsing topics, is consulting reference materials. Reference materials enable speakers to identify information on their topic in a short amount of time. This includes general reference materials such as **encyclopedias** that are helpful in providing detailed and precise facts, statistics, and general information on your topic. If you are unsure about how to define or narrow your topic, consult a reference source to help you understand the dimensions of your topic. When speakers understand the big picture, they can more intelligently narrow their topic.

After you have browsed through reference materials, you can make a more informed judgment as to what information you would like to further research. While most of us are familiar with hardbound volumes of reference materials, most reference materials are now contained online, which makes obtaining this information even easier.

Consider Asking for Help

When all else fails, ask for help. Talk to your friends, family, classmates, and your professor about your speech topic. In the process of discussing ideas, you might be directed to a possible topic. At the very least, you will be able to develop a list of possible ideas that you can further refine by one of the three brainstorming methods.

We have listed five general ways you can generate topic ideas for your speech. These methods are very useful in helping students generate topic ideas. It is important to remember that whatever method you use, allow your creativity to guide your generation of topic ideas. When you can uniquely perceive a topic, it is more likely that you will present your topic to the audience in a new and interesting manner.

REFINING YOUR TOPIC

After you have generated topic ideas, it is time to refine your topic. Refining a topic is important because you need to narrow down your topic to make your topic more manageable to research. We will discuss five guidelines to follow that will help you refine your topic. Following these guidelines will help you adapt your speech topic to the public speaking setting.

A Focused Topic

One problem speakers have is not effectively narrowing their topic to fit the time constraints of the public speaking situation. Even the topics we identified earlier need to be more focused and precise for the assigned speech. An example of a speech that can be further narrowed is the previous informative speech, *New Rides at Disney World*. There might be ten new rides at Disney World. If the speaker is giving a six to eight minute classroom speech, this is not enough time to properly cover, in detail, all ten rides. The speaker would be wise to narrow the topic to inform the audience of three or four new rides at Disney World. This is a more focused and precise speech topic that will make research and preparation much more manageable. Plus, the speaker will be able to fit the speech into the time constraints of the assignment.

A Topic That Interests You

Have you ever had to write a research paper about a topic in which you were not very interested? If you have, it was probably a very tedious and frustrating experience that you struggled to complete, because you did not care about the topic. The same holds true for public speaking. However, unlike a paper where your lack of enthusiasm is private, in a speech your lack of enthusiasm will be public. The audience will be able to perceive you are not interested in your topic by a lack of passion, a lack of preparedness, and an unpolished delivery. You will appear as though you are "going through the motions." You want to avoid this problem by picking a topic you are interested in so you will be motivated to prepare and deliver a good speech.

A Topic That Is Interesting to the Audience

In Chapter 4, we discussed how to use audience analysis to help you adapt your speech to the audience's interests. At this stage in the development of your speech, you will benefit from conducting an audience analysis. For example, if a speaker has a passion for exercise as a speech topic, the use of research databases can be used to tailor the topic to the audience. Thus, the speaker could research "exercise and college students" to determine what has been done, in addition to adapting the topic to the audience. Use the information you gathered from the audience to adapt your information to them so your speech is interesting and relevant to them. Furthermore, social media sites can be explored to determine more specific information about college students and exercise. Thus, when speakers take the time to adapt the topic (and specific information in the topic) identification can be achieved, which makes for a more relevant speech for the audience. As defined in Chapter 4, **identification** is any attempt by the speaker to establish some sort of common ground with the audience on an issue or problem.

A Topic That Presents New Information

In a speech class, some topics are more popular than others. Therefore, it is sometimes not possible to pick a totally new topic. However, just because you have a common topic, does not mean you have to present a speech that only repeats what the audience already knows about the topic. *It is your job as the speaker to incorporate new information into your speech that makes your speech interesting and keeps your audience's attention.* If you research your topic thoroughly, you will be able to discover new information on your topic that you can incorporate into your speech. Some topics, however, are so overdone that regardless of whatever new information you might find, the topic is a "turn off" to the audience. Students are commonly asked to avoid speech topics such as smoking, drunk driving, abortion, gun control, and capital punishment because most audience members have been saturated with information about these topics. Try to avoid cliché topics and concentrate on topics that can yield new information.

Select a Topic That Is Appropriate to the Situation

As a public speaker, you are responsible for meeting all the ethical, moral, social, and speech guidelines for your presentation. You should not try to intentionally offend or attack individuals or groups; you should not misrepresent information; and you should not plagiarize. You do not want to undermine your own credibility by not meeting the appropriate standards for the public speaking situation.

Another important part of meeting the appropriate standards of the public speaking situation is to have your topic conform to one of the three general purposes of a speech: to inform, to persuade, or to entertain. In Chapter 8, we further discuss the three general purposes of a speech and how they help you organize and outline your speech. However, at this stage of refining your topic, all you need to know is the general purpose of your speech. Your general purpose will help guide you in determining what specific information you will need when you research your topic. For the remainder of this chapter, we will talk about what sources you can consult to obtain more information on your topic. Once you obtain all your information, you will be ready to start organizing and outlining your speech, as discussed in Chapter 8.

INFORMATION LITERACY

Up until this point, we have discussed strategies for generating topic ideas. An important but often overlooked aspect of selecting and researching a topic is giving yourself enough time to locate, review, and identify information that you can use to build your speech. There are no "short cuts" to obtaining credible sources in order to construct a speech. When speakers are able to incorporate information from credible sources into their speech, it is an effective means for bolstering the speaker's **ethos** and **logos** in the presentation. Thus, we emphasize that speakers must go beyond "googling" a topic on the Internet and using the information for a speech.

Although the Internet provides a speaker with a wealth of information very quickly, the information obtained should be scrutinized thoroughly. Since information does not go through as rigorous a review process as sources that have been peer reviewed or reviewed by an editor (or an editorial board), information posted on a Web site can be inaccurate, altered, misrepresented, and/or plagiarized.[1] Also, some Web sites that might look credible are really sites produced by special-interest organizations who are pushing covert agendas. In addition, always be wary of information from individual homepages because the information might be biased, inaccurate, and dated. Finally, speakers need to be mindful that any information downloaded such as photos, text, and video clips are protected by the same copyright laws as printed material.

The accessibility of information on the Internet has shifted the gatekeeping and evaluative process from editors to individuals who are accessing information. Thus, the importance of evaluating information is even more critical.[2] This is why we stress conducting research for your topic using specialized research databases. By **database**, we are referring to a search engine that contains a specialized collection of information that can be accessed electronically (see the Online Research section that follows).

While researching a topic might seem like the least appealing aspect of public speaking, the skills learned are valuable and enhance one's ability to demonstrate information literacy. **Information literacy** is the ability for individuals to locate information from reliable sources, to evaluate the credibility of the information, and to incorporate it appropriately into a speech. We will discuss how to achieve information literacy by first discussing the types of sources followed by several tests of evidence individuals can employ to evaluate sources. We complete the chapter by addressing online research and strategies for researching a topic.

Type of Sources

An important step in achieving information literacy is to understand the categories for sources. Each category defines a level of credibility for the information. Speakers need to be aware of the type of source and the reliability/credibility of the information. Sources can be classified into three types: primary, secondary, and tertiary.

A **primary source** includes documents, physical objects, original works, or eyewitness accounts that were created during the actual historical time period that is being examined. When speakers have a primary source, they can observe the actual time period or event without the source being filtered through the interpretation of someone else. A few examples of primary sources include but are not limited to: speeches, interviews (legal proceedings, transcripts, etc.), data/statistical documents, creative works (novels, etc.), and broadcast transcripts.

A great advantage of a primary source is that individuals can observe and evaluate the original document in its entirety in order to reach their own conclusion. For example, the evidence an individual would obtain from viewing a speech of the President would be much more valuable than simply relying on newspaper articles of the President's speech. Newspaper articles will select specific parts of the President's speech, which influences the writing of the story and thus the evidence that can be gathered from it. Moreover, additional factors such as the type of newspaper and reporter bias will also impact the evidence presented in the article. Instead, if individuals viewed the actual speech of the President, they would be able to observe the speech in its entirety and make their own interpretation and evaluation of the speech

A **secondary source** is a document that was created after the actual time period that is being examined. A secondary source does not enable the researcher to observe the evidence in its entirety. Instead, secondary sources provide analysis, interpretation, and evaluation of a primary source. The authors of secondary sources offer explanations and descriptions of primary sources, often quoting them within the text of the work. It is not uncommon for a secondary source to use primary sources as evidence to present a particular opinion or point of view. A few examples of secondary sources include but are not limited to: biographies, journal articles, newspaper articles, etc. What makes a secondary source a credible source is the document undergoes peer review or an editorial review to ensure the accuracy of the information in the document before it is published.

Sometimes the line between a primary and secondary source is blurred, especially with news articles. However, if the source was recorded or commented on at the time it was happening and the individual can observe the evidence in its entirety, the source is a primary source. For example, although a newspaper article might include eyewitness accounts that were written at the time of the event, it would still be considered a secondary source. The article would be labeled as a secondary source because an individual would not be able to observe the eyewitness testimony in its entirety. Furthermore, the author of the newspaper article selected which testimony to include, exclude, and edit in the article. However, if the newspaper article simply listed the full interview testimony (without editing it), then it would be considered a primary source.

A **tertiary source** is evidence that defines, compiles, summarizes, and/or provides background information from other sources. If the primary purpose of the source is to summarize or provide background that comes from other sources (whether the sources are identified or not), then it is a tertiary source. A few examples of tertiary sources include but are not limited to: dictionaries and encyclopedias, Web pages, etc.

While tertiary sources are helpful for a speaker to initially identify research topics or search terms, they are a weak form of support for public presentations. Many tertiary sources do not meet the tests of evidence (that we discuss next) and they do not show an advanced level of research or information literacy. Tertiary sources can be consulted as a starting point, but it should not be considered "raw material" for the presentation.

Evaluating Evidence

The development of the Internet has provided instant access to information at any time of the day from any location. However, while information is more accessible, it is not always verifiable or accurate, which is why we stress that speakers need to be able to demonstrate information literacy. The more credible and accurate the source, the more credible the speaker will be when making a presentation. Thus, information literacy enables speakers to identify and locate the most credible sources on the Web. While there are a number of tests of evidence, we offer three as a starting point: authorship, bias, and currency. The ideas are listed on the following page.

EVALUATING WEB PAGES

Authorship:

+ Is the author (individual, organization, or corporation) of the Web page explicitly identified?

+ What is the background, expertise, and character (ethics) of the person or group who created the Web page?

+ Can the information presented be accepted as reasonable and/or objective?

+ Does the author incorporate support material (primary and secondary) research into the document?

Bias:

+ What is the individual's, organization's, or group's affiliation with the topic?

+ Are their self-interests involved?

+ Does the author incorporate opinions and support material from various sources or does the author only draw from a particular perspective?

+ Does the author narrowly pull information from sources or are ideas/opinions given complete context?

+ Does the author omit, downplay, ignore, or magnify information to support a specific idea?

Currency:

+ What is the date of the Web page?

+ Has the site been updated?

+ Are there broken links in the site (which is a sign that the site is not maintained regardless of the date)?

+ Is there a copyright date or publication date?

+ Is the information recent enough to be used in a presentation?

The tests of evidence help speakers identify credible sources on the Web. It is another approach for speakers to achieve information literacy. Ultimately, speakers that can research at an advanced level by using specialized research databases will locate credible information and demonstrate information literacy. We discuss this next.

RESEARCHING YOUR TOPIC: ONLINE RESEARCH

The tests for evaluating Web pages are helpful tools for speakers to locate credible sources. Sometimes students believe this limits their ability to find information for their speeches, but nothing can be further from the truth. There are a number of specialized research databases students can use to research their topics in order to identify appropriate sources. Specialized research databases meet the tests of evidence and provide information from sources that are credible. Credible sources can be placed into two categories: scholarly sources that are peer reviewed and popular sources that are editor reviewed. Scholarly sources are **peer reviewed**, which means individuals in a specific field have evaluated the information, verified its accuracy, and contribution to knowledge in order for it to be published. Academic (scholarly) journals fall into this category. Meanwhile, a popular source such as a magazine is either reviewed by an **editor** or **editorial board**. Typically, popular sources are available in print and/or online. Sources such as *Time* and *Newsweek* can be found in this category.

In addition, nonprofit organizations represent another source to locate reliable information. A speaker can access information from official business or government Web sites, and online news services that present information for the general public. Often these online sources end with the address: *.org, .edu,* or *.net*. However, these sources still need to be evaluated as *.org* is no longer limited to nonprofit organizations.

6

97

Online Research

Using a specialized research database meets the tests of evidence that yield sources that are credible due to peer review or editor review. Moreover, specialized research databases are indexed (by publication, date, topic, etc.), which allows for a systematic investigation of a topic.[3] Most times these databases are accessed by subscription, which is paid for by libraries. Thus, the databases accessed through your library enable you to identify primary and secondary sources for a speech.

While many of the subscribed databases such as EBSCOhost or ProQuest (which are a family of databases) can only be accessed through a library's online collection, free Internet search engines such as Google Scholar, Google News, and ERIC provide free alternatives that yield sources that are peer reviewed and/or editor reviewed. For example, Google Scholar is limited to scholarly sources and provides source results that are very similar to traditional research databases. However, researching a topic can be more time consuming as these free search engines often lack advanced search features, full-text is limited, and duplications can be present in search results.[4] In addition, the gatekeeping of sources for accuracy in Google Scholar is not as stringent as subscribed databases, so individuals should be aware to evaluate the source.[5]

Whether you are using a specialized research database or a free search engine such as Google Scholar or Google News, conducting a search is very similar—often by use of **Boolean operators** ("and" or "or"). Putting two terms together such as "hiking and Yellowstone Park" narrows a search, while using "or," such as "hiking or Yellowstone Park," expands it. This is a simple, yet effective means speakers can use as a starting point for finding information on a topic. Most databases offer more advanced search options such as searching by full-text, date, publication, keyword, or title. These are all tools that you can use to locate credible information. The more you use these databases and search options, the more effective you will be as a researcher who demonstrates information literacy.

Information literacy also means understanding the type of database and what type of information can be found in the database. Thus, there are categories or indexes in which topics can be researched. Briefly, we discuss a few of these indexes below.

Periodical indexes categorize magazines and scholarly journals. Magazines and scholarly journals are referred to as periodicals because these sources are published on a specific cycle, usually daily, weekly, monthly, or quarterly. Periodicals are the most frequently used database by public speakers. For example, EBSCOhost (although it is a collection of specialized databases) contains a host of indexes that can be searched, such as *Time, Newsweek, Sports Illustrated, People, Ebony*, and various journals.

Newspaper indexes are important sources of information because they are published daily. For example, the ProQuest Newspaper Index is a popular newspaper index that enables speakers to research several newspapers at once. In contrast, many major papers such as the *New York Times*, the *Washington Post*, the *Wall Street Journal*, the *Los Angeles Times*, and the *Christian Science Monitor* enable individuals to search for information from the paper from its own homepage. Among the many benefits of searching for information through newspapers—it allows the speaker to obtain "local information" on a topic that can be key in creating identification with an audience.

Book catalog: While books might be overlooked by many as a source, they can provide a great deal of depth on a given topic. Books can be searched through your library by options such as by keyword, subject, or by title to find a source. Speakers, however, should still keep the tests of evidence in mind when consulting books. Not every book is credible (especially self-published ones), and books, like other sources, should be evaluated by considering authorship, bias, and currency.

It must be noted that although we have discussed each index and/or catalog as distinct and separate entities, a trend among libraries is to provide databases such as Discovery Search, which pulls sources from different databases (periodical, newspaper, and books) at the same time. Thus, search results will yield different types of sources for a topic (such as books, magazines, and newspapers, etc.) instead of only providing results from a single type of source (such as only books or only newspapers, etc.).

From reading this chapter you should have a better idea of how to systematically select and research a topic. We began this chapter by explaining how to generate topic ideas, and then we made some suggestions for refining your topic. Then, we discussed the importance of information literacy and how it is a vital skill for evaluating sources for a presentation. We finished the chapter by discussing how to research a topic with an emphasis on online research via research databases. We close this chapter by providing an APA reference list that you can use to document your sources in your outline.

EXAMPLES OF REFERENCES

Here are examples of APA-style documentation for the most common references. If your source does not conform to any of these examples, consult the *Publication Manual of the American Psychological Association*.[6]

I. Periodicals

General Citation Format for Periodicals

Author, A. B., & Author, C.D. (year). Title of article. *Title of Periodical, volume,* page numbers. Doi: xx.xxxxxxxxxx

Journal Article, Single Author, with DOI

Gill, R. (2013). The Evolution of Organizational Archetypes: From the American to the Entrepreneurial Dream. *Communication Monographs, 80(3),* 331–353. doi: 10.1080/03637751.2013.788252

Journal Article, Two Authors, with DOI

Ono, K.A. & Jackson II, R.L. (2011). Civil discourse in the face of complex social issues. *Critical Studies in Media Communication, 28(1),* 1–7. doi: 10.1080/15295036.2010.545045

Journal Article, without DOI (when DOI is not available)

Stahl, R (2009). A clockwork war: Rhetorics of time in a time of terror. *Quarterly Journal of Speech 94(1),* 79–99. Retrieved from http://navigator-wcupa. passhe.edu/login?url=http://search.ebscohost.com/login.aspx?direct=true& db=a9h&AN=28552301&site=ehost-live&scope=site

Magazine Article

Stone, D., & Picon, M. (2010, October). How green is the Big Apple? *Newsweek.* 156, 60.

Magazine Article, No Author

Auto industry stages big-time comeback (2011, August). *USA Today Magazine.* Retrieved from http://web.ebscohost.com/ehost/detail?vid=7&sid= cf27dd57-ee69-405a-9b1e-ce14dbcd1da2%40sessionmgr112&hid=118& bdata=JnNpdGU9ZWhvc3QtbGl2ZSSzY29wZT1zaXRl#db=a9h& AN=64405665

Online Magazine Article

Munsey, C. (2012, February). Anti-bullying efforts ramp up. *Monitor on Psychology, 43(2).* Retrieved from http://www.apa.org/monitor/

Newspaper Article

Carr, D. (2012, February 27). Blurred line between espionage and truth. *The New York Times*, B1.

Online Newspaper Article

Dolan, M. (2013, October 17). Out of prison and into the unknown. *Los Angeles Times*. Retrieved from http://www.latimes.com/

Newspaper Article, No Author

Climate of uncertainty (2013, October 1). *Wall Street Journal*, A14.

Newspaper Editorial

A promising progress report (2012, October 22). [Editorial]. *The Washington Post*, A16.

II. Books

General Citation Format for Books

Author, A. B. (date). *Title of work*. Location: Publisher.

NOTE: For books published online only, use:

Author, A. B. (date). *Title of work*. Retrieved from http://www.xxxxxxxx

Author, A. B. (date). *Title of work*. doi: xxxxxx

Single Author

Lordan, E. J. (2010). *The case for combat: How presidents persuade Americans to go to war*. Santa Barbara, CA: Praeger.

Book with More than One Author

Chen, G. & Starosta, W.J. (2005). *Foundations of intercultural communication*. New York: University Press of America.

Edited Book

Burgchardt, C. (Ed.). (2010). *Readings in rhetorical criticism*, 4th ed. State College: Strata.

Book Chapter

Brown, T. (2011). Scripting the Black male athlete: Donovan McNabb and the double bind of Black masculinity. In R. Johnson II, & M. Hopson (Eds.), *Masculinity in the Black imagination* (pp. 147–166). New York: Peter Lang.

Reference Book

Encyclopedia Britannica, 15th ed. (2010). Chicago: Encyclopedia Britannica.

Entry in an Encyclopedia

Pajares, F. (2008). Positive psychology. In W. A. Darity Jr. (Ed.), *International Encyclopedia of Social Sciences* (Vol. 6, 385–386). Detroit: Thompson/Dale.

III. Nonprint Sources

General Citation Format for Nonprint Sources

Author, I., (date). *Title of work* [Medium]. Location of Publisher/Producer: Publisher/Producer.

Film

Netter, G. (Producer), & Hancock, J. L. (Director). (2009). *The Blind Side* [Motion Picture]. U.S.A.: Warner Brothers Pictures.

Music

Mars, B. (2012). Treasure. *On Unorthodox Jukebox* [CD]. New York: Atlantic.

Personal Interview

Jones, C. J. (2010, September 27). [Personal Interview]. Ohio University, 211 Lasher Hall: Athens, OH.

Speech

Beebe, S.A. (2013, November 23). *It's a Wonderful Discipline*. Washington, D.C. Address at the annual conference of the National Communication Association.

Television Broadcast

Cross, D. & Moore, C. (Executive Producers). (2014, February 12). *Anderson Cooper 360°* [Television broadcast]. Atlanta: Cable News Network.

Single Episode of a Television Series

Weddle, D., & Thompsen, B. (Writers), & Smight, A. (Director). (2010). Shock waves [Television series episode] *CSI: Crime Scene Investigation*. New York, NY: CBS.

VOCABULARY

Book catalog — a searchable research database that contains a collection of books.

Brainstorming — the process of generating as many speech topic ideas as possible.

Brainstorming by category — generating speech topic ideas by listing several topics on a piece of paper and then filling in related subjects underneath the topic.

Brainstorming by clustering — generating speech topic ideas by starting with one idea and then forming associations that radiate out from the original idea.

Brainstorming by narrowing — generating speech topic ideas by starting with a general topic and then making each general topic more specific.

Encyclopedia — reference material that provides detailed and precise facts, statistics, and general information on a topic.

Ethos — the audience's perception of the speaker's credibility, which includes the speaker's integrity, honesty, knowledge, and competence (see Chapters 12 and 13).

Information literacy — the ability for individuals to locate information from reliable sources, to evaluate the credibility of the information, and to incorporate it appropriately into a speech.

Identification — any attempt by the speaker to establish some sort of common ground with the audience on an issue or problem.

Newspaper index — a searchable research database that contains a collection of newspapers.

Logos — a systematic pattern of thought based on reasoning and evidence (see Chapters 12 and 13).

Peer-reviewed source — when individuals in a specific field have evaluated the information, verified its accuracy, and contribution to knowledge in order for it to be published.

Periodical index — a searchable research database that typically provides sources by genre such as magazines and newspapers that are published on a certain cycle, such as daily, weekly, monthly, or quarterly.

6

Primary source — includes documents, physical objects, original works, or eye-witness accounts that were created during the actual historical time period that is being examined.

Popular source — a well-known magazine or news source that is mass-produced and is typically available in print and/or online.

Reference materials — sources that provide general background information and facts on topics, such as encyclopedias, yearbooks, dictionaries, quotation books, biographic books, and atlases.

Secondary source — document that was created after the actual time period that is being examined. A secondary source does not enable the researcher to observe the evidence in its entirety.

Tertiary source — evidence that defines, compiles, summarizes, and/or provides background information from other sources.

REFERENCES

[1] Miriam Metzger, "Making sense of credibility on the web: Models for Evaluating Online Information and Recommendations for Future Research," *Journal of the American Society for Information Science and Technology* 58:3 (2007): 2078–2079.

[2] Metzger, 2079.

[3] Jerome V. DeGraff, Nicholas DeGraff, and H. Charles Romesburg, "Literature Searches with Google Scholar: Knowing What You are and are not Getting," *GSA Today 23, 10* (2013): 44–45.

[4] Linda Sebelhaus and Michelle Cawley, "Searching for News Online: Challenging Traditional Methods," *Online Searcher, 37, 2* (2013): 14

[5] DeGraff, DeGraff, and Romesburg, p. 45.

[6] *Publication Manual of the American Psychological Association*, 6th edition, (Washington, D.C.: American Psychological Association, 2010).

"It is terrible to speak well and be wrong."
–Sophocles

"There are no facts, only interpretations."
–Friedrich Nietzsche

"Statistics are no substitute for judgement."
–Henry Clay

"'For example' is not proof."
–Jewish proverb

"Get your facts first, and then you can distort 'em as much as you please."
–Mark Twain

This Chapter Examines:

+ argumentation

+ support material

As Sarah presented her speech on the importance of recycling, she explained why students need to help clean up the environment, and she gave a description of what it is like to live near a landfill. Sarah described this experience as, "Horrible! The smells, the odors; no one wants to have a landfill in their community. I have seen the situation, and it is horrible. If you lived there, you would agree with me; it is just so horrible. For these reasons, we should take an active role in cleaning up our environment. Recycling is very important, this is why everyone should recycle."

This description given by Sarah does not effectively convey to her audience what it is like to live near a landfill because she fails to clearly describe *why* living next to a landfill is awful. In fact, Sarah's description is dull, unimaginative, and vague. Often speakers know the information "in their heads," but they do not present **concrete** examples or **evidence** that give the audience a clear understanding of the topic, in this case what it is like to live near a landfill. Thus, it is your responsibility as a speaker to provide evidence, or what we broadly refer to as **support material**, which is the substance of any speech such as examples and facts that make your ideas more precise and concrete for your audience.

Using support material will make your ideas more descriptive and understandable for the audience. When you make any presentation, you should avoid vague language by supporting your ideas with vivid examples so your audience will interpret your ideas the way you intended to present them. When a speaker is not specific or descriptive, the speech will resemble Sarah's vague and abstract explanation of what it is like to live near a landfill. Using support material in a speech simply clarifies your ideas and information for the audience in a concrete manner.

When you research your topic, you want to locate and identify information that reinforces the main ideas of your speech. The sources you use to support your main ideas should be cited in your speech. When you **cite a source**, you are simply acknowledging the authenticity of your information by stating the author, name of the publication, title, and date of the source to the audience. There are several reasons why it is important for you to cite your sources in your speech. First, when you cite your sources, it builds your credibility as a speaker. Second, citing your sources bolsters credibility in your speech. The audience knows you are not conjuring up information. Instead, citing your sources indicates whether or not your information is believable, trustworthy, and accurate. It shows the audience that you have verifiable information that supports your ideas. Third, it prevents you from being accused of plagiarizing other works as your own. Anytime you have key information (anything that is not common knowledge), cite it in your speech. Remember that the more credible the sources you cite in your speech, the more believable your speech will be (see Chapter 6).

This chapter will explain how you can make your speeches more interesting, understandable, concrete, and vivid for your audience by using support material. Support material makes your ideas more precise and concrete for your audience.

Therefore, we will discuss support material in two steps. First, we will discuss argumentation and how the ideas expressed in a speech can be better understood through the concepts of claims, grounds (support material), and warrants. Then, we identify the types of support material such as examples, facts, statistics, testimony, narratives, and anecdotes that can be used in a speech.

Figure 7-1. Research

ARGUMENTATION

Up until this point, we have focused on the process and the preparation that is needed for speakers to construct a speech for presentation. We don't want to overlook, however, how the message (or argumentation) is constructed in the speech. **Argumentation** can be defined as the explicit and implicit messages that are supported with evidence and reasoning. Scholar Stephen Toulmin created a model of argumentation (the Toulmin Model) that illustrates sound reasoning/logic in a speech. Although the Toulmin Model of Argumentation consists of six parts, for our purposes, we will focus on the first triad of the model, which are the building blocks of argumentation: claims, grounds, and warrants.

Claim

The first part of argumentation is the **claim**, which is a statement alleged to be true. In any speech, speakers will make specific claims about a topic. Whether the claim is informative, persuasive, or entertaining, speakers are making statements that they want the audience to accept. We can use the following claim as an example:

Claim: The Eagles have the best fan base in Philadelphia.

The claim, "The Eagles have the best fan base in Philadelphia," is a specific assertion that a speaker could make. Whether the statement is accepted by the audience is dependent on the next concept in the Toulmin Model, the grounds.

Grounds

In any speech, all claims need to be supported by evidence. The evidence that is used to bolster the claim is referred to as the **grounds** (or proof). These two elements (claims and grounds) are the building blocks for logical argumentation. When claims are accompanied by grounds (or proof) the information in the speech is made more logically sound. For example, we can return to our previous example by including the grounds:

Claim: The Eagles have the best fan base in Philadelphia.
Grounds: Because each home game is sold out.

In the above example, the claim that the Eagles have the best fan base in Philadelphia is backed up by the proof of each home game being sold out. The grounds provides the logic for the claim and makes the claim more concrete. Notice how the claim can be understood by answering the question: "What is your point?" Meanwhile, the grounds answers the question: "What is your proof?" In any speech, speakers need to be aware of the claims they are making and how the claims are being supported by proof. In other words, effective speeches are ones in which a speaker's claims are supported by proof.

Warrant

A **warrant** is the reasoning that links the claim and the grounds. Warrants are general principles that represent a higher level of argument than claim or ground and they are not explicitly stated—but implicitly understood. We can once again return to our Eagles example to illustrate a warrant:

Claim: The Eagles have the best fan base in Philadelphia.
Grounds: Because each home game is sold out.
Warrant: Eagles fans are very passionate and loyal in supporting their team.

In this example, notice the implicit reasoning that further connects the claim (the best fan base) with the grounds (each game sold out). The warrant (the passion and loyalty of Eagles fans) strengthens the links between the claim and the grounds. It is a further explanation for why Eagles games are consistently sold out regardless of the play of the team. As any Philadelphian knows, there is a fanatical following that roots for the team when it is good and boos when the team is bad!

At this point, we can illustrate the first triad of the Toulmin Model (claim, grounds, and warrants) as means for constructing an effective argument. The model is helpful in illustrating how speakers can bolster their claims with grounds or proof. In other words, the statements (claims) made in speeches should be backed up with support material (grounds) to produce stronger and more logical arguments in the speech. We will discuss several different types of support material in the next section.

SUPPORT MATERIAL

The basic elements of the Toulmin Model depict how speakers can construct effective messages. Any speech will become more vivid and logical when claims are reinforced by grounds and warrants. The Toulmin Model enables speakers to be more strategic in constructing their speech. As speakers begin to work on outlining their ideas and refining them into claims, speakers should be mindful of how their claims are being supported. Speakers can bolster their claims by grounds, or what is commonly referred to as support material. In this section, we will discuss specific types of support material that can be used in a speech, such as examples, facts, statistics, testimony, narratives, and anecdotes.

7

Examples

One of the best approaches for supporting your ideas and making them concrete for the audience is through vivid examples. **Examples** are specific cases used to illustrate a point. If you consider Sarah's speech from the beginning of the chapter, she could have easily used an example to explain one of her ideas. In Sarah's case, she needs to explain in concrete terms how the smells are horrible. Here is how Sarah could have made this idea more concrete:

The smells coming from a landfill are horrible. Imagine the foul stench of a garbage can filled with decaying vegetables, soiled baby diapers, and yesterday's tuna fish. Now multiply that smell by 100,000 more garbage cans that are dumped every day in a landfill just 10 miles from your home. This smell is more oppressive than a dead skunk. This smell is powerful enough to penetrate your senses and resistant to being blown away by the wind.

In this revision of Sarah's speech, the audience has a much clearer understanding of what she means when she says the smell is horrible. Sarah compares the smell to the examples of a garbage can and a skunk to help the audience imagine the odor of a landfill. This description is more concrete, and the audience is not left to wonder what "horrible" means.

There are different types of examples speakers can use to support their ideas. The two most common types are factual examples and hypothetical examples. **Factual examples** are specific cases used to illustrate a point that actually occurred in real life. A factual example is a very effective form of support because you are using information that really happened. Audiences can identify with real examples because they are based on real life, which makes the examples relevant. Often real life is better than fiction because the unusual occurrences of life are a good way to gain your audience's attention. As in Sarah's speech, she is using a factual example to explain her experiences living next to a landfill.

On the other hand, **hypothetical examples** are specific cases used to illustrate a point that is based upon a composite of real life situations. When a speaker uses a hypothetical example, the speaker places the audience members in an imaginary situation to make a point of what could actually happen. The following is an example of a hypothetical example:

Picture yourself and your date after a romantic evening at your favorite restaurant. You decide to walk around town afterwards to enjoy the nice evening and to window shop. Later, you decide to stop at a small coffee shop to get some dessert. However, when you reach for your wallet, you discover that it is missing. You now realize that the person you bumped into earlier picked your pocket. This hypothetical situation might be uncommon to you, but if it happened, would you know what to do?

As you can see, hypothetical examples are effective when they can create a specific situation where the audience must mentally process your information as they continue to imagine the situation. Using hypothetical examples is another way to maintain the audience's interest and attention.

When using hypothetical examples, it is important that the hypothetical example is based on actual situations or facts. If the hypothetical example is too extreme, or if it is not very representative of the situation, the audience will reject the example. If the audience rejects the example, they might also reject your speech. For example, consider a speaker who is presenting an informative speech on the hidden dangers of tropical vacation spots. The speaker could use a hypothetical example of being eaten by an anaconda in the Amazon rainforest. This example would not be very effective because being eaten by an anaconda snake in the Amazon rainforest is very uncommon and definitely not representative. However, the hypothetical example of a group of tourists who became ill for their entire vacation because they did not get the proper shots before their tropical vacation is a more likely example.

Although factual and hypothetical examples are a great way to keep your audience's interest, you want to follow a few guidelines when using them. First, make sure the example is relevant and appropriate to your topic. Don't include an example just to include one. The example should clarify or reinforce an idea or concept for the audience. Second, the example should be representative of the situation. You do not want the example to be too extreme. The audience will not perceive an extreme example as believable or within the realm of probability. Third, make sure you describe the example accurately so the audience fully understands the point you want to make.

Facts

Another way speakers support their message is by using facts. A **fact** is any information that can be verified as true. For example, it would be a fact to say that George Washington was the United States' first president. We could check several sources to verify that Washington did serve as the nation's first president, from 1789–1797. However, if a speaker stated, "George Washington was the nation's greatest president," this statement would not be a fact; it would be an opinion. Trying to determine if he was our greatest president is a value statement that cannot be verified as true. All you can do is acquire public opinion about this value statement. You cannot confirm the statement as fact.

When used within a speech, facts are a quick way for a speaker to define, clarify, inform, reinforce, shock, and enlighten an audience. Facts can point out the unusual, the unknown, the overlooked, and the unique aspects of a topic that would be of interest to the audience. For example, consider the following facts that could be incorporated into the speech we outline in Chapter 8 about Yellowstone Park:

- Yellowstone Park has the greatest concentration of thermal features such as geysers and hot springs in the world.

- Old Faithful erupts every 35 to 120 minutes for 1.5 to 5 minutes.

- Yellowstone Park has the greatest concentration of large wildlife such as elk, bison, mule deer, grizzlies, moose, bighorn sheep, and pronghorn antelope in the lower 48 states.

- The best time to view Yellowstone's wildlife is in the spring and autumn.

All these facts are key points that the speaker could make in the speech about Yellowstone Park at different strategic places in the speech (see Chapter 8 on organization). The facts provide specific information for an audience to understand.

As support material, facts should be used with caution. One of the guidelines you want to follow as a speaker is to not overuse facts. Nothing can be more boring for an audience than listening to a speech that lists fact, after fact, after fact. When you do this, you are not giving a presentation by conveying ideas to an audience. Instead, you are reciting a list that involves no prior pre-planning. When using facts, don't overuse them—try to incorporate them with other forms of support to keep your presentation interesting and vivid. Also, make sure you do not confuse opinion for fact. **Opinion** is simply a person's expressed point of view. When a speaker uses an opinion as fact, the speaker has misled the audience into believing a point of view rather than a verifiable fact. Avoid this error by making sure you can verify your facts, and explicitly state when you are using opinion so you do not mislead the audience.

Statistics

Statistics are similar to facts in that statistics are also a quick way to make a point and support your ideas. **Statistics** are simply numbers that are used to represent or clarify information. Instead of saying a lot of people experience car theft, which is vague, this idea can be clarified by using a statistic. A speaker can simply say that every 30 seconds a car is stolen. A statistic is a quick reference that places a numerical value on information. Without the statistic, the audience would be left to wonder how much is "a lot."

Although statistics are very easy to identify and use, there are several dangers in using them in a speech. First, you want to make sure your statistic is truly representative of the point you are trying to represent. For example, what if the car theft statistic used above came from a report on tourist crime in Mexico? In this case, the speaker has not only been unethical, but the statistic is not truly representative of car thefts that occur in the United States.

Second, make sure your statistic precisely examines what you are claiming it does. You must consider what the statistic is measuring. Did the statistic come from a study of high-crime areas as opposed to tourist or low-crime areas? These are key aspects to consider because you do not want to use a statistic about car theft in Peoria, Illinois, and generalize it to the country as a whole. Instead, understand how the statistic was acquired and use it in a comparative way. You can acknowledge that the statistic only represents a certain situation, but it does point out that car theft can occur.

Third, simplify your statistics. Sometimes numbers are hard for the audience to understand. For example, if you say one billion people live in China, it is accurate, but a large number like "a billion" might not make an impact on the audience. Instead use a comparison to help your audience understand. You can say one billion people live in China, which means one in seven people on the earth live in China. This makes the information more tangible for the audience. In addition to these concerns, do not overuse statistics in a speech. You should incorporate the most compelling and clearest statistics that help you clarify the idea or convey the most striking information.

Testimony

"Ask not what your country can do for you, but what you can do for your country."

This quotation from President John F. Kennedy's Inaugural Address in 1961 illustrates another form of support—testimony. **Testimony** is a direct quotation from someone who is acknowledged as an authority or expert on a given subject. Often this is referred to as **expert testimony**. Whenever you are going to use testimony as support material, you want to use the most credible person as a form of support. When you use a highly respected person as a form of support, it enhances your credibility as a speaker, and it legitimizes your information.

You must be aware that the credibility of a person's testimony will vary from situation to situation. For example, if you were giving a speech about golf, it would be appropriate to use a quotation from Tiger Woods as he explains some aspect of golf. However, if you were giving a speech on space travel, Tiger Woods would not be the best source to use (even if he did speak about it). There are many other people who have been in space who would represent a more credible source, such as John Glenn. Also, keep in mind that some speakers are perceived as more credible across various audiences regardless of the topics, due to the speaker's integrity, trustworthiness, and expertise. For example, testimony from Colin Powell on almost any political subject would be more credible than Paris Hilton.

In addition to expert testimony, speakers often use personal testimony. **Personal testimony** is speaking from your own experience. Suppose you are giving a speech on how to take better photographs, and you have been a photo technician for the past five years. You can acknowledge your credibility on the subject to the audience, and you can explain your experience taking and developing photographs. The advantage of personal testimony is that it personalizes the information for your audience by providing living proof from your own experience with the subject.

7

As with other forms of support, testimony has its weaknesses. The primary weakness is that expert testimony can always be contradicted by other expert testimony. Therefore, it is always wise to use testimony in conjunction with another form of support. Do not support a claim solely by testimony. When using testimony, you want to follow a few guidelines.

First, make sure the person you are quoting is credible. Again, the more highly credible your source, the more credible you will be perceived as a speaker, and the more credible the audience will perceive your information. Second, make sure the person has expertise. Do not confuse credibility with expertise because they are not the same concept. **Credibility** deals with the audience's perception of a speaker as honest, trustworthy, competent, and dynamic, whereas expertise deals with how much knowledge, training, education, and experience a person has in relation to a topic. As you can imagine, a speaker can be considered an expert, but not be perceived as credible. Third, make sure the quotation you are using is within the speaker's area of expertise. As we mentioned above, it's appropriate to use a quotation from Tiger Woods about golf, but it would be not be as credible to use a quotation from Tiger Woods about space travel.

Narratives

Narratives are stories you tell within a speech. Narratives are not as verifiable as other forms of support, but they are effective in getting the audience mentally and emotionally involved in your speech. Most people enjoy good stories, and for this reason narratives are an excellent way to keep your audience's attention. Narratives can be as detailed, descriptive, and developed as needed. They add a different spice to your speech. In addition, narratives allow speakers to engage their audience with nonverbal communication such as gestures and movement. Speakers who are familiar with their story can explain it, while still maintaining effective eye contact with the audience.

When considering using a narrative in your speech, keep the following guidelines in mind. First, make sure the story is appropriate and relevant to your topic. There is nothing worse than a speaker who tells a long story that is unrelated to the speaker's topic. In this case, there is a good possibility the speaker will lose the audience because the audience is trying to make sense of the story and how it relates to the speech. For this reason, make sure the narrative is relevant.

Second, make sure you know the progression of the story. All stories have a beginning, a middle, and an end. Whenever you miss a part or key parts in that progression, it can undermine the whole story. Think back to the last time you were listening to a story or a joke, and the person forgot part of the story or worse yet, forgot the punch line. You probably felt frustrated that you did not get the "whole story." Your audience will experience the same frustration with a poorly told narrative if all the necessary parts are not present.

Third, make sure you know the main point of the story and how it relates to the main point of your speech. Ideally, the story will have the same main point as your speech. An example of this would be speakers who use the story of Rosa Parks and her decision to stand up for civil rights in order to orient the audience to the main idea of their speech, which is standing up for your rights. Sometimes the story does not directly relate to the topic, but the story does reflect a similar theme that will be developed in your speech. For example, maybe the speaker refers to the same Rosa Parks story to talk about a related topic, that of making important decisions.

Fourth, try to use as much detail and vividness as possible when you are telling the story. The development of the story is what the audience likes to hear. Try not to omit important details because this could undermine the story. Plus, the more descriptive the speech is, the more the audience will work mentally to create an image of your speech in their minds. When an audience is mentally processing and following your narrative, this keeps an audience interested and involved in your speech.

Anecdotes

An **anecdote** is when you use humor to make a point. One way you can distinguish anecdotes from narratives is that anecdotes are much shorter than narratives. Also, anecdotes always use humor to express an idea, whereas a narrative is much longer and might or might not use humor to illustrate a point. Anecdotes function the same way as narratives in that they rely on a story to keep the audience mentally involved. However, another difference is that anecdotes are more risky to use than narratives because anecdotes rely on humor. With anecdotes, a speaker risks the chance that the audience might not like the humor, won't understand the humor, or will find the humor inappropriate. This can cause a speaker to panic and lose concentration, which can disrupt the delivery of the entire speech.

Whenever you use an anecdote, you have to make sure the short story is humorous, appropriate, and relevant to your topic. It is always helpful to test out your anecdotes on your roommates, family members, or co-workers before you present them in a speech so you can determine whether the story is appropriate or not. Also, more importantly, be prepared if the anecdote fails. Keep your composure and continue to give your speech. You might want to follow the failure with a joke about that failure and then move on. This shows the audience that you are still in control of the situation. The key is not to dwell on it, because it might ruin your concentration and hamper the delivery of your speech. As for guidelines, the same guidelines that apply for narratives also apply for anecdotes.

7

In this chapter, we have given you the reasons why it is important to incorporate support material into your speech. We have discussed the building blocks of argumentation through three of the basic concepts from the Toulmin Model: claims, grounds (or support material), and warrants. Then, we identified several different forms of support you can use in a speech to make your ideas more precise and concrete. In addition, we explained various guidelines for using different types of support material in your speech. Remember that using support material in a speech gives you the advantage of making your ideas more clear, understandable, and vivid for the audience.

VOCABULARY

Anecdote — a brief story that uses humor to make a point.

Argumentation — the explicit and implicit messages that are supported with evidence and reasoning.

Citing sources — acknowledging the authenticity of your information by stating the author, name of publication, title, and date of the source for the audience.

Claim — a statement alleged to be true.

Concrete example — an illustration that refers to specific objects or information. Concrete examples are more precise in meaning and less open to different interpretations.

Credibility — the audience's perception of a speaker's integrity, honesty, and competence.

Example — a specific case used to illustrate a point.

Expert testimony — a direct quotation from someone who is acknowledged as an authority on a given subject.

Fact — information that can be verified as true.

Factual example — a specific case used to illustrate a point that actually occurred in real life.

Grounds (or proof) — the evidence that is used to bolster the claim.

Hypothetical example — a specific case used to illustrate a point that is based upon a composite of real life situations.

Narrative — a story within a speech.

Opinion — a person's expressed point of view.

Personal testimony — speaking from your own experience.

Statistics — numbers that are used to represent or clarify information.

Support material — the substance of any speech such as examples, facts, statistics, testimony, narratives, and anecdotes that make a speaker's ideas more precise and concrete.

Testimony — a quotation or opinion from a person.

Toulmin Model — a model of argumentation that illustrates sound reasoning/ logic in a speech; three concepts from the model include: claims, grounds, and warrants.

Warrant — the reasoning that links the claim and the grounds.

7

ORGANIZING YOUR MESSAGE 8

"Let all things be done decently and in order."
-Corinthians 14:40

"We put things in order—God does the rest. Lay an iron bar east and west, it is not magnetized. Lay it north and south and it is."
-Horace Mann

"Good order is the foundation of all things."
-Edmund Burke

"Order is heaven's first law."
-Alexander Pope

This Chapter Examines:

+ culture and organization

+ how to determine your purpose

+ how to determine your main points

+ how to determine your organizational structure

+ how to include support material

+ how to determine your connections

Malik is a pre-med student who is looking forward to his anatomy class this semester. He wants to be a doctor, and this class offers him an opportunity to learn his "craft" from the renowned Dr. Benjamin Rode. Dr. Rode has been a distinguished medical doctor for over 25 years, and he has been awarded many honors throughout his career. After two weeks in class, however, Malik is struggling to understand Dr. Rode's lectures. The primary problem is that Dr. Rode never completes a single thought. He conveys some information, and then he rambles from story to story. While the stories are interesting, it is difficult to determine what information is important and what is not. Malik hopes he will figure it out soon because the first examination is next week.

This hypothetical example illustrates a common problem that occurs between a speaker and listener in the communication process—the speaker fails to organize a concise and understandable message for the audience. Research clearly shows that students dislike instructors who are disorganized in thought, shift from subject to subject, or speak on extended tangents.[1] When a speaker delivers an unorganized message in this manner, it is easy for an audience to mentally "tune out" a speaker and thus ignore the information the speaker is trying to communicate. To avoid this problem, organize your ideas and deliver a structured speech so your audience can understand your message.[2]

Delivering an organized speech benefits both you and your audience. First, organized speeches enable your audience to understand, follow, and remember your message more easily. Moreover, audiences perceive speakers who present organized speeches as more competent and trustworthy.[3] Second, when you organize your information, you are able to remember your ideas more clearly so you can be more confident about your delivery.[4]

This chapter explains how you can effectively organize your message for a public presentation. Next, you will be shown the process of organizing a presentation, which includes: identifying your presentation purpose, determining your main points, organizing your main points, including support material for your main points, and connecting your main points. Before we talk about how to organize a message, we briefly discuss culture and organization.

CULTURE AND ORGANIZATION

Throughout this textbook, we acknowledge the importance of considering the cultural backgrounds of audience members when preparing a presentation due to the multicultural mosaic of ethnicities, nationalities, religions, and languages that comprise American society. As we discuss in Chapter 4, speakers must be familiar with different cultural values and how these values shape people's perceptions, interpretations, and the attribution of meaning. In public speaking, culture plays an important role in how individuals use logic to organize the content, evidence, and reasoning of a speech. **Logic** (or logos) is a systematic pattern of thought based upon reasoning and evidence. Logic includes the main ideas, content, evidence, and reasoning of a speech, as well as the considerations of organization (see Chapters 12 and 13 for a further discussion of logic/logos).

Almost all public speaking textbooks in American culture (this one included) emphasize Western culture's linear logic for organizing speeches. Linear logic is based upon presenting information in a linear sequence where the content, evidence, and arguments proceed from beginning to end in a straight line.[5] **Linear logic** pragmatically states a central idea, which is followed by specific evidence and examples that directly relate to the main idea. With linear logic, one point is directly related to the next point as the message is specifically "spelled out" for the audience. In Western cultures, when all information is linked in a linear progression from beginning to end, the speech is considered to demonstrate sound reasoning and logic.

However, logic and organizational patterns vary from culture to culture. What is considered to be logical, well reasoned, and organized in one culture can be perceived as illogical, devoid of reasoning, and disorganized in another culture.[6] Individuals from different cultures and co-cultures value different types of logic, which produces different types of reasoning and organizational patterns. The different types of logic affect how individuals from different cultures communicate with one another and with others outside their culture. For example, in Japan, it is customary to begin a speech with an apology.[7] At a conference held in Japan, an American scholar began his speech with a sincere apology (he apologized for knowing little about the topic and little about Japanese culture, and he hoped he would not be wasting anyone's time). At the conclusion of his speech, many

8

listeners complimented him on his apology and said it was the best one they had heard from someone outside their culture. In collectivistic cultures, like Japan (where the group is more important than the individual), an apology reinforces the cultural values placed on fitting in with others, being relationship oriented, and maintaining obligations.

Non-Western cultures do not demonstrate linear logic, but configural logic when communicating with another person or when presenting information. **Configural logic** is based upon presenting information in a spiral or cyclical pattern where information jumps from idea to idea with content, evidence, and arguments used as needed to support specific ideas.[8] Whereas linear logic can be thought of as information that proceeds in a line, configural logic can be thought of as information that proceeds through a progression of dots. Configural logic is a cultural value that is often found in high-context cultures. In a **high-context culture**, the meanings of a communication message are imbedded in the situation, the relationship of the individuals, and the implicit norms, beliefs, and values of the culture. Therefore, speakers are able to move in and out of ideas easily, because the audience already understands the embedded meaning in the context of the message and can "connect the dots" without explicit information necessary in linear logic.

In Eastern cultures, such as China, Japan, and Korea, the configural logic organization pattern is often referred to as indirection because the topic is discussed in a tangential way. It is common for speakers to talk around the topic, but not directly mention it. As Chen and Starosta explain, the topic is described as what it is not, rather than what it is.[9] Since indirection takes place in high-context cultures, the audience is able to interpret more meaning from the context and is able to make logical connections without explicit explanations. An example of indirection can be illustrated by an Eastern folktale. In this folktale, a young man from a lower-class family is interested in a young woman from a high-class family. The mother of the young man makes an appointment to meet with the mother of the young woman to determine if her son might pursue the relationship. The two mothers exchange pleasantries and cordially talk about village life, the weather—everything except their children. How did the mother of the young man know that the mother of the young woman did not approve of their relationship? The mother of the young woman served bananas and tea to the young man's mother to indirectly communicate that the relationship between their two children was incompatible and unacceptable. By knowing the cultural norms of the society (bananas are not served with tea), the two women were able to communicate using configural rather than linear logic.

Likewise, African American culture uses configural logic as information is often organized in spirals. A message is commonly presented in spirals, returning again and again to the same points, but from different perspectives. Many studies have identified the configural logical organizational pattern within the African American culture from traditional African American preaching to the rap lyrics of hip-hop music.[10] The configural logical organizational pattern is illustrated by cultures with strong oral traditions (cultures that place a great emphasis on speaking) that demonstrate a variety of linguistic techniques such as metaphors, indirection, signifying, and personal experience when communicating.

Chen and Starosta identify additional cultures that value configural logic such as Russian, Spanish, and Arabic cultures. Identifying these differences demonstrates that we can't assume that everyone inherently knows how to organize information by linear logic and that culture does influence logic and organizational patterns. We believe that through third-culture building, people from cultures and co-cultures who do not practice linear logic can incorporate some aspects of their configural logic into a presentation that emphasizes linear logic. **Third-culture building** involves a speaker and audience creating a new culture that draws from and extends the norms and values from the independent cultures. Through third-culture building, the speaker, instead of presenting a speech spirally, will take specific elements from configural logic and insert them into a linear logic presentation.

The reason why we favor third-culture building with an emphasis on linear logic for the organization of speeches is practicality. Since the dominant culture creates the norms for society, all members of society must be able to communicate effectively based upon a "common standard" that cuts across cultural differences. Sometimes audience analysis and ceremonial speeches (see Chapter 15) provide speakers with a greater flexibility when it comes to organization. If a specific audience analysis or ceremonial speech does not call for configural logic, then we suggest using linear logic in preparing presentations. The process of organizing a speech by using linear logic is the focus of the rest of the chapter beginning with a discussion of how to determine your purpose.

8

HOW TO DETERMINE YOUR PURPOSE

The first step in constructing an organized message is to identify the purpose of your presentation. The purpose of your speech clarifies the goals of the speech, guides your selection of information, and establishes the tone of your presentation. In this next section, we explain and describe three aspects of determining the purpose of your speech: the general purpose, the specific purpose, and the thesis statement.

General Purpose

The **general purpose** is the overall objective a speech can accomplish. There are three general purposes of a presentation: to inform, to persuade, or to entertain. While any presentation can incorporate all of these general purposes, presentations usually have one primary general purpose. Once you know the general purpose of your presentation, you can begin to understand what type of speech you will present, what type of information you need to gather, and what goals you can set for your speech.

GENERAL PURPOSES	
To inform	To provide understanding or to increase knowledge
To persuade	To shape, reinforce, or change the audience's attitude/beliefs/values/behaviors
To entertain	To use humor, satire, and irony to amuse an audience

Specific Purpose

While the general purpose identifies the type of speech a speaker will present, the **specific purpose** is the precise goal your speech will accomplish. The specific purpose is based upon the general purpose of the speech. More specifically, the specific purpose should take the conceptual idea of the general purpose and make it more concrete. The following example illustrates how the specific purpose is more concrete than the general purpose of the presentation.

TOPIC	GENERAL PURPOSE	SPECIFIC PURPOSE
Yellowstone Park	To inform	To inform the audience of Yellowstone Park's unique ecosystem
Yellowstone Park	To persuade	To persuade the audience that Yellowstone Park's unique ecosystem needs to be saved
Yellowstone Park	To entertain	To entertain the audience by illustrating humorous events that can occur while camping at Yellowstone Park

Thesis Statement

Once you have determined the general and specific purposes, it is important to develop a thesis statement for your speech. The thesis statement defines the main idea of the presentation. The thesis statement should be complemented and developed by all the information in your presentation. For example, if the thesis statement for your speech is, "Yellowstone Park's geysers and hot springs are world famous for their variety," then your information must support this main idea. You would not, therefore, include information about the park's controversial grey wolf repopulation program because that goes beyond the scope of your thesis statement. However, speaking about Old Faithful would be appropriate because Old Faithful is a famous geyser, which is directly related to your thesis. The following example highlights the general purpose, specific purpose, and thesis statement of a presentation on Yellowstone Park.

TOPIC	Yellowstone Park
GENERAL PURPOSE	To inform
SPECIFIC PURPOSE	To inform the audience of Yellowstone Park's unique ecosystem
THESIS STATEMENT	Yellowsone Park offers many natural wonders that can be explored at any time of the year

The general purpose, specific purpose, and thesis statement help you establish a foundation for your speech. Conceptualizing these speech elements allows you to determine what type of speech you have, what the goal of the speech is, and what the main idea of the speech is. The next section describes how you progress from this foundation to developing the main points of your speech.

8

HOW TO DETERMINE YOUR MAIN POINTS

Any speech is composed of three parts: the introduction, the body, and the conclusion. Often these three general parts of a speech are referred to as **basic speech structure** because in the introduction you "tell them what you are going to tell them," in the body you "tell them," and in the conclusion you "tell them what you already told them." We will start with the development of the body, because the body of the speech is often planned first. In Chapter 9, we discuss how to introduce and conclude your speech. However, your immediate task is to divide the body of your speech into main points.

Divide Body into Main Points

For the most part, the information from your research, plus your general purpose, specific purpose, and thesis statement will guide how you divide your topic into main points. Continuing with the Yellowstone Park example, suppose you divide this topic into three parts:

A. *The wildlife of Yellowstone*

B. *Yellowstone's geysers and hot springs*

C. *Activities*

As the example above shows, the three points not only divide the topic, but they form the beginning of a skeleton of the body of the speech. Plus, each main point is a separate idea that does not overlap with any other idea.

Limit Your Main Points

When you are dividing your main points, you want to carefully consider how many points you will attempt to discuss in your speech. As a rule, speakers should limit their main points from two to five. There are many reasons why you want to limit the number of main points in your speech. One reason you want to limit your main points from two to five is that it is easier for the audience to follow a speech that has a limited number of ideas than a speech that has many ideas. In addition, remember your time constraints. It is much easier to prepare a speech that has a few main points than a speech that has many. Also, limiting the number of main points prevents you from including too much information in the speech.

Remember that it is important for you to determine what information is relevant for your speech and what information is irrelevant and can be eliminated. For example, talking about Yellowstone Park's entire ecosystem for an informative speech would be unrealistic. However, if the speaker divides the topic into three categories in relation to Yellowstone Park's ecosystem (as the above example illustrates), the speaker would have a much more realistic speech topic. The speaker will still have to limit the amount of information for each main point, but the speech will be a great deal more manageable.

Use Parallel Structure

When developing the main points for your speech, construct the main points in **parallel structure**. Using parallel structure simply means that the main points are repeated in the same grammatical structure of phrases, words, or sentences. For example, consider the Yellowstone Park example from above.

NOT PARALLEL IN STRUCTURE	PARALLEL IN STRUCTURE
A. The wildlife of Yellowstone	A. Yellowstone Park's wildlife
B. Yellowstone's geysers and hot springs	B. Yellowstone Park's geysers and hot springs
C. Activities	C. Yellowstone Park's activities

As you can see, parallel structure aligns the grammatical structure of the main points. It is far easier for the audience to follow and remember your information when your main points are constructed in a parallel way. Unlike other forms of communication, such as reading, where a person can reread information if they are confused, a speech does not offer this opportunity. Once the listener is lost, it is impossible for the listener to revisit the lost information. Therefore, parallel structure helps the audience identify main points, clarify information, and retain information.

Balance

The final aspect you want to consider when you are developing your main points is **balance**. A speech is balanced when the information for each part of the speech (introduction, body, and conclusion) has the right amount of development and emphasis. The introduction should be about 10% of the speech, the body about 80%, and the conclusion about 10%.

One way to check the development of each main point is to check how much sub-dividing you have included for each main point. If you have a great deal of information for two main points but very little for another main point, try to balance out your information. In this case, eliminate information in the first two points or add more information to the third point. In general, you want each main point to be proportionally balanced within your speech. This is especially true for speeches with only two main points, such as a problem-solution or cause and effect speech. In these cases, you want your information as equal as possible. If your information is not balanced in a problem-solution or cause and effect speech, your speech will seem unbalanced to the audience. Here are some guidelines for balance:

8

SYMMETRICAL PATTERN		DESCENDING PATTERN		ASCENDING PATTERN	
Introduction	10%	Introduction	10%	Introduction	10%
Main Point #1	20%	Main Point #1	35%	Main Point #1	20%
Main Point #2	40%	Main Point #2	25%	Main Point #2	25%
Main Point #3	20%	Main Point #3	20%	Main Point #3	35%
Conclusion	10%	Conclusion	10%	Conclusion	10%

These are rough estimates, but this gives you a good idea of how to maintain balance within your main points so your speech is well developed. Also, it is a good way to help you tailor information for your given time constraints. In the next section, we will show you how to place your main points into an organizational structure that best conveys your information.

HOW TO DETERMINE YOUR ORGANIZATIONAL STRUCTURE

Whether your speech is successful or not is largely determined by how well the audience understands and retains your information. Your speech will be enhanced greatly by selecting an organizational structure that complements your information. *Your job as a speaker is to identify what type of information you have and to decide which organizational structure best explains your information.* We will identify different ways you can organize your main points, but first we discuss the three principles of organization that underline these structures.[11]

Three Principles of Organization

Osborn and Osborn identify three principles that explain how we process information: the principle of similarity, the principle of proximity, and the principle of closure.[12] We will look at each principle separately.

The **principle of similarity** means we tend to group together information that shares common elements or is alike in some regard. If your topic is "sharks" you can divide the topic by types, by location, or by size. The key is that you group the topic by some type of common relationship. This principle is the basis for the topical organizational structure that will be discussed further in the next section. A topical organizational structure can be developed from natural divisions within the topic such as the colors that comprise the spectrum of a rainbow or customary divisions such as organizing college students into academic ranks—freshmen, sophomores, juniors, and seniors. Anytime you have information that shares common relationships, organize your information by topic.

The **principle of proximity** is the tendency to organize information according to how it occurs in time or space. In short, any information that has a chronological order or is located within a physical setting should be organized by proximity. Any speech that emphasizes a process, such as demonstration speeches, historical development speeches, or explanation speeches, should be organized by how these events occur over time, which is a sequential organizational pattern. It is much easier to explain a process when you follow its chronological order. Imagine how difficult it would be to explain the events of 9/11 by topic. Your audience would miss important details, especially the origin of the attacks and the evolution of how various agencies responded. By proceeding in sequence your audience will understand the beginning, the middle, and the end.

On the other hand, if your topic is the Hawaiian Islands, you would most likely use spatial structure rather than chronological structure to convey your information. You would organize the information according to how each island is physically located, one next to another, in the Pacific Ocean. The key with spatial organizations is to start in one direction and then proceed in a deliberate manner to the end, such as left to right, one point in a circle and around, or east to west. Whenever information is related in a chronological order or physical location, use the principle of proximity to organize your main points.

The **principle of closure** is based on our affinity for completion. We prefer definite beginnings and definite endings. Think back to the last time you were watching a good television program only to have it end as a "to be continued" episode. You probably were frustrated because you did not have closure and had to watch the following week to find out what happened. This concept also applies to making presentations. Each organizational structure needs to have closure, but there are two organizational structures that especially call for closure: cause and effect and problem-solution. In both cases, you are presenting a beginning by identifying either a cause or problem, and then you offer closure by suggesting an effect or a solution. The principles of similarity, proximity, and closure help you organize your main points. Following these principles also enhances your ability to construct a speech for your audience that is understandable. Next, we will expand upon the organizational structures that organize your main points.

Organizational Structures

The organization of your speech should not be taken lightly. You want to structure your main points so the information will make the most sense for your audience. We will identify eight common organizational structures in which a message can be structured.

As previously mentioned, a **time-sequence** organizational structure organizes information as it occurs over time. Whenever you present information that follows a chronological order or occurs over time, a time-sequence organizational structure should be used. Usually demonstration or "how to" speeches such as explaining how to make a picture collage, how to surf the net, or how to perform CPR fall into this category. Organizing information by time-sequence is very effective because the audience can better understand a process or event when it is carefully broken down into its chronological order.

USUALLY INFORMATIVE	EITHER INFORMATIVE OR PERSUASIVE	USUALLY PERSUASIVE
Time-sequence	Topical	Problem-solution
Spatial	Cause and effect	Motivated sequence
	Climactic or anticlimactic	Position-options-proposal

Spatial organizational structures organize information as it is located within a physical setting or location. This organizational structure is ideal when speaking about a place or setting such as the points of interest of a city or how something is physically laid out such as a building plan. A spatial organizational structure helps the audience visualize the location or setting, and they can better understand the relationship between the items. Remember that spatial organizations start in one direction and then proceed in a deliberate manner to the end.

The **topical** organizational structure is the most flexible and most widely used organizational structure. Organization by topic divides a subject into natural or customary divisions. It is highly flexible because speakers can choose the most important aspects of their subject from its natural or customary divisions. Anytime your subject seems too broad, divide it into topics, and then determine what are the most important or most interesting aspects of the subject you want to present to the audience. For instance, referring to the shark example, possible topical speeches include three types of predator sharks or three types of North Atlantic sharks, and so on.

The **cause and effect** organizational structure identifies the conditions that create a problem and the outcomes that can result from the conditions. A cause and effect organizational structure is appropriate when you want to analyze a topic for your audience. Some appropriate cause and effect organizational structures would be the cause of acid rain and its effects on the environment, or the cause of road rage and its effects on a person's driving. Whenever you choose a cause and effect organizational structure, spend a proper amount of time on the causes (about 2/3) and the effects (1/3).

Climactic and anticlimactic organizational structures refer to where the most important main points are located. In a climactic structure, the strongest main point is located last in the body as the speaker works toward a climax in his or her speech. An anticlimactic structure means the opposite—the strongest main point is located first. Placing the most important information first is strategic when you are speaking to a neutral or hostile audience and you want them to listen to your perspective. In addition, climactic and anticlimactic speeches can be used in conjunction with other structures. For example, you can have a climactic topical organizational structure or an anticlimactic problem-solution organizational structure.

The **problem-solution** organizational structure is a persuasive structure whereby the speaker identifies a problem and then offers a solution to solve the problem. The persuasion is accomplished in two steps. First, the speaker convinces the audience through evidence that there is a particular problem that is affecting many people. Second, the speaker then tries to convince the audience of the best solution(s) to the problem. An advantage of this type of organization is it allows the speaker to develop the speech in two parts. It is up to the speaker to determine how much time to spend on each part. If the problem is well known, the speaker might want to spend more time on the solution. If the problem is not well known, the speaker might want to spend equal time on the problem and the solution.

Monroe's motivated sequence was developed by Alan Monroe. It is a five-step sequential method in motivating an audience to a specific action.[13] These five steps include attention, need, satisfaction, visualization, and action. The **attention step** is where the speaker tries to gain the audience's attention and establish the importance/relevance of the topic to the audience. The **need step** is where the speaker articulates how the audience is affected by a problem in order to convince the audience there is a need for change. In other words, the speaker shows the audience there is a need for action. The **satisfaction step** is when the speaker shows the audience how they can resolve the problem. The speaker convinces the audience that the proposed solution will bring the most satisfaction. The **visualization step** is where the speaker gives the audience an image of how the solution solves the problem. This can be done in a positive way by explaining the positive results the audience will receive by taking action, or it can be done in a negative way by explaining the negative consequences the audience will experience if they do not take action. Finally, the **action step** is where the speaker makes a persuasive appeal for the audience to act on the request. The speaker wants the audience to make a commitment and requests the audience to act on the request.

The **position-option proposal** organization is similar to the Motivated Sequence except the speaker provides the audience with several options. Then, the speaker persuades the audience to adopt one particular option. The first step is to establish the current position or current state of affairs. When the speaker describes the current condition or current state, the problems of the current condition are exposed and/or the causes of the current state are provided. The second step is to give the audience options. The speaker articulates several options the audience can take to solve the current problem. The final step is to persuade the audience to adopt one proposal by explaining how the proposal has more strengths and less weaknesses than the other options. This way the audience can see why they should be supporting the speaker's proposal.

8

We have explained several ways you can organize the main points of your speech. When choosing an organizational structure for your speech, you want to choose the organizational structure that best fits the type of information you want to present to your audience. Once you have determined your organizational structure, you can begin to decide how you want to support your main points.

HOW TO INCLUDE SUPPORT MATERIAL

The main points of a speech cannot stand by themselves. Each main point should be reinforced with support material. As we discussed in Chapter 7, **support material** is the substance of any speech such as examples and facts that verify a speaker's information and make the speaker's ideas more precise and concrete. Including support material for your speech allows you to develop and explain your ideas more completely. Plus, when you use support material in your speech, you are able to verify the claims you make in your main points. If we return to the Yellowstone Park example, we can illustrate how support material develops the body of the speech.

What the following example illustrates is how support material helps develop the speech. The use of facts, examples, narratives, and testimony verifies claims about the park's wildlife, geysers and hot springs, and activities. Without support material, this speech would be vague and abstract because there would not be any specific information explaining the three points of the speech. *The key when selecting support material is to choose support that is appropriate and that specifically backs up the point you want to convey.* Avoid adding support material that does not support your claim. This could lead you off track, and your information will appear to be out of place to your audience. Likewise, your speech can appear to be out of place if you do not make clear connections between main points. How to make connections between main points in a speech is discussed next.

A. Yellowstone Park contains a variety of wildlife
   1. Name variety and types of large mammals
      a. Types
      b. Grey wolf reintroduction story
   2. Explain best seasons to view the wildlife
      a. Spring
      b. Autumn
B. Yellowstone Park contains famous geysers and hot springs
   1. Old Faithful
      a. Facts
      b. Personal story
   2. Mammoth Hot Springs
      a. Facts
      b. Myths
C. Yellowstone Park contains many activities for visitors
   1. Scenic drives
      a. The Grand Loop
      b. Driving tips
   2. Hiking
      a. Popular hiking areas
      b. Hiking tips
   3. Camping
      a. Different campsites
      b. Camping tips

8

HOW TO DETERMINE YOUR CONNECTIONS

One feature of public speaking that is often overlooked by speakers is how they link one main point to the next main point. When the connection between main points is done correctly, it results in smooth transitions that are pleasant to hear and subtly move the audience along. However, when the connections between main points are not done well or not done at all, the audience can get lost in the speech. In this case, information blends together, and it is difficult to distinguish how your speech is progressing. When you do not provide connections, a speech can be a free-flowing fountain of ideas devoid of direction and without indication of what is important or what is of interest. Do not let your speech be a free-flowing fountain. You have the ability to direct the flow of your information, to signal when you are changing ideas, and to indicate when a point is important. Incorporating smooth transitions separates good speakers from average speakers. In the next section, we will discuss several connections and transitions you can incorporate into your speech to help organize it and direct the flow of your speech.

Signposts

Signposts are statements that indicate what information will be covered and in what order the information will be covered. Often, signposts are used in conjunction with the preview of the speech (see example below). In short, signposts forecast the sequence in which the main points will appear in the speech. The following example is a signpost that occurs in conjunction with a **preview** to indicate the sequence of the main points in a speech. Notice how the signpost is constructed in parallel form:

> *I will inform you of three aspects of Yellowstone Park's natural wonder.*
>
> *First, I will describe the variety of Yellowstone Park's wildlife.*
>
> *Second, I will explain the unique features of Yellowstone Park's geysers and hot springs.*
>
> *Third, I will highlight Yellowstone Park's enjoyable activities.*

Notice that signposts are always numbered. This helps the audience understand what information you will cover and in what order you will cover it.

Transitions

Transitions are statements that connect the previous idea to the new idea. More specifically, the transition links the idea the speaker is finishing to the idea the speaker is beginning. When transitions are used, they function as bridges that move the audience from the end of one idea to the new idea. An example of a transition is illustrated by a student speaker who links two ideas in her informative speech on heart attacks—treatments and preventions:

> *Although there are many innovative treatments for people who have suffered heart attacks, why suffer a heart attack when there are many preventions that people can take to lower their risk of a heart attack?*

What this example illustrates is how the speaker is moving the audience from the previous idea she completed, treatments, to the new idea, preventions. In this way, the audience knows what information will be discussed next. Without transitions, the speech will sound disorganized with ideas and information popping up out of nowhere.

Another type of transition is the internal summary. The **internal summary** reviews the information the audience has already heard. These summaries are used when information is complex or when a speaker has covered a lot of information. In these cases, instead of simply moving to the next point, summarize what has already been covered to refresh the audience's memory of what they have heard. For example:

> *Now that I have explained the different types of wildlife that inhabit Yellowstone Park, and the unique features of Yellowstone Park's geysers and hot springs, I'd like to describe the various activities Yellowstone Park offers visitors.*

The example illustrates how the speaker recapped the first two main points of the speech before the speaker moved on to the third main point. Internal summaries are especially useful when you are leading up to a climactic ending or when you are trying to build a persuasive case.

8

Internal Previews

While internal summaries review what was heard, **internal previews** forecast what the audience will hear next. This is helpful when the audience is going to hear several subpoints in a row. Internal previews operate in a manner similar to the preview of a speech, but they occur in the body of the speech. Internal previews can be combined with transitions.

[Transition] *While Yellowstone Park contains numerous wildlife, it also contains a variety of geysers and hot springs.*

[Internal preview] *I will discuss the park's three most popular thermal features: first, I will elaborate on the unique features of Old Faithful; second, I will describe the characteristics of Norris Geyser Basin; and third, I will explain the unusual aspects of Mammoth Hot Springs.*

The completion of our discussion on connections ends this chapter on how to organize your message. Organization starts with identifying the general purpose, the specific purpose, and the thesis statement. After you develop a thesis statement, you need to determine what your main points will be, which is often influenced by what type of information you have in relation to the principles of similarity, proximity, and closure. These principles underlie several organizational patterns. Once you have your main points arranged by an organizational structure, you need to consider support material for your main points and how to connect the main points to keep your ideas flowing smoothly.

From reading this chapter you now know how to construct, develop, and outline the body of a speech. Outlining the body of your speech will help you organize your ideas and enhance your ability to make an effective presentation. Once the body of the speech is organized, you can start developing the introduction and conclusion to your speech, which will be discussed in the next chapter.

VOCABULARY

Anticlimactic organization — organizational pattern that places the strongest information first in the body of a speech.

Ascending pattern — organizational pattern in which the least amount of information is contained in the first main point with the amount of information increasing with each succeeding main point.

Balance — when all parts of the speech, the introduction, the body, and the conclusion, have the right amount of development and emphasis.

Basic speech structure — the three general parts of any speech, which are the introduction, the body, and the conclusion.

Cause and effect organization — organizational pattern that identifies the conditions that create a problem and the outcomes that can result from the conditions.

Climactic organization — organizational pattern that places the strongest information last in the body of a speech.

Configural logic — based upon presenting information in a spiral or cyclical pattern where information jumps from idea to idea with content, evidence, and arguments used as needed to support specific ideas.

Descending pattern — organizational pattern in which the most amount of information is contained in the first main point and then the amount of information decreases with each succeeding main point.

General purpose — one of three general overall objectives a speech can accomplish such as to inform, persuade, or entertain.

High-context culture — the meanings of a communication message are imbedded in the situation, the relationship of the individuals, and the implicit norms, beliefs, and values of the culture.

Internal preview — a statement that forecasts the information the audience will hear. Internal previews serve the same function as a preview, but occur in the body of the speech.

Internal summary — a statement that reviews the information the audience has already heard before connecting to the new idea.

Linear logic — based upon presenting information in a linear sequence where the content, evidence, and arguments proceed from beginning to end in a straight line.

Logic — (or logos) is a systematic pattern of thought based upon reasoning and evidence.

Monroe's motivated sequence — a persuasive organizational pattern that involves five steps: attention, need, satisfaction, visualization, and action.

Parallel structure — repeating the same grammatical structure of phrases, words, or sentences for clarity.

Position-option proposal — a persuasive organizational pattern that involves three steps: acknowledging the current situation (position), expressing options that can improve the situation (options), and offering one option as the best (proposal).

Preview — a statement that indicates the main points of a speech.

Principle of closure — a psychological way of organizing information by providing a clear beginning and ending.

Principle of proximity — a psychological way of organizing information according to how it occurs in time or space.

Principle of similarity — a psychological way of organizing information together that shares some common relationship or is alike in some regards.

Problem-solution — organizational pattern that organizes information by first identifying a problem and then by offering a solution to the problem.

Signposts — statements that indicate what information will be covered and in what order it will be covered.

Spatial organization — organizational pattern that organizes information as it is located within a physical setting.

Specific purpose — the goal of a speech.

Support material — the substance of any speech, such as examples, facts, statistics, testimony, narratives, and anecdotes, that make a speaker's ideas more precise and concrete.

Symmetrical pattern — organizational pattern in which main points are balanced.

Thesis statement — the main idea of the presentation.

Third-culture building — involves a speaker and audience creating a new culture that draws from and extends the norms and values from the independent cultures.

Time-sequence organization — organizational pattern that organizes information as it occurs in time.

Topical organization — organizational pattern that organizes information by dividing the topic into natural or customary divisions.

Transitions — statements that connect the previous idea to the new idea.

REFERENCES

[1] Patricia Kearney, Timothy G. Plax, Ellis R. Hayes, and Marily J. Ivey, "College Teacher Misbehaviors: What Students Don't Like About What Teachers Say and Do," *Communication Quarterly* 39 (1991): 309–324.

[2] The majority of research that explains how structured and organized messages are better understood and remembered by audiences was published in the 1960s and 1970s. Some articles include: Christopher Spicer and Ronald E. Bassett, "The Effect of Organization on Learning from an Informative Message," *The Southern Speech Communication Journal* 41(1976): 290–299; Earnest Thompson, "Some Effects of Message Structure on Listeners' Comprehension," *Speech Monographs* 34 (1967): 51–57; Arlee Johnson, "A Primary Investigation of the Relationship Between Organization and Listener Comprehension," *Central States Speech Journal* 21 (1970): 104–107.

[3] Ernest Thompson, "An Experimental Investigation of the Relative Effectiveness of Organizational Structure in Oral Communication," *Southern Speech Journal* 26 (1960): 59–69.

[4] Harry Sharp, Jr. and Thomas McClung, "Effects of Organization on the Speaker's Ethos," *Speech Monographs* 33 (1966): 182–183.

[5] Mark P. Orbe and Tina M. Harris, *Interracial Communication* (USA: Wadsworth, 2001), 223.

[6] Guo-Ming Chen and William J. Starosta, *Foundations of Intercultural Communication* (Needham Height, MA: Allyn and Bacon, 2001), 144–146.

[7] Everett Rogers and Thomas Steinfatt, *Intercultural Communication* (Prospect Heights, IL: Waveland Press, 1999), 88–89.

[8] Orbe and Harris, 223; Chen and Starosta, 146.

[9] Chen and Starosta, 145.

[10] John R. Rickford and Russell J. Rickford, *Spoken Soul* (New York: John Wiley & Sons, 2000); Smitherman, G. *Talkin' that talk* (New York: Routledge, 2000).

[11] Michael Osborn and Suzanne Osborne, *Public Speaking*, 4th ed. (New York: Houghton Mifflin, 1997), 210–213.

[12] Ibid.

[13] Douglas Ehninger, Bruce E. Gronbeck, and Alan H. Monroe, *Principles of Speech Communication*, 9th brief edition (Glenview, Illinois: Scott, Foresman and Co., 1984), 249.

8

INTRODUCTIONS AND CONCLUSIONS 9

"...speech is like a love affair. Any fool can start it, but to end it requires considerable skill."
-Lord Mancroft

"If you haven't struck oil in your first three minutes, stop boring!"
-George Jessel

"If you want a happy ending, that depends, of course, on where you stop your story."
-Orson Welles

This Chapter Examines:

- creating an introduction

- creating a conclusion

After researching the speech topic of the weather phenomenon, El Niño, Billy prepared for his presentation. He organized and outlined his ideas, and he practiced the delivery of his speech. Not only was Billy prepared, but he was excited to share his research with the audience. On presentation day, Billy started his speech by stating, "I will tell you all about El Niño." As he began to present his information he noticed the blank looks of boredom on the audience members' faces. Billy did not let this distract him; he continued with his speech until he was ready to end the speech. However, he was unsure how to end the speech, so he abruptly ended his last thought and simply said, "Thank you."

This example illustrates the importance of beginning and ending your speech with an effective introduction and conclusion. No matter how interesting, unique, or captivating your topic is, all speeches need an effective introduction and conclusion. Introductions and conclusions are "bookends" that subtly build interest for your speech and wrap up the speech in a captivating manner. This chapter explains how you can develop an effective introduction and conclusion for your speech.

CREATING AN INTRODUCTION

Creating an effective introduction is important. As Billy's example illustrates, if you do not introduce your information appropriately the audience can be "turned off" to your topic or you can lose your audience before you even proceed into the main points of your speech. Introducing your speech is very important and should not be taken lightly. A creative introduction will pique the audience's curiosity and establish a tone for your speech. Good introductions are like appetizers that increase the audience's appetite for your speech. Any introduction should demonstrate four functions: gain attention, relate the topic to audience, establish credibility, and preview the organization of the speech. Each function will be explained.

Figure 9-1. Introduction

Gain Attention

For any introduction, your first priority is to gain the audience's attention by sparking curiosity for your topic and increasing the audience's interest in your topic. You can accomplish these objectives by gaining the attention of your audience in your introduction. Sometimes the attention step is referred to as the attention-getter. Consider the following attempt to gain the audience's attention:

> *Hi, my name is Bob Thornton, and I will be talking about a mysterious bacteria that is invading river systems in the United States called the "Red Tide."*

While this introduction is clear, it does not grab the audience's attention, because it fails to increase audience curiosity for the topic. Avoid unimaginative and uncreative introductions that do not gain the audience's attention. *Instead, you want to be as creative as possible to gain the audience's attention.* The following example shows how a speaker can construct a more developed attention-gaining introduction that builds interest in the topic:

> *Imagine yourself vacationing in Florida during winter break. It's a sunny day of 85°. You are in a small sailboat with your best friends, leisurely enjoying your favorite snacks and beverages. The water is clear enough for you to see all types of marine life, including the endangered manatee, which you see gently floating in the water. As the temperature begins to rise, you decide to dangle your legs in the water to cool off and enjoy the day. That evening, however, you notice red rashes and a burning sensation on your legs. Little did you know that you had been exposed to a new bacteria that is beginning to invade river systems and inland water areas. You had just been exposed to the Red Tide.*

This hypothetical example illustrates how a more developed story gains the audience's attention. The hypothetical example invites the audience to think along with the story as the speaker develops the scene and the conditions that lead into the speech. For each introduction, you want to gain the audience's attention first and then proceed into your topic. It is a more effective way to introduce your topic. Here are some additional ways you can gain the audience's attention to start your speech.

Ask a Rhetorical Question

Beginning your speech with a rhetorical question is a quick and efficient way to lead into your topic and to get your audience mentally involved in your speech. The rhetorical question is usually a question the speaker does not expect the audience to explicitly answer. For example, a speaker might ask, "How many people here have had difficulty finding parking on campus?"

9

However, sometimes the speaker does want to receive a more explicit response from the audience by asking audience members to raise their hands. The speaker can simply direct the audience by saying, "By a show of hands, how many people have had difficulty finding parking on campus?" Regardless of what you want to accomplish with your rhetorical question, you want to make sure you pause after the question so the audience can think about the question. Too often speakers ask the question and then proceed into their speech without allowing the audience to think about their question. Rhetorical questions are more effective when you allow the audience to mentally think about the question before you continue with the rest of your speech.

Begin with a Quotation

Starting with a quotation is an effective way to gain the audience's attention because a quotation can accurately sum up a theme that you will develop in your speech. Also, quotations can sometimes articulate a feeling, mood, and idea better than you can. For example, consider this introduction that started with a quotation:

> *"Four score and seven years ago our fathers brought forth on this continent a new nation conceived in liberty, and dedicated to the proposition that all men are created equal." These words spoken by Abraham Lincoln over 100 hundred years ago still capture so eloquently the fundamental ideals that make this country so great—equality.*

In this example, a student is using the words of Abraham Lincoln to introduce the topic of equality. Although this example uses a well-known quotation from Lincoln's Gettysburg Address, quotations do not always have to be from prominent persons or from significant events. Quotations can be used from almost any type of source. The key is to use a quotation that is appropriate for the situation. Naturally, it would make more sense to include a quotation from the Secretary of State if you were talking about United States foreign policy. However, if you want to show the average American's perspective on United States foreign policy, you could use a common citizen's quotation. Regardless of who you quote, make sure the statement is clear, unambiguous, and that it directly relates to your topic. As a speaker, make sure to acknowledge the source of the quotation so there is no mistake that the words spoken are not your own.

Use Striking Information

Sometimes the most effective way to gain audience attention is to use a striking fact, statistic, and/or example. A speaker might want to start with a graphic picture or state a dramatic statistic. When a speaker starts with striking information, the audience understands the relevance of the topic right away. For example, consider this opening, which also asks a rhetorical question:

For those of us who drive to campus, I have one question for you. Do you know whether your car is secure? If you drove to class today and parked it in one of the lots, you expect your car to be there waiting for you after class in the parking lot. But will it be there? This is a legitimate question because it is estimated that a car is stolen every 30 seconds in many parts of this country, and most thefts take place in under a minute.

In this case, the speaker uses a striking statistic to get the audience focused on the significance of the topic, car theft. Whenever you want to make a strong point to start your speech, use striking information to gain the audience's attention.

Tell a Story

Humans have always enjoyed good stories. Stories are a way to keep the audience mentally involved in your speech, as they draw the audience into your information. The story we discussed earlier about the Red Tide is a good example of how a speaker can get an audience mentally involved with a story. Stories work well when they are interesting and relevant to your main point. Never tell a story that has no connection to your speech, and make sure that you know the story. It is very frustrating for an audience to listen to a story that does not make sense or is told in a disjointed, confusing manner. There are many ways a speaker can tell a story. Two common ways speakers incorporate stories into a speech are by creating a "visualization" and by telling a generic story.

When speakers use a visualization, they are asking the audience to mentally participate in imagining a situation or in thinking back to a certain experience. Visualizations are great because they allow everyone in the audience to get involved without anyone leaving his or her seat. Using a generic story is another good way to begin your speech. When speakers use a generic story, they talk in general terms, which allows the audience to think in different directions. Then, the speaker clarifies the information, which illustrates to the audience a new way to think about the topic. For example, here is how a speaker used a generic story to begin a speech:

All of you have used this drug. It's white, powdery, and at one time or another we have all used it to help us cope. You say you haven't? Well, I guarantee you have. I have used it, and I'm not afraid to admit it. What drug am I referring to? It is caffeine. In its purest form it's white and powdery, and it is included in many foods and beverages, and many of us use it to get through the day.

9

As you can see, using a generic story influences the audience to wonder what the speaker is referring to. Once the speaker clarifies the generic story, the audience has been effectively linked to the topic.

Start with a Demonstration

Another way to gain your audience's attention is to start with a brief demonstration. Having the audience watch you do something is a good way to make a point. Sometimes when you show some process to the audience, it is more effective than trying to simply explain the process. For example, one student started her speech by demonstrating sign language. Then, she told the audience what she had signed, which lead into her topic on sign language.

Sometimes the demonstration can have a surprise, such as asking for a volunteer. Whenever you are going to start with a demonstration, keep these ideas in mind. First, avoid using any type of firearm, weapon, or any other sharp objects that could injure your audience or yourself. Second, make sure you plan the demonstration and keep it brief. This includes planning to make sure the audience will be able to see the demonstration. Third, if you are using a volunteer, ask someone in advance to be your volunteer so your speech will proceed smoothly.

Use Humor

Using humor as a way to introduce a topic is a very effective way to gain an audience's attention. Moreover, it "breaks the ice" with the audience, and it relaxes the audience by putting them into a good mood to listen to your speech. The difficulty with using humor is that the humor must be funny and in good taste. Also, if the humor backfires, this can make speakers nervous or it can distract speakers from proceeding smoothly into their speech. Whenever you are using humor, make sure it is well planned out, that you know how to properly deliver it, and that you know all the parts of the message.

Show a Media Clip

Media clips can be helpful in gaining the audience's attention. A media clip often grabs the audience's attention and it can have more impact than what the speaker can simply state. When using a media clip to introduce your speech, it is helpful to give a brief introduction of the footage before you show it. For example, you might introduce a media clip by saying, "I would like to begin this presentation by showing you a scene you might have experienced before." After the short clip is finished, you should clarify what the audience saw and relate it to your topic. When speakers do not link the media clip to their topic, it can make the footage seem unrelated to the topic. Also, make sure the media clip is short and to the point. You do not want to show a long segment for an attention-getter that constitutes half of your speech. Rather, you want the media clip to give the audience just a taste of the topic. When you are planning to use a media clip, make sure the footage is cued to the proper place so the footage will be ready to be shown for your presentation.

The examples we have provided are some of the common ways a speech can be introduced to your audience. Keep in mind that the examples are not an exhaustive list. Creativity is the best attention-gaining device. Strive to create a unique and interesting attention-getter that builds curiosity for your speech. Avoid stale and boring introductions such as, "Hi, my name is…" or "Today I will talk about…" These are not effective ways to gain your audience's attention or create curiosity and interest for your topic. *Remember that it is your job as a speaker to think of creative ways to gain your audience's attention.*

Relating Topic to Audience

A second function of introductions is to relate the topic to the audience. Sometimes this is referred to as establishing **common ground** because the speaker explains how the topic directly relates to the audience. In other words, the speaker's and audience's common interests are linked by a "common bond," which is the topic. When you can establish common ground or the **rationale** for a speech, it clarifies the speech's relevance to the audience. While the primary function of the attention-getter is to gain attention, establishing common ground explicitly states why this topic is important and relevant for the audience to hear. Never assume the topic alone will be of interest to an audience because the audience might think they have already heard everything they want to hear about your topic. By stating why your topic is important and how your topic is relevant to the audience, you can clarify how your speech is different from other similar speeches the audience might have already heard.

Establish Credibility

A third function of an introduction is to establish the credibility of the speaker on the topic. This can be done in two ways. First, the speaker can tell the audience of their experience or their expertise in the topic they are speaking about. For example, if a student gave a speech on photography, he can establish his credibility by saying:

> *As a photo technician the past five years at Casio and Casio Studios, I have developed many pictures, and I would like to share some pointers I have learned to help you avoid common mistakes in picture taking.*

9

Remember that establishing your credibility is not "bragging" or "talking down" to your audience. It is an essential element in any speech. When you establish your credibility in a speech, it tells the audience you have personal experience with the subject, and you have gained valuable knowledge from this experience. Another way speakers can demonstrate credibility in a speech is by **citing** information from credible sources to illustrate to the audience that they have researched the topic and they are knowledgeable about the topic.

Preview the Organization of the Speech

Finally, the fourth function of an introduction is to define your **thesis** and **preview**—the main points of the speech. This way the audience knows specifically what the speech will be about and in what order the speech will develop the thesis. For example, here is a sample thesis and preview:

> [Thesis] *Taking better pictures is easy once you know what common errors to avoid.*
>
> [Preview] *In order for you to understand how to take better pictures, first, I will explain the different film speed options; second, I will discuss how light affects your pictures; and third, I will provide several tips on how to avoid common photography mistakes.*

Notice how each main point starts with a **signpost** that indicates the order in which the main points will be presented. Providing a clear thesis and preview helps the audience understand and follow the progression of your ideas. Without a clear thesis and preview, the speech has no direction, and your audience will get lost. Once an audience is lost, the effectiveness of your message wanes.

We will now return to our Yellowstone Park example to show how a speaker can organize the introduction of this speech to lead into the body of the speech that we have already developed in Chapter 8.

I. Introduction
   A. Attention-Getter: Start with a short media clip of some scenic views of Yellowstone Park
   B. Common Ground: Everyone has taken a vacation or has enjoyed the scenic views of their favorite park. Yellowstone Park offers as many, if not more scenic views than any park you have visited.
   C. Credibility: I have taken two vacations at Yellowstone Park, and each time I have experienced new natural wonders.
   D. [Thesis]: Yellowstone Park offers many natural wonders that can be explored any time of the year. [Preview]: To better understand Yellowstone Park's natural wonders, first, I will elaborate on the variety of wildlife that live in the park; second, I will discuss the unique geysers and hot springs found in the park; third, I will explain several activities you can enjoy in the park.

This example shows how a speaker can introduce a speech on Yellowstone Park. As you can see, it is a developed and structured introduction that gains attention, establishes common ground, articulates credibility, and forecasts a thesis and preview. Once you have successfully created an introduction for your speech, the last step is to finish the construction of your speech by providing a conclusion.

CREATING A CONCLUSION

Conclusions are an opportunity for you to wrap up the speech by reminding the audience of the ideas you talked about, by restating the relevance of your speech, and by bringing closure to your speech. Conclusions are just as important as introductions. When constructed well they bring the speech to a close without a speaker ending the speech by saying, "That's it," or "I'm done," or "The end." We will discuss three functions of a conclusion and how you can incorporate these functions into your speech to make an effective conclusion. These three functions are to review main points, reinforce your message, and provide closure.

9

Review Main Points

The beginning of your conclusion is where you review the main points of your speech. After you finish the last point of your body, use a transition to link to your review. A **review** is when the speaker simply restates the main points of the speech in the same order they were previewed and discussed in the body. For example, a review of the Yellowstone Park speech might be:

> *In this speech, I have provided you with a better understanding of Yellowstone Park's natural wonders by elaborating on the variety of wildlife that live in the park, by discussing the unique geysers and hot springs found in the park, and by explaining several activities you can enjoy in the park.*

When you give the audience a review, it signals to them that the speech is coming to an end. It also allows for a smooth transition from the body to the conclusion without trite phrases such as, "In conclusion…" or "In summary…"

Reinforce Message

After the main points of the speech are reviewed, you should restate the relevance of the speech to the audience. Reinforcing your message reiterates for the audience what the speech was about and what valuable knowledge the audience has gained from your speech. For the Yellowstone speech, the audience has gained valuable information about the natural wonders of the park that can be experienced at any time in the year. When you reinforce your message to the audience, you remind the audience of the importance and relevance of your speech.

Provide Closure

Finally, provide closure to your speech. A very simple way to provide closure is to end your speech the way you began. If you started your speech with a quotation, end with a quotation; if you started with a story, end with a story. When you end the way you began, this is an indication to the audience that you are ending the speech because the audience recognizes that this is how you started. A closure is also referred to as a clincher. A **clincher** provides a fitting and memorable end to the speech by linking back to the attention-getter. Finishing with a similar attention step allows your speech to come full circle. Good speech structure can be compared to taking a trip; you start from one destination; you follow highways to a point; then, you return and end up where the trip started.

III. Conclusion

A. [Thesis]: I have explained how Yellowstone Park offers many natural wonders that can be explored year round [Review] by elaborating on the types of wildlife that live in the park; by discussing the unique geysers and hot springs found in the park; and by explaining several activities you can enjoy in the park.

B. Reinforce Message: You now are more aware of what Yellowstone Park offers to visitors who want to explore its natural wonders. The next time you are planning a vacation, you should consider Yellowstone Park.

C. Clincher: End by showing more media clips of Yellowstone Park's scenic views.

From reading this chapter, you understand the importance of developing an introduction and conclusion. When you take the time to develop an introduction and conclusion, it will help you present a more effective speech. We have explained the functions of introductions and conclusions along with providing examples of how to outline and develop an introduction and conclusion. Finally, we have included a sample outline of the Yellowstone Park speech to show you what a completed outline looks like.

9

I. Introduction

    A. **Attention-Getter:** Start with a short media clip of some scenic views of Yellowstone Park

    B. **Common Ground:** Everyone has taken a vacation or has enjoyed the scenic views of their favorite park. Yellowstone Park offers as many, if not more scenic views than any park you have visited.

    C. **Credibility:** I have taken two vacations at Yellowstone Park, and each time I have experienced new natural wonders.

    D. **Thesis:** Yellowstone Park offers many natural wonders that can be explored any time of the year. **Preview:** To better understand Yellowstone Park's natural wonders, first, I will elaborate on the variety of wildlife that live in the park; second, I will discuss the unique geysers and hot springs found in the park; third, I will explain several activities you can enjoy in the park.

II. Body

    A. Yellowstone Park contains a variety of wildlife

        1. Name variety and types of large mammals

            a. Types

            b. Grey wolf reintroduction story

        2. Explain best seasons to view the wildlife

            a. Spring

            b. Autumn

    B. Yellowstone Park contains famous geysers and hot springs

        1. Old Faithful

            a. Facts

            b. Personal story

        2. Mammoth Hot Springs

            a. Facts

            b. Myths

    C. Yellowstone Park contains many activities for visitors

        1. Scenic drives

            a. The Grand Loop

            b. Driving tips

        2. Hiking
            a. Popular hiking areas
            b. Hiking tips
        3. Camping
            a. Different campsites
            b. Camping tips
III. Conclusion
    A. **Thesis**: I have explained how Yellowstone Park offers many natural wonders that can be explored year round [**Review**] by elaborating on the types of wildlife that live in the park; by discussing the unique geysers and hot springs found in the park; and by explaining several activities you can enjoy in the park.
    B. **Reinforce Message**: You now are more aware of what Yellowstone Park offers to visitors who want to explore its natural wonders. The next time you are planning a vacation, you should consider Yellowstone Park.
    C. **Clincher**: End by showing more media clips of Yellowstone Park's scenic views.

VOCABULARY

Attention-getter — a function of the introduction in which the goal is to grab the audience's attention and build interest for your topic.

Citing sources — acknowledging the authenticity of your information by stating the author, name of publication, title, and date of the source for the audience.

Clincher — a function of the conclusion that provides a fitting and memorable end to the speech by linking back to the attention step.

Common ground — when the speaker explains to the audience how a topic relates to the audience to establish a common interest between speaker and audience (similar to the concept of rationale).

Credibility — the audience's perception of the speaker's integrity, honesty, and competence.

Preview — a statement that indicates the main points of a speech.

9

Quotation — a direct statement made by a person.

Rationale — the benefits and significance of the topic to the audience (similar to the concept of common ground).

Review — a statement that restates the main points of a speech.

Rhetorical question — a question asked by the speaker to the audience that is not expected to be answered.

Signpost — a statement that indicates what information will be covered and in what order it will be covered.

Thesis — the main idea of the speech.

DELIVERY 10

"A thing said walks in immortality / if it has been said well."
–Peter Pindar

"I distrust the incommunicable; it is the source of all violence."
–Jean-Paul Sartre

"When the eyes say one thing, and the tongue another, a practical man relies on the language of the first."
–Ralph Waldo Emerson

This Chapter Examines:

+ the four types of delivery

+ vocal delivery

+ nonverbal delivery

+ practicing the speech

As Jocelyn waits to deliver her speech, she thinks about all the time and effort she spent selecting, researching, organizing, outlining, and preparing her speech. Jocelyn is enthusiastic about her presentation, because she believes the audience will find it interesting and unique. When Jocelyn finally walks to the front of the classroom to deliver her speech, however, she stumbles over a few words, she incorporates vocal fillers such as "ah" and "um," and she shifts her eye contact from the back wall to her notes. After she finishes her speech, Jocelyn is disappointed because she knows she had interesting information, but she did not complement her information with a strong delivery.

Many people can identify with the difficulty Jocelyn had delivering her speech. Delivery is a critical aspect in public speaking, because unpolished delivery can undermine speech content even if it is organized and interesting. What happened to Jocelyn illustrates that excellent speech content does not guarantee a successful speech. All speakers must practice delivering their speech for the presentation to be effective. In fact, it takes several practices for speakers to become comfortable with the speech and the ideas they will present. No matter how experienced the speaker, practice is essential for success. The only way to perfect your delivery is through practice, practice, and more practice. As you practice your speech, you will become more familiar with the information, you will be less nervous, and your ideas will flow more smoothly.[1]

A speaker's delivery is effective when the speaker can articulate a message in a clear and interesting manner without distracting vocal utterances or nonverbal movement. In fact, a strong delivery enhances the content of the speech because the audience can focus on what is said instead of how it is said. Developing an effective delivery is a challenge for every speaker. In time, speakers will develop a style with which they feel the most comfortable.

Figure 10-1. Effective Delivery

Whatever your style, you want to demonstrate a mixture of a **formal delivery** (an organized delivery that is achieved through preparation and planning) and an **informal delivery** (a conversational and spontaneous delivery). Speakers who demonstrate the strengths of both a formal and informal delivery are perceived to be effective speakers.[2]

In this chapter, we will discuss how delivery impacts the public speaking situation. More specifically, we will identify the four common types of delivery. Second, we will describe various aspects of the vocal delivery and offer some suggestions for improving your vocal delivery. Next, we will explain the components of the nonverbal delivery and offer some helpful hints for improving your nonverbal delivery. Finally, we will offer some guidelines for practicing your speech.

THE FOUR TYPES OF DELIVERY

Although there are endless types of speaking occasions, there are four primary types of delivery. Some types of delivery are more formal, where the speaker prepares and plans an organized and precise message. Other types of delivery are more informal, where the speaker can demonstrate a conversational and spontaneous delivery.

Memorized Speaking

When a speaker delivers a speech word for word from memory it is called **memorized speaking**. In this type of speaking, not only are the words memorized, but all aspects of the vocal delivery (such as voice inflection) and nonverbal delivery (such as gestures and movement) are memorized. To deliver a memorized speech, a speaker must endlessly practice the speech until all aspects of the speech are mastered. Although memorized speaking seems tedious and time consuming, in ancient times this style was the primary type of delivery. In fact, ancient orators used to memorize complex speeches that would last for several hours. Today, however, there is little need for memorized speeches. Only short presentations such as acceptance speeches, introductions, or toasts are commonly memorized.

One advantage of a memorized speech is that a speaker can demonstrate excellent delivery skills such as eye contact, gestures, movement, and vocal inflections. However, you can only achieve this if you concentrate on delivering ideas to your audience rather than recalling memorized words. There are many disadvantages to memorized speaking. First, speakers can easily forget their speech. All it takes is forgetting one word, one phrase, or one sentence to cause the speaker to forget the entire speech. Second, since it is very difficult to demonstrate delivery skills

10

(because the speaker is concentrating on the words), the speech can lack gestures, movement, and vocal inflection unless the speaker has practiced over, and over, and over again. Third, memorized speeches can intensify nervousness since the speaker knows that everything is dependent on memory.

Manuscript Speaking

When a speaker delivers a speech that has been already written out word for word it is called **manuscript speaking**. Commonly, manuscript speaking occurs when a speaker needs to be precise and accurate. Examples of manuscript speeches include the State of the Union Address, court rulings, or any type of prepared statement about an important subject. These speeches are delivered from a manuscript because the speakers do not want to be misunderstood or have their words taken out of context. Although manuscript speaking might seem easy, it is very difficult. Since speakers have the text in front of them, it is easy to *read* the speech instead of *delivering* the speech to the audience. Whenever manuscript speaking is required, you must practice vocal and nonverbal delivery to make your speech appear to be conversational and spontaneous.

The advantage of manuscript speaking is that speakers have the text of the speech in front of them so memorization is not necessary. Since the text is in front of the speaker, the speaker will be more confident and less nervous. However, there are many disadvantages to manuscript speaking. First, manuscript speaking often results in a monotone delivery that is not conversational and lacks vocal variety. Second, the speaker tends to read the speech, which limits audience eye contact. Third, nonverbal delivery suffers as the speaker tends to be anchored to a podium, which makes the speaker appear more stiff and less natural. Fourth, since speakers are speaking from a prepared text, they can't easily adapt to audience feedback. Thus, the speaker is more likely to "stick to the text" and less likely to respond to audience needs.

Extemporaneous Speaking

When a speaker plans and prepares a speech ahead of time and delivers a speech from an outline or notes it is called **extemporaneous speaking**. This is the most common delivery style because it incorporates the best of the formal style (organization, preparation, and planning) with the informal style (conversational, spontaneous, and vocal variety). The advanced planning and preparation allows the speaker to gain confidence for delivering the speech, and it allows the speaker to use a variety of delivery skills because the speaker is speaking from notes rather than from memory or from a manuscript. In extemporaneous speaking, the exact wording can change from presentation to presentation, but not the general ideas of the speech. The ideas and the order of the speech are always the same. Extemporaneous speaking allows speakers to develop confidence with their speech as they practice from an outline.

There are many advantages to extemporaneous speaking. First, it allows for a maximum use of delivery skills. A speaker can appear conversational and spontaneous, while demonstrating direct eye contact, gestures, and movement. Second, speakers have the freedom to adapt to audience feedback. Third, extemporaneous speaking allows for the delivery of an organized message since you have prepared ahead of time. Fourth, preparing for the speech ahead of time allows for greater confidence. The one disadvantage of the extemporaneous speech is the amount of time that is spent organizing, researching, and practicing the delivery. If speakers do not give themselves enough time to practice, they might not be able to confidently deliver their speech.

Impromptu Speaking

When the speaker gives a presentation with little or no preparation it is called **impromptu speaking**. How can someone give an impromptu speech? Usually the speaker's experience and knowledge allow the speaker to speak on a topic. For example, you might be on a job interview, and although you might not know ahead of time the specific questions you will be asked, you answer the questions well because you are talking from experience. This example points out that sometimes the speaker has no choice but to give an impromptu speech—answering questions in class, offering your opinion at a meeting, and introducing yourself or others.

Whenever you are in an impromptu speaking situation, it is wise to keep your ideas simple and concise. Moreover, you want to articulate a clear and direct message without "placing your foot in your mouth." If you are giving an impromptu speech in a classroom situation here are few ideas to keep in mind. First, remember that the impromptu speech is your opportunity to demonstrate effective vocal and nonverbal delivery skills. Since you are speaking with little or no preparation, strive to demonstrate a conversational delivery, eye contact, gestures, movement,

Figure 10-2. Impromptu Delivery

10

159

and enthusiasm. Second, don't be afraid to be original. You do not have to remember every specific piece of information about your topic. Rather, you can rely on your own personal experiences and knowledge to help you talk about the topic. Third, notice what is occurring in the speaking situation. Don't be afraid to respond to the situation. If there were other speakers who spoke before you, you can respond to what a previous speaker said. You can also comment on the audience and the occasion as well as your topic.

There are several advantages to impromptu speaking. When an impromptu speech is successful, the speaker will have demonstrated an excellent knowledge of a topic, which can impress an audience. Impromptu speeches help improve the speaker's ability to think quickly. Also, impromptu speeches allow speakers to perfect delivery skills. The obvious disadvantage of impromptu speaking is that a speaker's mind can go blank. The speaker can forget information or not be able to comment on the topic at all. Second, a speaker can mistakenly say something inappropriate. Third, since there is little preparation, the speakers' delivery can be poor as they might have difficulty thinking of what to say or have difficulty managing their nonverbal delivery. Fourth, nervousness can increase as the speaker waits to speak.

VOCAL DELIVERY

In the public speaking situation, how you present your information can sometimes be more important than the information itself. We say this because if the audience is distracted by **vocal fillers** (utterances such as *ah* and *um*), fast speaking, **monotone delivery** (the same speaking volume, pitch, and rate), or soft voice projection, it will be difficult for your audience to concentrate on your message. In order to present your ideas in a clear and fluent way, make sure you work extensively with your **vocal delivery** as you practice your speech. Your vocal delivery consists of the vocal qualities of volume, pitch, rate, pause, and enunciation that help you present your message in an interesting, fluent, and vivid manner. Each of these vocal qualities will be expanded upon to illustrate how you can incorporate them successfully into your speech.

Volume

When making a presentation, you want to deliver your speech at an appropriate volume. **Volume** is the loudness and softness of your voice. Sometimes speakers mistakenly assume that to be heard they have to speak at the same volume level for each speech. However, this is not always the case. Effective speakers are skillful in adjusting their speaking volume to the speaking situation. For example, if you are giving a presentation in a large auditorium with no microphone, you will need to project your voice at a louder volume. Whereas, if you are in a small room with only five other people, you can use your normal conversational volume to speak.

Many novice speakers have to work on projecting their voice at a louder volume for their message to be heard by everyone in the audience. Although a strong projection is necessary for a public presentation, do not confuse projecting your voice with shouting. Shouting is when you are screaming at an audience. Not only is screaming very difficult for an audience to tolerate, but it can strain your vocal chords and make your voice hoarse. Projecting your voice is when you amplify your normal conversational voice so it carries to a further distance. Speakers can achieve an appropriate volume level by simply raising their conversational voice, not by shouting.

When observing experienced speakers, you will notice that their volume is not constant throughout a speech. The speakers' volume stays at an audible level, but the speakers raise or lower their volume for impact and effect. For example, raising your volume helps a speaker show intensity. If a speaker subtly raised the volume on the sentence, "He did it!" with the highest volume on the word *it*, the speaker would be conveying intensity in their message. On the other hand, speakers can lower their volume to indicate seriousness. For example, if speakers consistently lower their volume on the sentence, "I only wanted to say hello," with the lowest volume occurring on the word *hello*, this signals a serious tone. Changing the volume in your speech is an effective way to incorporate vocal variety into your speech.

You can practice projecting your voice at an audible level by recording yourself practicing your speech, projecting your voice at different volumes. When you review the recording, identify which voice projection best carried your voice at a conversational tone. When you establish your voice projection, begin to practice your speech and take notice of any sentences that can be raised or lowered to produce **tonal meaning**.

Pitch

Another way to incorporate vocal variety into your presentation is to vary your pitch. The vocal quality of **pitch** is the highness or lowness of sound. An easy way to distinguish between volume and pitch is that volume involves the level of your voice, whereas pitch refers to the articulation of sound. When you draw out the sound of a word such as, *Ouch!* or *Yes!* you have altered the pitch of the word. Usually change in pitch is referred to as **voice inflection**. When you vary the pitch of sounds in your speech, this is another way to add vocal variety to your speech. Plus, varying your pitch allows you to convey tonal meaning, and it makes your

10

message more pleasing to hear. Changing the volume level and pitch of your message also allows you to avoid monotone deliveries.

One way to include pitch variation into your speech is to isolate key phrases in your speech that can be vocally emphasized to help you illustrate meaning. For example, here are some key sentences that use vocal inflection to emphasize a point.

It was this *long*.

This *is* the best part.

I do not want to go.

Each of the italicized words indicates how voice inflections help the speaker convey a particular meaning. After you have incorporated necessary inflections into your speech, record yourself, and play it back. Adjust the vocal inflection as needed to help you convey the tonal meaning you want.

Rate

The **rate** is the speed at which a person speaks. It is common for novice speakers to speak quickly. Usually a quick speaking rate is caused by nervousness. Once you are able to become more comfortable and confident, you will be able to control your speaking rate. In fact, changing the speaking rate in your speech can convey certain tonal meaning. For example, faster rates indicate happiness, fear, anger, and surprise. Meanwhile, slower rates convey sadness or disgust.[3] However, you want to avoid a constant speaking rate that speeds through information. When this occurs the speaker is not communicating with the audience. Instead, the speaker is talking *at* and not *to* the audience. Usually, the audience will "tune out" fast speakers because it is too difficult to follow the speakers' message.

When preparing for your speech, you can monitor your speaking rate by recording your speech. When listening to the recording, you can determine whether your speaking rate is appropriate, too fast, or too slow. Here are some suggestions for those who need help with a speaking rate that is too fast or too slow. The best suggestion for fast deliveries is to incorporate more pauses into your delivery. You should pause before or after transitions, pause after major changes in ideas, and pause to indicate important ideas. When you incorporate pauses throughout the speech, the pauses help slow down your speaking rate. Second, imagine your audience knows nothing about your topic. Usually, when we are conveying new information to people (such as giving directions), we tend to take our time to help the person retain the information. You want to duplicate this same principle in public speaking. It is appropriate to infer that the audience knows little about your topic because your audience most likely will not know as much about your topic as you do. On the other hand, if your delivery is too slow, practice until you know it very well. Once you thoroughly know your ideas, you will be able to proceed through your information more quickly. Second, eliminate any long pauses you might have in the speech.

Pauses

A **pause** is a deliberate brief silence. Pauses are subtle vocal qualities that can help the speaker convey a tonal meaning. When used in public speaking, pauses can serve a practical and dramatic function. As a practical function, pauses allow speakers to slow down their delivery and to maintain a normal breath cycle. In order to serve this practical function, the pause needs to be before or after transitions or at the end of a sentence. A pause in the middle of a sentence will disrupt the flow of the speech and make the speaker appear unprepared. As a dramatic function, pauses can draw the audience into the speech. A dramatic pause allows the audience to think about the idea and pay closer attention to what will be said.

When preparing for your speech, it is a good idea to include pauses at major transitions in your speech in order to maintain your normal breath cycle. If you record your practice speech, you can decide for yourself where you can use pauses for either practical or dramatic effect.

Enunciation

The United States consists of many different cultures. In fact, the statistics indicate that 20 million Americans are recent immigrants to the United States, 32 million Americans' first language is not English, and 14 million Americans are not fluent in English.[4] When you also consider the regional differences in how people say words, this demonstrates how enunciation fluctuates not only from co-culture to co-culture, but from region to region. For example, English as it is spoken in Boston, Massachusetts, has a different flavor than English spoken in Mobile, Alabama. **Enunciation** is the generally accepted way to pronounce and articulate words. Perfecting your enunciation is important, because a speaker can lose credibility quickly by not pronouncing or articulating words correctly. We will explore both pronunciation and articulation in more detail.

The generally accepted way to vocally produce a word is called **pronunciation**. When you look up a word in the dictionary, it lists the word's generally accepted pronunciation. For example, take the word *arctic*, which is commonly mispronounced *ar-tic* rather than correctly pronounced *arc-tic*. This mispronunciation might not seem significant, but imagine if a campaigning politician incorrectly pronounced the name of a town, or a newscaster mispronounced a person's name. While these are honest errors, the credibility of the speaker can be damaged, especially if mispronunciations occur frequently. Usually mispronunciation occurs

10

when a speaker is covering a topic that is highly technical or has a lot of jargon. The key is to detect these mistakes in practice, and make sure you know how to pronounce words before your actual speech.

The generally accepted way to vocally produce sounds crisply and distinctly is called **articulation**. Poor articulation usually occurs from the deletion or substitution of certain sounds. For example, saying *runnin'* instead of *running* is caused when a speaker deletes the *g* from the word. Also, if someone says *budder* instead of *butter*, they have substituted the *d* sound for the *t* sound. Our everyday conversation is filled with examples of how we delete and substitute sounds. Again, do not carry these errors into the public speaking setting. Eliminate errors by catching them in practice sessions before you give the actual speech.

Conversational Delivery

When you project your volume at an acceptable level, adjust your pitch by using voice inflections, maintain a steady speaking rate, incorporate pauses into your speech, and use correct enunciation, you have achieved **vocal variety**. When you achieve vocal variety, you have achieved a conversational delivery that conveys a natural speaking tone that is clear, vivid, and pleasing to hear. Most importantly, your conversational delivery brings your words and meanings to life, which allows you to keep your audience's interest.

NONVERBAL DELIVERY

In Chapter 1, we discussed how messages are composed of two parts—verbal and nonverbal. Nonverbal communication is important in helping us communicate and interpret meanings. For these reasons, you want to demonstrate sound nonverbal delivery in your speech so the audience will be able to focus on your message and not on distracting movements. We will discuss the important nonverbal delivery aspects of appearance, breathing, eye contact, facial expressions, gestures, and movement.

Appearance

In our society **appearance** does matter. People form impressions of us based upon our physical looks and external artifacts such as clothing and jewelry. How others perceive you is very important in public speaking. Based upon how you choose to present yourself, your appearance can either enhance or undermine your credibility as a speaker. The more well-dressed and well-groomed the person, the more favorably the person will be perceived by the audience.[5] Therefore, you should strive to make a favorable impression on your audience. This does not mean on speech day you should necessarily dress as if you are going on a job interview, but you do want your clothing to make a good impression on the audience. Avoid wearing clothing or jewelry that is distracting to your audience or that undermines your credibility such as ripped up jeans, revealing clothes, baseball caps, or lots of glittering jewelry. Sometimes speakers do wear clothing to reinforce the topic of their speech. For example, it would be appropriate for a speaker to wear a karate outfit if the speaker was giving a demonstration speech on karate kicks. Otherwise, use common sense when choosing attire for your presentation, and keep your clothing simple, neat, and sharp.

Breathing

We often do not think about breathing. In fact, **breathing** is an involuntary action that we are not supposed to think about. As we discussed in Chapter 2, nervousness makes your muscles tight which prevents your diaphragm from fully contracting and drawing in enough air to maintain a normal breath cycle. When this happens the speaker can sound monotone and out of breath as the speaker gasps for air. As you are waiting for your speech, practice deep breathing. You will know if you are deep breathing if you place your hand on your stomach and you feel your stomach muscles move forward when you take a breath. If you do not feel your stomach muscles move forward, you are not deep breathing. You will have to take deep breaths to fill your lungs with enough air to maintain a normal breath cycle. A fresh supply of air in your lungs can help you avoid gasping for air, which destroys any chance for vocal variety in your delivery.

Eye Contact

What separates effective public speakers from ineffective public speakers? It is eye contact. Effective **eye contact** is when a speaker looks directly into the eyes of the audience while giving a speech. When speakers make eye contact with the audience, they are able to convey their message to people instead of to the floor, to their notes, or to the back wall. Although eye contact varies from culture to culture, in the public setting, you want to make direct eye contact with your audience.

Public speakers should not be intimidated by making eye contact because eye contact has many benefits. First, it allows the speaker to personalize the message to the audience. Looking at audience members makes them feel like you are speaking to them (which you are). Second, eye contact maintains the attention of the audience. When we look at people, they tend to look back at us. Making direct eye contact is a way to keep audience members involved in your speech. Third, strong eye contact demonstrates confidence and improves your credibility as a speaker.

10

When you are practicing eye contact, concentrate on looking into audience members' eyes. Practice conveying thoughts to people, not to the back wall or to your notes. If you do not have a practice audience with whom you can practice eye contact, draw a face on several pieces of paper and tape them to the back wall at eye level. You can simply practice your speech alternating from face to face. Avoid eye contact that is only briefly maintained for a short amount of time. This will make your eye contact appear to be shifty, as if you are unsure of yourself. Instead, concentrate on conveying a thought or an idea to a person. Once you have conveyed a thought to one person, you can move on to the next person.

Facial Expressions

An effective way to communicate our emotions is through our **facial expressions**. A friendly smile or an angry look can sometimes communicate these feelings more effectively than words alone. Your facial expressions must complement the verbal message in your presentation. This is especially true when you are attempting to communicate emotional appeals. If you are giving a persuasive speech and you want to convey intensity, your facial expression should complement your vocal delivery and the content of your message. It is hard to elicit emotional responses when your facial expressions don't match the vocal delivery or content.

When practicing your speech, try to record yourself so you can review your facial expressions. If this is not possible, practice your facial expressions in front of a mirror so you can identify if your facial expressions are complementing the vocal delivery and the content of the message. If you find any inconsistencies between your facial expressions and your vocal delivery or content, practice to make your facial expressions complementary. Most of the time your emotions and feelings will naturally complement the vocal delivery and content, especially as you relax and become more familiar with your speech.

Gestures

One of the hardest nonverbal aspects for a speaker to manage or incorporate into a speech are gestures. A **gesture** is any movement by the head, arms, or hands that complements or reinforces a message. The most common gestures are hand gestures. Hand gestures are also the most awkward to demonstrate in a speech because speakers often have difficulty knowing what to do with their hands during a speech. The best advice is to allow your hands to naturally gesture. A natural gesture means your gestures are out in front of you for all to see (as opposed to being at your sides) and your gestures are large, as in a natural conversation. When you naturally gesture, your hand gestures will look smoother instead of looking awkward and mechanical. For moments when you are not gesturing, keep your hands at your sides rather than holding your hands behind your back or in front of you.

Practice your hand gestures in front of a mirror. Make sure you keep your hands in front of you and that your movements are large enough for the audience to see. You can also incorporate gestures to complement and reinforce your message. For example, if a speaker said, "It will not start, it will not run, it will not work," the speaker can use a hand gesture to punctuate the *not* in each phrase to complement the intensity of the speaker's message. Also, a speaker can reinforce a message. If a speaker said, "It was this high," the speaker can use her two hands to illustrate the height of the object.

Movement

When speakers use **movement** in a speech, it shows they have a mastery of the subject, they are in control of their speech, and they can engage the audience. Movement also makes the speech more vivid. In addition, movement allows the speaker to release nervous energy. The most common form of movement is the transitional walk. A **transitional walk** is when the speaker walks during a transitional phrase in the speech. Transitional walks are another way to indicate that the speech is moving from one idea to the next. For example, if a speech has three main points, the speech will have four major transitions (the preview, the transition between points #1 and #2, the transition between points #2 and #3, and the review) that the speaker can move on. When using transitional walks, never turn your back toward the audience, and when you reach your next destination, pivot so you are still positioned toward the center of the audience. As the diagram below indicates, speakers simply move to the next location in the room when they start to give their transition.

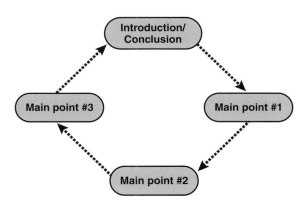

The diagram illustrates that the speaker has used transitional walks to form a diamond figure on the floor. When transitional walks form a figure such as this, it is also referred to as **platform movement**. Platform movement means the speaker is walking in a predetermined pattern. There are a number of patterns a speaker can make depending on the number of transitions in the speech and the creativity of the speaker. Usually, with platform movement, speakers finish the speech in the same spot that they began the speech to signal to the audience the conclusion of the speech.

Although platform movement allows a speaker to move in a set pattern, more experienced speakers find platform movement too constricting and will instead use transitional walks in various tangents. When speakers walk on a tangent, they vary the distance and angle when they are moving. In this case, the speaker is not interested in making a pattern but in using movement to indicate a change in thought.

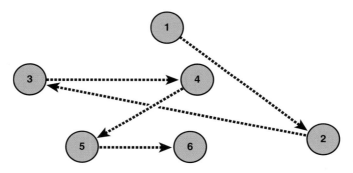

When using transitional walks, make sure that you actually walk. This means taking about five to six steps for each transitional walk. If you make your transitional walk any shorter, you will appear to be tentative instead of taking a natural walk. Also, it is very important the speaker does not pace because pacing can be very distracting for the audience. If you limit your walking to transitional phrases, then you will eliminate any chance of pacing.

Dynamic Delivery

When a speaker can demonstrate the aspects of appearance, breathing, eye contact, facial expressions, gestures, and movement, the delivery is dynamic, lively, and engaging. Demonstrating a dynamic delivery is an effective way to keep your audience's attention by perfecting the incorporation of vocal and visual elements into your speech. Practice these aspects to help your delivery to be more effective.

PRACTICING THE SPEECH

This chapter has provided hints to help you improve important aspects of your vocal and nonverbal delivery. Although these delivery skills seem like a lot to incorporate into a speech, you will find through practice that some aspects will come naturally, while others will take some work. As you practice, concentrate on the delivery skills that need improving. As you develop the ability to perfect an aspect of delivery, move on to the next one. How quickly you perfect certain delivery aspects depends on the person. It might take all semester to finally perfect some skills, but that is the nature of public speaking. You learn from experience and practice. We conclude this chapter by leaving you with more helpful hints for practicing your speech.

Start with an Outline

Once you have completely developed your speech, put together a **preparation outline** that includes all parts of the speech (introduction, body, conclusion). The preparation outline should also include all the necessary support material and examples that will be presented in the speech. Make sure all parts of the speech are balanced and have the proper support material for each main point.

Develop Notecards

When you have completed the preparation outline, transfer information onto a **key word** outline on notecards. Begin to practice the entire speech out loud. Include all transitions, support material, examples, and source citations. Work to familiarize yourself with the material so you can eventually give the speech while only looking at your notecards 10% to 20% of the time. Concentrate on grasping ideas so your delivery will flow smoothly.

Practice in Front of a Mirror

When you have perfected an extemporaneous delivery, record yourself and review your presentation to polish your vocal delivery. Then, practice in front of a mirror to monitor your nonverbal delivery. After each practice session, work on the parts of your delivery that need to be improved upon for the actual speech.

10

Practice in Front of an Audience

When you feel confident with your vocal and nonverbal delivery, deliver your speech in front of an audience (such as friends and family). Continue to work on perfecting your delivery skills, and ask questions of the audience about your content and delivery. Make adjustments as necessary.

Duplicate the Actual Speaking Environment

Before you give your presentation, practice your speech a final time in a place that is similar to the setting in which you will give the speech. This will allow you to become familiar with your speaking environment and it will give you a better idea of what to expect.

In this chapter, we have discussed various aspects of delivery to help you improve your presentations. We identified the common speaking styles that a speaker can use, and we explained the strengths and weaknesses of each. We informed you of the various components of the vocal delivery and how you can incorporate these qualities into your own speech. We also discussed nonverbal delivery and how to enhance your own nonverbal delivery in the public setting. Finally, we have provided additional tips on how to practice for a presentation. From reading this chapter, you should be able to work on and improve your own delivery for your presentation.

VOCABULARY

Appearance — the combination of physical looks and external artifacts such as clothing and jewelry that can influence how people perceive us.

Articulation — the generally accepted way to vocally produce sounds crisply and distinctly.

Breathing — an involuntary expanding and contracting of the lungs that provides the body with oxygen.

Conversational delivery — conveying a message by using the voice's natural, everyday speaking tone.

Dynamic delivery — when a speaker successfully demonstrates the nonverbal aspects of appearance, breathing, eye contact, facial expressions, gestures, and movement to produce a lively and engaging delivery.

Enunciation — the generally accepted way to pronounce and articulate words.

Eye contact — when the speaker looks directly into the eyes of audience members.

Facial expressions — manipulations of the face that are an effective way to communicate emotions and feelings. Usually, facial expressions are involuntary.

Gestures — any movement by the head, arms, or hands that help complement or reinforce a message.

Key word outline — a speaking outline that includes all parts of the speech (introduction, body, conclusion) along with support material examples that is limited to only key words.

Monotone delivery — when the entire speech is delivered in the same speaking volume, pitch, and rate.

Movement — using purposeful movement to engage the audience and to signal to the audience a change in idea or to signal a dramatic effect.

Pause — a deliberate brief silence.

Pitch — the highness or lowness of sound. Also called voice inflection.

Platform movement — when a speaker's transitional walks follow a predetermined pattern.

Preparation outline — a rough draft of a speech that includes all parts of the speech (introduction, body, conclusion) in addition to all the necessary support material and examples that will be presented in the speech.

Pronunciation — the generally accepted way to vocally produce a word.

Rate — the speed at which a person speaks.

Tonal meaning — when we emphasize a word to indicate the meaning of a message (see Chapter 11).

Transitional walk — when a speaker walks during a transitional phrase in the speech to indicate a change in idea.

Vocal delivery — the vocal qualities of volume, pitch, rate, pauses, and enunciation that help a speaker present a message in an interesting, fluent, and vivid manner.

Vocal fillers — making utterances such as *ah* and *um*.

Vocal variety — using a conversational delivery that is clear, vivid, and pleasing to hear by demonstrating the vocal qualities of volume, pitch, rate, and enunciation.

Voice inflection — see pitch.

Volume — the loudness and softness of your voice.

10

REFERENCES

[1] John O. Greene, "Speech Preparation Processes and Verbal Fluency," *Human Communication Research 11* (1984): 61–84.

[2] Stephen E. Lucas, *The Art of Public Speaking*, 11th edition, (Boston: McGraw-Hill, 2009), 244.

[3] Lucas, 249.

[4] Guo-Ming Chen and William J. Starosta, *Foundations of Intercultural Communication*, (Lanham, MD: University Press of America, 2007), 6.

[5] Michael Osborn, Suzanne Osborn, and Randall Osborn, *Public Speaking: Finding Your Voice*, 9th edition, (Boston: Allyn and Bacon, 2012), 265–266.

LANGUAGE AND COMMUNICATION 11

"One of the difficulties in the language is that all our words from loose
using have lost their edge."
 —Ernest Hemingway

"Communication is something so simple and difficult that we can never
put it in simple words."
 —T. S. Matthews

"It is a luxury to be understood."
 —Ralph Waldo Emerson

This Chapter Examines:

+ language as symbolic communication

+ language and meaning

+ effective language

+ colorful language

+ incorporating rhythm

+ avoiding offensive language

A motorist was driving on the Merritt Parkway outside New York City when his engine stalled. He quickly determined that his battery was dead and managed to stop another driver who agreed to push his car to get it started. "My car has an automatic transmission," he explained, "so you'll have to get up to 30 to 35 miles per hour to get me started." The second motorist nodded and walked back to the car. The first motorist climbed into his own car and waited for the Good Samaritan to pull up behind him. He waited and waited. Finally, he turned around to see what was wrong. There was the Good Samaritan—coming at his car at 30 to 35 miles per hour! The damage to his car amounted to $2,400.[1]

This example illustrates how easily two people can miscommunicate with one another. The interaction seemed like a simple, straightforward message that was sent and received. The problem, however, was that the language used to convey the message was not precise enough in meaning for the "Good Samaritan" to interpret the intended meaning of the first driver. As a result, instead of one driver helping another driver by pushing his car, one driver ended up ramming the other driver in a rear-end collision.

This scenario also highlights how important it is to select language carefully when you are in a speaking situation. Think of your own interactions and conversations. How many times have you either interpreted a message incorrectly or stated something vaguely that led to miscommunication? While you might be able to correct meaning in an interpersonal conversation, it is not as easy to correct meaning in a public speaking situation. Words are like toothpaste; once they come out, it is impossible to put them back into the "tube." This is why language is an important aspect to consider when you make a presentation. This chapter will discuss ways in which you can use language more effectively in order to construct messages that are more precise in meaning. Before we can explain how you can use language more effectively in the public setting, you need to understand the principles behind how language works.

LANGUAGE AS SYMBOLIC COMMUNICATION

Language is something we use every day, but we seldom consider how language is used in the communication process. Usually, we assume that when we speak the English language, we will *automatically* achieve mutual understanding between both persons. Not until we experience miscommunication do we fully understand that communication is a **symbolic process**. Communication as a symbolic process means the language we use to communicate is based upon an association between a symbol (words) and a referent (concepts, objects, feelings, thoughts, ideas).[2] The **semantic triangle** pictured here diagrams how language functions. The semantic triangle illustrates that symbols are only a representation of a concept. Language then is dependent upon knowing the correct symbols for certain referents. The more precise our symbols are, the more likely the receiver will interpret the message as the source intended. For example, if you attempt to describe an aircraft carrier as *big*, the word *big* is a vague descrip-

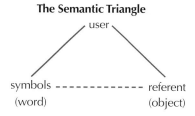

The Semantic Triangle

tion because there is no universal standard for what constitutes *big*. What is *big* to one person could be small or medium to another. However, if you decided to describe the size of an aircraft carrier by comparing it to the size of three football fields, you would have provided a more precise meaning for the audience that is not as open to interpretation as the description of simply *big*.

As we will illustrate in this chapter, our words alone do not constitute meaning; meaning is determined by agreement and negotiation between people. Words do not contain meaning; they only represent a concept. Meaning is dependent on people. In fact, meaning rests in people, not in words. We will describe two principles to keep in mind when using language.

Symbols Are Arbitrary

The first principle of language is that symbols are **arbitrary**. The arbitrary nature of language means that words gain meaning through common agreement. In fact, every word in our language has gained meaning through common agreement. As the semantic triangle illustrates, there is no direct association between the word C-A-T (the symbol) and the fury, little four-legged animal with a long tail (the referent). We only know this association through common agreement. The word CAT only means furry, little, four-legged animal because we all agree that it does.

The arbitrary nature of language is easily highlighted by regional differences where people give different *names* to the same object. One of the best examples involves the word *pop* or *soda*. In the East, a carbonated soft drink is commonly referred to as *soda*, whereas in the Midwest the same object is referred to as *pop*. If you are an Easterner traveling through the Midwest and you stop for a *soda*, people might look at you funny and say, "You mean *pop?*" This shows that language is an arbitrary association between a symbol and a referent. The name for the object (*soda/pop*) is an arbitrary association, which is why there are two different terms for the same object.

Symbols Are Ambiguous

The ambiguous nature of language is the second principle of language, which means that words have multiple meanings. Words do not have only one use. All you have to do is take a look at a dictionary to see that most common words have many different definitions. Therefore, how the word is used and the context it is used in can determine the meaning of the word.

Consider the different meanings the word *fast* has:

A man is *fast* when he can run rapidly.

But he is also *fast* when he is tied down and cannot run at all.

And colors are *fast* when they do not run.

One is *fast* when s/he moves in suspect company.

But this is not quite the same thing as playing *fast* and loose.

A racetrack is *fast* when it is in good running condition.

A friend is *fast* when s/he is loyal.

A watch is *fast* when it is ahead of time.

To be *fast* asleep is to be deep in sleep.

To be *fast* by is to be near.

To *fast* is to refrain from eating.

A *fast* may be a period of noneating—or a ship's mooring line.

Photographic film is *fast* when it is sensitive (to light).

But bacteria are *fast* when they are insensitive (to antiseptics).[3]

This example highlights how words have multiple meanings and that meaning is influenced by the context. Words also acquire new meanings over time. Since language is an ever-developing and evolving symbolic process, how we use words is always changing, which can lead to miscommunication. For example, the common meaning for *pot* was a container you put a plant into or cooked food with. Today, we commonly use the word to refer to marijuana. A *rap* used to be a knock on the door; now we commonly think of *rap* as a genre of music. The list goes on and on. The meanings of words change over time, which can increase miscommunication.

The principles of arbitrariness and ambiguity are important to keep in mind when you are attempting to decide what language to use in your presentation. The language you use and how you use it in your speech greatly influences how the audience interprets your message. We will take a closer look at the meaning that can be derived from language.

LANGUAGE AND MEANING

Mutual understanding is achieved between two people when both communicators interpret the same meaning from the message. This is why it is important for speakers to choose their language very carefully and strategically. Language can influence the meaning of a message in a variety of ways. Here we will discuss four different types of meaning: denotative, relative, connotative, and tonal meaning.

Denotative Meaning

The common dictionary meaning of a word is referred to as **denotative meaning**. Denotative meaning is the explicit meaning of words or what the words mean at face value. For example, suppose you bought a new suit and the first time you wear the suit your best friend says, "Wow! You look great!" The obvious denotative meaning, the explicit meaning, is a compliment, that you look great in your new suit. Denotative meaning always refers to the common usage of words, the explicit meaning of words. Speakers can ensure that the audience interprets the same denotative meaning they intend by defining unfamiliar terms or by clarifying for the audience how they are using the word in a different way from its common usage.

A good example of how language conveys denotative meaning recently occurred at a local college when the campus law enforcement agency changed its official name from "public safety" to "university police." The name change represented a different denotative meaning for the campus law enforcement agency. Instead of being perceived as a campus watchman as the "public safety" name suggests, the new name of "university police" symbolized a legitimate police force that has the power to "enforce the law."

Relative Meaning

On the other hand, **relative meaning** refers to the implicit meaning of the word. It is the opposite of what the word means at face value. For example, consider the previous new suit illustration. Suppose you tripped and fell into a muddy ditch while wearing your new suit. Then, you run into your best friend who says, "Wow! You look great!" In this situation, you would know the friend was using relative meaning and was actually making fun of you by implying, "You look like a mess." However, notice how the denotative meaning of the statement was actually a compliment ("You look great!"). In most situations, you would know the real meaning of the statement was relative meaning, which was to make fun of your appearance ("You look like a mess!"). One common example of relative meaning is sarcasm. When speakers use sarcasm, they are using the opposite meaning of the words. You should always be careful when using sarcasm because sarcasm can lead to miscommunication, especially if you do not know the other person very well.

Connotative Meaning

The personal and subjective meaning that words and phrases can evoke is called **connotative meaning**. Connotative meaning comes from emotional attachments we associate with certain words. Often the emotional attachments evoke a past memory when we hear the word. For example, take the word, "Thanksgiving." For many people, "Thanksgiving" evokes positive emotional and subjective meanings that are associated with past memories of the holiday such as being with family members. For others, however, "Thanksgiving" can have negative connotations. Some people get depressed during the holidays because they might not have family, they might not have significant others to be with, or they might come from a dysfunctional family. These examples point out that the memories and emotions associated with words can be very powerful in motivating and inspiring an audience. For this reason, speakers try to include words in their speeches that generally have positive associations, such as freedom and liberty.

Tonal Meaning

When we emphasize a word to indicate the meaning of a message it is referred to as **tonal meaning**. Tonal meaning is similar to how we use italics in written communication to accent the meaning. In the case of verbal communication, voice inflection accents the meaning of a word. For example, consider the phrase, "John is going?" You can say this phrase with the your pitch rising on the word *going* to indicate a question. However, if you emphasize the word is in the middle of the phrase, you are not indicating a question, but you are stating a fact, "John *is* going." We use tonal meaning all the time to indicate the meaning of a message. You can use tonal meaning in your speeches for effect and to make your vocal delivery more dynamic and less **monotone**.

EFFECTIVE LANGUAGE

Now that we have covered how language functions and how different meanings can be conveyed through language, we can discuss ways you can make your language more precise, vivid, and accurate for your presentations. The goal is to construct a presentation that will result in a high level of mutual understanding between you and your audience. You should avoid making presentations that can lead to misunderstanding, confusion, and miscommunication.

Use Concrete Words

The common problem with our use of language is that we are often too vague or abstract in our choice of words. When you are abstract, the audience might or might not interpret your intended meaning correctly. For example, suppose you described the eruptions of Old Faithful in Yellowstone Park by saying:

> *It shoots water into the air, and some comes down as mist. It is amazing how it erupts like clockwork.*

This vague description leaves a lot to be explained and clarified for the audience. You could make your description more concrete for the audience by saying:

> *Old Faithful is the world's best-known geyser, and it is located in Yellowstone National Park. A geyser is a naturally occurring spring that periodically propels hot water and steam upward. In fact, every 30 to 120 minutes, Old Faithful shoots water 15 to 30 feet in the air for 1.5 to 5 minutes. It is truly amazing to see.*

In this second example, the meaning of the statement is more precise, because concrete words are used to describe Old Faithful. **Concrete** words refer to specific objects or information. Concrete words help you produce more precise meaning and are less open to different interpretations. On the other hand, **abstract** words are less precise and more vague in their description. For example, consider the following words:

Abstract words: *high, progress, peacekeeper*

Concrete words: *15 feet, constructing a new mall, U.S. Marine*

Despite the vividness of concrete language, sometimes a speaker does want to use abstract words to make general appeals to the audience. However, anytime you are supporting ideas or explaining information, you should use concrete language such as comparisons, contrasts, descriptions, and explanations. Using concrete words make your ideas much more clear for the audience.

Direct and Indirect Language

The benefit of using concrete words is that you will be using direct language. **Direct language** is using specific words to describe concepts or ideas. Meanwhile, **indirect language** is using abstract words to describe concepts or ideas. Whether you choose to use direct or indirect language is important because this can greatly influence the meaning of your message. For example, large corporations and the government often use indirect language to put a positive spin on information or to neutralize a negative description. In the corporate world, you hear indirect language such as "the company is downsizing to keep up with the competition," which directly translates to "since we are losing money, we needed to cut costs, so we fired workers." Or the stock market experienced an "economic correction," which directly translates into "the stock market lost points, and stock values declined, and you probably lost money." In a public speaking situation, you do not want to use indirect language because it will appear as if you have something to hide. Use direct language to increase preciseness and mutual understanding between you and your audience.

Comparison and Contrast

One of the best ways you can be more concrete and direct is to use comparisons and contrasts to clarify ideas. A **comparison** is when you show the similarity between two concepts or objects. Usually with a comparison, you are comparing something the audience is familiar with to something they are less familiar with. Meanwhile, a **contrast** is when you show the differences between two concepts or objects. With a contrast, you are usually contrasting unfamiliar aspects of two similar concepts or objects.

Comparisons and contrasts help the audience visualize and conceptualize ideas. For example, if you are talking about the size of the moon you can say it is 2,162 miles in diameter. However, simply stating the diameter of the moon probably will not help the audience truly understand its size. If you used a comparison, you could help the audience understand this number better. You could say, "The moon is 2,162 miles in diameter. However, you can better understand the moon's diameter by comparing it to the Earth. If the Earth was a basketball, then the moon would be a baseball." This comparison better illustrates the moon's size to the audience by using the familiar objects of a basketball and baseball.

Contrasts also help the audience visualize and conceptualize ideas for the audience. For example, a speaker attempting to distinguish a jaguar from a leopard could say, "Jaguars are more stocky and muscular with a shorter tail than the leopard." While this statement is accurate, it is hard for the audience to picture the difference because more descriptive language is needed. Instead, the speaker would be wise to use a contrast:

While most people confuse the appearance of jaguars and leopards, knowing the difference between these two large cats is quite simple when you consider the following differences. First, jaguars are found in Central and South America. Leopards are found in Africa. Second, these cats can be distinguished by their coats. The jaguar's coat is comprised of dark spots that have internal markings within the spot. The leopard's coat only has dark spots with no internal markings.

This second example illustrates how the speaker used a contrast to better distinguish the two cats to the audience (notice that the speaker would probably need a presentational aid to further clarify the idea; see Chapter 14). In pointing out the differences, the audience can better visualize the idea the speaker is trying to present.

Whenever you are preparing a presentation, you always want to make sure you have selected the most appropriate language. You can be more effective with your language by using concrete words, direct language, and comparisons and contrasts. These language devices will help your message be more precise and clear.

Figure 11-1. Language

COLORFUL LANGUAGE

While you want to be clear, direct, and concrete with language, it does not mean your language has to be dull. In fact, you want to use colorful language that creates images, makes creative associations, and maintains your audience's interests. Consider the following example from Frederick Douglass:

Great streams are not easily turned into channels, worn deep in the course of ages. They may sometimes rise in quiet and stately majesty, and inundate the land, refreshing and fertilizing the earth with their mysterious properties. They may also rise in wrath and fury, and bear away, on their angry waves, the accumulated wealth of years of toil and hardship. They, however, gradually flow back to the same old channel, and flow on as serenely as ever. But, while the river may not be turned aside, it may dry up, and leave nothing behind but the withered branch, and the unsightly rock, to howl in the abyss-sweeping wind, the sad tale of departed glory. As with rivers so with nations.

While Douglass could have conveyed his message in a more concrete way, he would have lost the impact of his more embellished speech. The key is to include language devices that help enhance the delivery style of the concrete message. In

Douglass's case, he was using colorful language to motivate audience members to take action against hypocrisy: all men are created equal, yet the institution of slavery was still flourishing. We will discuss two ways in which you can make your language more colorful by using metaphors and similes.

Metaphor

A **metaphor** is an implied comparison that does not use the words *as* or *like*. Often a metaphor compares two unlike concepts in order to redefine meaning. In other words, metaphors redefine a referent by comparing it to another unlike concept. For example, consider the historical example provided by Winston Churchill as he characterized the new post–World War II reality facing Europe and America:

> *It is my duty, however, to place before you certain facts about the present position in Europe. From Stettin in the Baltic to Trieste in the Adriatic an iron curtain has descended across the continent.*

In Churchill's address, which would become known as the "Iron Curtain Speech," he could have said that the governments of Eastern Europe were now under Soviet control or that the people of Eastern Europe had lost many freedoms. Both of these statements would be true. However, by using the metaphor of the *"iron curtain"* that has *"descended across the continent,"* Churchill was able to convey his idea with more impact. The *"iron curtain"* metaphor and the action of *"descending across the continent"* created a more vibrant mental picture for his audience. Even today, after the fall of the Soviet Union, the metaphor the "iron curtain" continues to define and distinguish the political, social, and economic philosophies of western and eastern Europe and their historical allegiance to either the United States or Russia.

Furthermore, this example illustrates how metaphors add vividness to the concepts or ideas that you are presenting. In short, metaphors can make your ideas more persuasive and more interesting. Whenever you use a metaphor, make sure the comparison you are making is compatible, appropriate, and consistent. You do not want to state inappropriate metaphors because the audience might not understand the comparison. Also, you do not want to have inconsistent metaphors because the audience can get confused. For example:

> *The plane soared reminiscent of an eagle swooping down on prey and raining down like a LeBron James jump shot.*

This example is an inconsistent metaphor or a **mixed metaphor**, because the comparison is making more than one comparison at a time. To avoid confusion, the metaphor should use either the eagle metaphor or the sports metaphor, but not both.

Simile

Similar to metaphors, a **simile** is a direct comparison between two concepts, objects, or ideas that use the words *as* or *like*. Similes also compare two unlike concepts, objects, or ideas by pointing out the similarities between the two concepts. However, instead of implying the relationship between concepts as with metaphors, a simile makes a direct connection between two ideas for the audience. For example, consider a historical simile made by Thomas Jefferson:

> *Written laws are like a spiders' webs; they will catch the weak and poor, but are torn to pieces by the rich and powerful.*

Jefferson used a simile to compare a spider web to the American legal system. In Jefferson's opinion, the law operates like a spider web; it is able to catch small creatures but is annihilated by large ones. This point is more descriptive with the simile than it would have been without it. We use similes all the time to help us describe information. We say things such as, "He fell like a tree," and "Her grin was as wide as the Cheshire Cat's." The key is to make clever and creative comparisons that help you explain the idea or concept you are talking about.

When using similes, follow the same guidelines we mentioned for metaphors. However, regardless of whether it's a metaphor or a simile, don't be afraid to incorporate these language devices into your speech. Metaphors and similes help make your language more concrete, vivid, and interesting for the audience.

INCORPORATING RHYTHM

Not only can language be colorful, but language can also be memorable and eloquent when the speaker articulates certain sounds, words, and phrases within a speech. How well speakers arrange their language can create a unique rhythm that is very distinctive and pleasing to hear for the audience. **Rhythm**, which is also referred to as a speaker's **cadence**, is a stylistic use of language that utilizes vocal aspects such as rate, pitch, and volume that make a speech more memorable and vivid. We will discuss three aspects of rhythm: repetition, alliteration, and antithesis.

Repetition

A common strategy speakers use to add rhythm to their speech is by incorporating repetition into their delivery. **Repetition** is when a speaker reiterates the same words or phrases at the beginning or at the end of consecutive sentences. Repetition adds rhythm to the speech as the speaker can emphasize an idea and make it more memorable. Also, when a speaker successfully uses repetition in a speech, it is an effective way to motivate and inspire an audience. One of the best examples of how a speaker used repetition to motivate and inspire an audience was the Reverend Dr. Martin Luther King, Jr. in his "I Have a Dream" speech during the March on Washington in 1963:

> *Let freedom ring from the snowcapped Rockies of Colorado!*
>
> *Let freedom ring from the curvaceous slopes of California!*
>
> *But not only that; let freedom ring from Stone Mountain of Georgia!*
>
> *Let freedom ring from Lookout Mountain of Tennessee!*
>
> *Let freedom ring from every hill and molehill of Mississippi.*
>
> *From every mountainside, let freedom ring!*

King's passionate repetition served as a wake-up call for America to live up to all its inalienable rights: life, liberty, and the pursuit of happiness for all citizens. His repetition motivated and inspired listeners to actualize the goal of full equality for all.

We can see repetition being demonstrated by Hillary Clinton when she spoke at the United Nation's World Conference on Women:

> *What we are learning around the world is that, if women are healthy and educated, their families will flourish. If women are free from violence, their families will flourish. If women have a chance to work and earn as full and equal partners in society, their families will flourish.*

In this short example, Clinton used two repeated phrases, "if women are" and "their families will flourish," to illustrate how empowering women will have a positive impact on their families. Clinton used the repetition to make a logical argument that as women do well, their families will do well. The repetition not only enables the audience to anticipate what Clinton will say but also reinforces the logical connection between the well-being of women and their families. When repetition is used in a speech it can build further identification between the speaker and the audience.

Alliteration

A second rhetorical strategy that speakers use to make their delivery more rhythmic is alliteration. **Alliteration** is when a speaker uses language that repeats the same sound to highlight an important idea in a speech. When speakers use alliteration, they are making a point in a rhythmic way to the audience. The repetition of the same sound allows the speaker to use vocal emphasis to rouse the emotions of an audience. Barack Obama speaking at the Fort Hood Memorial Service provides a good example:

> *This generation of soldiers, sailors, airmen, Marines, and Coast Guardsmen have volunteered in the time of certain danger. They are part of the finest fighting force that the world has ever known. They have served tour after tour of duty in distant, different, and difficult places.*

Notice that Obama could have described the military men as a brave and courageous force who served in many far and hostile locations. Although these words generally describe the same characteristics, the alliteration that Obama used expressed their service and sacrifice with more impact.

Antithesis

Finally, a third rhetorical strategy speakers incorporate into their delivery to establish a rhythm is antithesis. **Antithesis** is when a speaker combines two contrasting ideas to illustrate a point. In essence, antithesis takes one idea and turns it into a new idea for the audience to contemplate. One of the most famous is illustrated from John F. Kennedy's 1961 inaugural address:

> *Ask not what your country can do for you, ask what you can do for your country.*

Another example can be illustrated from Martin Luther King, Jr. who stated during the civil rights movement:

> *We must learn to live together as brothers or perish together as fools.*

You can see how antithesis changes generally accepted ideas to enable the audience to contemplate the new meaning that is derived from rephrasing the original idea. It is the contrasting phrases and/or ideas that gain the audience's attention and make the speaker's point more memorable.

Repetition, alliteration, and antithesis are three different ways in which you as a speaker can incorporate rhythm into your speech. Adding rhythm to your speech enhances its vividness and colorfulness. Moreover, rhythm helps the speaker avoid a monotone delivery.

AVOIDING OFFENSIVE LANGUAGE

We have discussed how speakers can use language to make ideas more concrete, memorable, and vivid. Speakers can also misuse language and offend audience members. Therefore, it is vital that all speakers be aware of and avoid the use of offensive language when making a presentation. Whether the offense was intended or not, overt or covert, multicultural audiences are very unforgiving when it comes to being offended. As we discussed in Chapter 4, speakers must be intimately familiar with not only different cultural values, but how these values shape perception, interpretation, and the attribution of meaning. Multicultural audiences expect that speakers are knowledgeable and sensitive to their cultural values, perceptions, and interpretations. For example, Donald Sterling, owner of the Los Angeles Clippers, made derogatory comments about African Americans that caused a national backlash. In response, the National Basketball Association fined Sterling 2.5 million dollars and banned him for life from the N.B.A.[4]

The controversy surrounding Sterling's statement emphasizes the power of language. Historically the dominant culture has enacted and maintained its power by labeling others. Most of the time labels are constructed to maintain social power and to remind the dominant culture of the social inferiority of other cultures and ethnicities.[5] This is why co-cultures such as African American and Latino cultures consider self-definition to be very important. Co-cultures want the ability to define themselves instead of having others define them. Therefore, given the power of language in the public sphere, we will discuss three types of offensive language speakers should avoid: stereotypes, sexist language, and marking language.

Stereotypes

Oversimplified characteristics attributed to an entire group of people are **stereotypes**. In general, stereotypes are perceived when a speaker makes a claim beyond the facts to a statement that has no valid basis. Stereotypes reveal the speaker's prejudice and beliefs towards a group of people.[6] **Prejudice** is an attitude towards a group of people that directly affects the way the person holding the stereotype treats the group of people. One difficulty with stereotypes is every single one of us harbors stereotypes because they are learned through socialization from parents, friends, religion, and personal experiences. The media such as television, radio, film, newspapers, and books also contribute to our stereotypes. Another difficulty with stereotypes is they are often based upon half-truths that are generalized to an entire group without allowing for individual variations.

Stereotypes can vary based upon type and intensity. The type of stereotype refers to whether the stereotype is positive or negative. For example, positive stereotypes of police officers might be that they are hardworking, self-sacrificing, and helpful. Negative stereotypes might be that they are aggressive, undisciplined, and trigger-happy. Although negative stereotypes receive the most attention (because they construct unfavorable images of groups), positive stereotypes are also problematic because they mask individual differences. Approaching a tall person and asking them basketball questions can be just as offensive as placing a negative stereotype upon that person. Positive stereotypes are well intended but demonstrate a lack of sensitivity and understanding of individual differences. For example, statements such as "African Americans are very athletic" or "Chinese Americans are very smart" might appear to be "positive," but they still perpetuate a troubling stereotype due to the general label that is being applied to the entire group. Again, avoid these types of statements to prevent yourself from offending your audience.

Stereotypes can be overt or covert. Although overt stereotypes are not as common in public speaking, when they are uttered they demonstrate a complete lack of sensitivity and understanding. The best way to avoid overt stereotypes is to eliminate statements that make absolute claims about an entire group. Therefore, speakers should avoid blanket assumptions such as "All athletes are dumb"; "All women like to watch soap operas"; and "All men are pigs." Covert stereotypes such as the Lott example are sometimes more difficult to identify and eliminate because they are imbedded in personal perceptions, interpretations, and beliefs about reality. The best way to eliminate covert stereotypes is to become more knowledgeable and understanding of cultural differences (through books, personal relationships, and empathy) as we explain at the end of this chapter.

Sexist Language

Making gender assumptions by using masculine terms to the exclusion of feminine terms when referring to both men and women is called **sexist language**. Historically, white men have controlled the development of language and how language is used to label and describe people, places, and ideas.[7] As a result, the masculine form of a word is taken as the standard, while the feminine form is derived from it. In addition, most words associated with men are more flattering and perceived as more positive than words associated with women. This might seem trivial, but sexist language indicates power relationships between men and women (where men maintain power) and language influences how people perceive gender roles.[8] For example, when the words *judge*, *doctor*, and *construction worker* are used, people tend to think of men, whereas when the words *secretary*, *nurse*, and *elementary school teacher* are used, people tend to think of women.

Speakers can eliminate sexist language from presentations by making their language more gender-neutral. **Gender-neutral language** is when language is made less sexist by eliminating gender stereotypes (such as using police officer instead of policeman) and the use of the generic *he*. For example, instead of using masculine terms such as *mankind* and *man-made*, use more appropriate terms such as *human life* and *human made*. In addition, eliminate the use of gender stereotypes when referring to professionals. Instead of *mailman* use *mail carrier*, and instead of *congressman* use *member of congress*. Moreover, speakers should eliminate the overuse of the generic *he*. Speakers can avoid this by referring to the person in the plural form. For example, instead of saying, "When a lawyer makes *his* final argument," say, "When lawyers make *their* final arguments." Using more gender-neutral language is an effective way for speakers to make their language more inclusive for a multicultural audience. Speakers do not want to alienate audience members; speakers want to reach as many audience members as possible.

Marking Language

When speakers make unnecessary reference to human characteristics such as gender or ethnicity when referring to a person, they have used **marked language**. When a person uses marked language, it implies a negative stereotype against the person being marked. It implies the person is an exception to the rule or that the person does not possess the necessary intelligence or education for a particular occupation. For example, if a sportscaster said, "Robert Griffin III, the African American quarterback of the Washington Redskins," this would indicate an unnecessary marking. Instead, it would be more appropriate to simply say, "Robert Griffin III, quarterback of the Washington Redskins." To avoid marked language do not make references to someone's gender or ethnicity when it is not relevant to your topic. However, when gender or ethnicity is an important point of your comment, then certainly do not hesitate to indicate gender or ethnicity. For instance, if a speaker is acknowledging the first woman discussed in the Bible they would simply say, "Eve, the first woman mentioned in the Bible…"

Eliminating stereotypes, sexist language, and marking language involves making a behavioral change. To change behavior, speakers need to be equipped with the correct knowledge and understanding of cultural differences. There are several ways a speaker can gain knowledge and understanding of cultural differences. One way is to read about different cultures to become aware of and knowledgeable of different cultural values and norms and how these impact communication. Speakers should also read historical works from different cultural perspectives to understand how different cultural perspectives were formed in reaction to the dominant culture. Speakers can also develop personal relationships with people of color to further break down stereotypes. When equipped with knowledge and understanding speakers can practice empathy when engaged with a multicultural audience. **Empathy** involves demonstrating respect and understanding for another by projecting yourself into the other person's position. In order for empathy to be effective, the person has to be genuine and mindful not to make quick judgments. Empathy involves the commitment to becoming comfortable with cultural differences.[9] When empathy is achieved then the communication context is ready for third-culture building. **Third-culture building** involves a speaker identifying common universal values that help the speaker and the multicultural audience create a new culture that draws from and extends the norms and values from independent cultures (see Chapter 4).

This chapter has reviewed the principles of language and discussed the meanings derived from language to give you a better idea of how language can impact the effectiveness of your message. We have explained ways your language can be more effective by using concrete words, direct language, comparisons, and contrasts. In addition, we have discussed how your language can be more colorful and rhythmic. Finally, we have outlined how to avoid offensive language. In understanding language, you will be more aware of how to construct precise messages that will help you and the audience reach mutual understanding.

VOCABULARY

Abstract words — language that is less precise and more vague in its description. Abstract words are less precise in meaning and more open to different interpretations.

Alliteration — when a speaker uses language that repeats the same sound to highlight an important idea in a speech.

Ambiguity — the second principle of language that means words have multiple meanings.

Antithesis — when a speaker combines two contrasting ideas to illustrate a point.

Arbitrariness — the first principle of language, which means words gain meaning through common agreement.

Cadence — see rhythm.

Comparison — pointing out the similarities between two concepts or objects.

Concrete words — when language refers to specific objects or information. Concrete words are more precise in meaning and less open to different interpretations.

Connotative meaning — the personal, subjective, and emotional attachments we associate with certain words or phrases.

Contrast — pointing out the differences between two concepts or objects.

Denotative meaning — the common dictionary meaning of a word. It is the explicit meaning of words or what the words mean at face value.

Direct language — using specific words to describe concepts or ideas.

Empathy — involves demonstrating respect and understanding for another by projecting yourself into the other person's position.

Gender-neutral language — when language is made less sexist by eliminating gender stereotypes (such as using *police officer* instead of *policeman*) and the use of the generic *he*.

Indirect language — using abstract words to describe concepts or ideas.

Marked language — when a speaker makes an unnecessary reference to human characteristics such as gender or race when referring to a person.

Metaphor — an implied comparison that does not use the words "as" or "like."

Mixed metaphor — making more than one comparison to describe the same concept or idea.

Monotone delivery — when the entire speech is delivered in the same speaking volume, pitch, and rate.

Prejudice — forming an attitude towards a group of people that directly affects the way the person holding the attitude treats the group of people.

Relative meaning — the implicit meaning of the word. It is the opposite of what the words mean at face value.

Repetition — when a speaker reiterates the same words or phrases at the beginning or at the end of consecutive sentences.

Rhythm — the stylistic uses of language through vocal aspects such as rate, pitch, and volume that make a speech more memorable and vivid. Also known as a speaker's cadence.

Semantic triangle — a diagram that illustrates how language is composed of symbols that are only a representation of the concept.

Sexist language — making gender assumptions by overusing masculine terms when referring to men and women.

Simile — a direct comparison between two concepts, objects, or ideas that uses the words "as" or "like."

Stereotype — an oversimplified characteristic attributed to an entire group of people.

Symbolic process — this describes how communication functions; communication is based upon language, which is an association between a symbol (words) and a referent (concepts).

Third-culture building — involves a speaker identifying common universal values that help the speaker and the multicultural audience create a new culture that draws from and extends the norms and values from independent cultures.

Tonal meaning — when we emphasize a word to indicate the meaning of a message.

REFERENCES

[1] William V. Haney, *Communication and Interpersonal Relations* (Homewood: Irvin, 1986), 250.

[2] Alfred Korzybski, *Selections from Science and Sanity* (Ann Arbor: Edwards Brothers, 1990).

[3] Haney, 256.

[4] Mike Bresnaham, Ben Bolch, and James Rainey, "The Donald Sterling Furor; Banned for Life" *Los Angeles Times* (30 April 2014), A1.

[5] Mark P. Orbe and Tina M. Harris, *Interracial Communication* (USA: Wadsworth, 2001). 54–56.

[6] Guo-Ming Chen and William J. Starosta, *Foundations in Intercultural Communication* (Needham Height, MA: Allyn and Bacon, 1998), 39.

[7] Lea Stewart, Pamela Cooper, Alan Stewart, and Sheryl Friedley, *Communication and Gender* (Boston: Allyn and Bacon, 1998), 58.

[8] Stewart, Cooper, Stewart, and Friedly, 61.

[9] Chen and Starosta, 42.

INFORMATIVE SPEAKING 12

"The most powerful factors in the world are clear ideas in the minds of energetic men of good will."
-J. Arthur Thomson

"he obligation to endure gives us the right to know."
-Jean Rostand

"ince we cannot know all that is to be known of anything, we ought to know a tle about everything."
-Blaise Pascal

This Chapter Examines:

+ the nature of informative speaking

+ guidelines for informative speaking

+ the artistic proofs and informative speaking

+ the types of informative speeches

+ the basic, skeletal, and sample outlines of the informative speech

---

Nineteen years ago, almost to the day, we lost three astronauts in a terrible accident on the ground. But we've never lost an astronaut in flight: We've never had a tragedy like this. And perhaps we've forgotten the courage it took for the crew of the shuttle; but they, the Challenger Seven, were aware of the dangers, but overcame them and did their jobs brilliantly. We mourn seven heroes: Michael Smith, Dick Scobee, Judith Resnick, Ronald McNair, Ellison Onizuka, Gregory Jarvis, and Christa McAuliffe. . .We will never forget them, nor the last time we saw them, this morning, as they prepared for their journey and waved good-bye and "slipped the surly bonds of earth" to "touch the face of God."

These words spoken by President Ronald Reagan in 1986 illustrate how he chose to inform the American public of the Challenger disaster. This example also highlights how Reagan was able to not only inform the audience, but he kept the audience's attention throughout his national address by using descriptive and colorful language. Although Reagan's example represents a formal speech in which he had the time to develop his ideas and thoughts, in our daily lives we commonly engage in informal informative speaking.

There are a number of ways we engage in informal informative speaking with others, such as discussing news-related information (current events, the weather, sports, financial reports), explaining new information (interesting topics we might have read, heard, or seen on television), giving advice (buying a house, managing personal relationships), giving directions, and receiving training for a new job. All of these examples represent some of the different ways we engage in informative speaking. In addition, the increase of technology such as cell phones, e-mail, social media, and the Internet, has provided more channels for us to participate in informative speaking and more opportunities for us to share information with others.

In this chapter, we will discuss how you as an informative speaker can present your information in an interesting, creative, and memorable way. Therefore, we will discuss how you can make your informative speech more interesting and vivid for your audience. Specifically, this chapter will cover the following topics: the nature of informative speaking, guidelines for informative speaking, the artistic proofs and informative speaking, the types of informative speeches, and the basic, skeletal, and sample outlines for the informative speech.

THE NATURE OF INFORMATIVE SPEAKING

In today's society we have a need to share and exchange ideas with others. If you think about your own day, you can probably think of many conversations where you were either sending or receiving information. Although we commonly participate in informative speaking, we are usually not aware of the nature of informative speaking. We will further discuss the nature of informative speaking by defining its purpose and by distinguishing it from persuasive speaking.

What Is Informative Speaking?

Informative speaking is when a speaker attempts to increase the audience's understanding or knowledge on a given topic. In other words, informative speaking focuses primarily on presenting the audience with new, relevant, and interesting information. The speaker's job is to present information clearly and accurately so the audience can learn something new. Therefore, audience analysis (as discussed in Chapter 4) is very important in informative speaking. If the audience is not given new, relevant, and interesting information, it will be difficult to present an effective informative speech.

Distinguishing Informative from Persuasive Speaking

For speakers to present an informative speech, they need to know the "boundaries" for informative speaking. It is important to know the distinction between informative and persuasive speaking because there is a fine line between these two types of speaking. When you are beginning your process of selecting an informative topic you should keep the following distinctions in mind.

INFORMATIVE SPEAKING		PERSUASIVE SPEAKING	
Purpose	To provide understanding or increase knowledge	**Purpose**	To shape, reinforce, or change the audience's feelings, attitudes, beliefs, or behaviors
Topic	Noncontroversial	**Topic**	Controversial
Opinion	Not used to persuade	**Opinion**	Is used to persuade
Appeal	No call to action	**Appeal**	A call to action

The first distinction between informative and persuasive speaking involves their purposes. In the informative speech, the speaker is not *intentionally* trying to change a feeling, attitude, belief, or behavior. Instead, the speaker is simply presenting information for the audience's understanding or knowledge. On the other hand, the persuasive speaker is definitely trying to change a feeling, attitude, belief, or behavior.

Another helpful distinction to remember between the two types of speaking is that informative speeches usually present topics that are noncontroversial. Controversial topics tend to take the informative speaker out of the "informative mode" of simply presenting information to the audience and into the "persuasive mode" of making arguments to persuade the audience to a certain action. This is why topics such as "abortion," "the death penalty," "legalizing drugs," "gun control," or "censorship in America" are difficult topics to discuss in an informative speech or panel presentation. These topics are more appropriate for a persuasive presentation in which the speaker takes a perspective and expresses personal opinions or feelings about such issues.

Our last statement leads into the next distinction between informative and persuasive speaking: the opinion of the informative speaker is not used to persuade the audience. However, in the persuasive speech, the speaker does use opinion to persuade the audience. This is a very fine distinction that speakers sometime cross. The key is *intention*. For example, the informative speaker is not intentionally using opinion to persuade the audience, "I think rollerblading is the best way to stay in shape." Notice how the speaker stated her opinion, but she was not intentionally persuading the audience to buy rollerblades to exercise.

The final distinction between informative and persuasive speaking is the call to action. Informative speaking does not include a call to action, whereas persuasive speaking does. A **call to action** is a speaker's specific appeal to the audience to respond to the speaker's persuasive goal. Usually, in the conclusion of persuasive speeches, speakers directly tell the audience the behavioral response they want: "I want everyone here to consider what I have said today and stop buying imported clothing." Meanwhile, the informative speaker does not make a call to action in the conclusion: "Imported clothing is an interesting topic that you now better understand and know more about."

These distinctions between informative and persuasive speaking help define the boundaries for each type of speaking. These boundaries will also help you in selecting an informative topic for your presentation. Remember that the key is intent. The informative speaker does not attempt to persuade the audience.

GUIDELINES FOR INFORMATIVE SPEAKING

For an informative speech to be effective it has to have more than simply information. As an informative speaker, you need to present your information in a creative and interesting way so you will be able to keep the audience's attention throughout your speech. You also need to help the audience understand and remember your information if you want to reach your goal of increasing the audience's understanding or knowledge on the topic. We discuss several approaches for maintaining interest and attention of the audience for the informative speech.

Select a Relevant Topic

Although we talked about topic selection in Chapter 6, we reiterate some of that information here to emphasize the importance of selecting an appropriate topic for your informative speech. Remember that you are the *expert* or *teacher* when you are presenting information to your listeners. The audience will look to you as the authority who has information to convey for their benefit. Therefore, it is important to select a topic you find interesting, and try to talk about something with which you have familiarity and experience. Also, you should consider choosing a topic with which you have specific training or background. This will most surely make you feel more comfortable because you already know something about the topic you will be discussing.

In addition, when considering informative topics, your topic should be relevant to your audience. One of the best ways to ensure your topic is relevant to your audience is by having the topic fulfill one of two needs. Your topic should be either a *need to know* or *neat to know*. A *need to know* topic presents information to an audience that is critical or vital to know about such as "how to reduce your risk of heart disease." Meanwhile, a *neat to know* topic presents information to the audience that is purely interesting for the audience to know about such as "the building of the pyramids." In both cases you are fulfilling certain needs that make the topic relevant to the audience.

When you make the topic relevant to the audience, you as the speaker are establishing the **common ground** or the **rationale** for your speech. If your audience believes that a topic will benefit them in some way (e.g., save time or money, reduce the risk of heart attack, save a life in an emergency situation), they will be far more likely to listen attentively. Let's say a speaker is very knowledgeable about automobiles. This speaker might decide to give an informative speech entitled, "How to Rebuild Your Carburetor." However, this might be of minimal use or interest to the audience and the topic is probably far too technical for their level of experience. Instead, the speaker would be wise to revise the topic and talk about either, "What to Look for When Buying a Good Used Car," or "Automobile Safety," or

"Automobile Troubleshooting: What to Do if Your Car Breaks Down." In this case, the speaker is still able to use his expertise and knowledge about automobiles, while providing the audience with a practical and useful topic. See Chapter 4 on audience analysis to further understand how you can adapt your topic to your audience.

Make Your Information Memorable

One way you can ensure an effective informative speech is by making your presentation memorable. When you take the time to plan what you say, how you say it, and how you present it, your informative speech will be greatly enhanced. There are a number of approaches you can follow to make your informative speech memorable. As the speaker, you should strive to incorporate as many of these approaches as possible into your informative speech.

Incorporate Support Material

Support material is the substance or material found in all speeches. As we discussed in Chapter 7, support material includes examples, facts, statistics, testimony, narratives, and anecdotes that are used to verify information. When you use support material in your speech, your ideas will be more descriptive and understandable for the audience. Any speech or group presentation that does not contain evidence or support material will simply consist of opinions and lack any real substance demanded by the audience. While your listeners might be interested in your personal viewpoints and opinions, it is simply human nature to demand "proof" on behalf of the speaker. Support material helps the speaker meet that demand. You should review Chapters 7 and 8 to see how support material is incorporated into a speech to make your ideas more concrete, vivid, and interesting.

In order for speakers to meet the audience's demand for proof, they will have to consult other information on their topic. Therefore, you will need to conduct solid research to gather useful information and evidence for the audience. As we have mentioned in Chapter 6, you should take full advantage of all resources available to you, from your library to the Internet, to find support material for your informative speech. A well-documented speech will provide far more valuable information and knowledge for your listeners than a speech lacking substantial support material.

Incorporate Colorful and Rhythmic Language

One of the greatest myths about informative speaking is that the speech has to be dull, uncreative, and uninteresting. This is far from the truth. Informative speeches should use colorful language that creates images, makes creative associations, and maintains the audience's interests. As the Reagan example illustrates in the beginning of this chapter, informative speeches can use lively and colorful language. We have already discussed in Chapter 11 how to use colorful language such as metaphors and similes to make your ideas more interesting and vivid. You should review this chapter for ideas on how to use colorful language in your informative speech.

Speakers can also make their speeches more memorable and eloquent by articulating certain sounds, words, and phrases within a speech. Rhythm, or cadence, is a stylistic use of language that uses vocal aspects such as rate, pitch, and volume that make a speech more memorable and vivid. In Chapter 11 we discussed three aspects of rhythm: repetition, alliteration, and antithesis, that speakers can use in a speech to intensify their ideas and to reinforce important information. We also suggest you review this information in Chapter 11 for ideas to incorporate rhythm into your speech.

Incorporate Presentational Aids

Another creative way you can make your informative speech more interesting and memorable is by using a **presentational aid**. A presentational aid is any physical device or material that speakers use in a speech to enhance, clarify, and/or reinforce the verbal message. Presentational aids enable a speaker to present information in creative ways. For this reason, presentational aids are a very effective way to gain your audience's attention and to make your speech memorable.

In addition to gaining the audience's attention and interest, presentational aids help take some of the pressure off the speaker. In Chapter 14, we discuss the purpose, rules, functions, types, and guidelines for using presentational aids. You should read this chapter and then decide if a concept or idea in your presentation can be enhanced by the use of a presentational aid. If you do decide your speech would benefit from a presentational aid, use Chapter 14 as a guide for how to incorporate the presentational aid into your speech.

Incorporate Audience Involvement

One aspect that separates great informative speeches from average speeches is audience involvement. Effective public speakers seek ways to involve the audience in the informative speech. When you can get your audience to participate in your speech you turn the audience from passive members to active members. People usually learn more when they are actively participating in your presentation.[1] As you develop your speech, you should not only consider the language and/or presentational aids you might use in your speech, but you should also think of ways to involve your audience.

Over the years, we have witnessed many presentations that have effectively involved the audience in an informative speech. For example, one speaker gave an informative speech on sign language. The speaker involved the audience by teaching them how to make various signs. After the speaker demonstrated how to make a sign, the speaker had the audience make the sign. It was a very effective method the speaker demonstrated in having the audience participate and learn in the speech. Another example involved a speaker who gave an informative speech on Tae-Bo. The speaker had the audience try a few of the moves that she had demonstrated in the speech. Again, it was another great example of how to involve the audience in the presentation.

Figure 12-1. Audience Involvement

Present Balanced Information

For any informative speech to be effective, it needs to present balanced information. This means that the information is tailored to the time constraints, there is a mixture of various support material, and it is adapted to the audience's knowledge level. This last point is important because you do not want to present information that overestimates or underestimates the audience. There is nothing more frustrating for an audience than attempting to listen to a presentation that is "over the audience's head" or a presentation that repeats basic knowledge that everyone knows. As an informative speaker your ideas should be adapted to the audience and you should include new information on your topic which is explained clearly. One way to present balanced information in an informative speech is to avoid information overload and underload.

Avoid Information Overload

Remember that you can only reach your goal of increasing the audience's understanding or knowledge on a topic if you present your ideas clearly. If you present far more ideas in your speech than is necessary or if you present your information by using a great deal of technical language or jargon, your audience will experience information overload. **Information overload** is when the audience receives too much information or is presented with too much technical language or jargon for the audience to understand.

Information overload can be a problem with any speech, but it can be solved easily. First, tailor your speech to your time constraints. Often, speakers try to include too much information into their speech. Instead, narrow down your topic and present less, but more detailed, information. Also, try to include a variety of support material. Informative speeches can be very boring when the speaker only presents fact, after fact, after fact. You should use a variety of support material within your speech, such as narratives and examples, to keep your speech interesting.

Avoid Information Underload

Another problem for informative speakers is information underload. **Information underload** is when a speaker underestimates the knowledge of the audience and presents basic information the audience already knows. Most of the time information underload is caused by speakers who have not done an audience analysis and/or careful research on the topic. In either case, this type of informative speech is doomed for failure. You want to avoid information underload by conducting an audience analysis. In Chapter 4, we discussed how you can analyze your audience to adapt your message to your audience. Also, make sure that you give yourself plenty of time to research the topic to discover the interesting and new information about your topic that you would like to share with your audience.

Following these guidelines for informative speeches will make your informative speech more interesting, colorful, and memorable. When you can construct an effective informative speech that maintains the audience's attention you will be more likely to reach your goal as an informative speaker. Another way speakers help themselves reach their goal for their informative speech is to demonstrate the artistic proofs of ethos, pathos, and logos in their presentation.

THE ARTISTIC PROOFS AND INFORMATIVE SPEAKING

The Greek philosopher Aristotle has often been called "the father of speechmaking." He is credited with the discovery of many central elements and components of public speaking, and he provides valuable advice for what constitutes an effective speaker in his treatise, *Rhetoric*. Perhaps Aristotle's greatest contribution is the three "proofs" of public speaking. These essential ingredients—ethos, pathos, and logos—have withheld the test of time and today remain as a foundation of all speeches and oral presentations.

Ethos

Aristotle defined the credibility of the speaker as ethos. **Ethos** is the audience's perception of the speaker's credibility, which includes the speaker's integrity, honesty, knowledge, and competence. Ethos represents the image of the speaker in the eyes of the audience. Does the speaker have a positive or a negative image? Is the speaker perceived as honest, trustworthy, knowledgeable, competent, and sincere? The reputation and experience of all speakers is very important if they are to be successful. Ethos might also be "earned" by a speaker who demonstrates thorough preparation and a respect and understanding of the audience, along with showing a genuine interest in the topic for the audience. In general, ethos is such a significant aspect of informative speaking, many experts in the field argue that if you can't establish ethos or credibility with the audience, you will never be successful in meeting your objectives as a speaker.

One way to establish ethos or speaker credibility is to briefly mention your personal experience with your topic early in the speech. This serves to reassure your listeners that you truly are qualified and knowledgeable. This is not "bragging" or "talking down" to your audience. When a speaker establishes credibility, it allows the listeners to judge the expertise and knowledge of the speaker. For example, a speaker discussing the topic of "personal computers" might indicate that they have had several years of experience with computers. A speaker who selects the topic, "How to Perform CPR in an Emergency Situation," might mention extensive training and state certification in CPR procedures to demonstrate speaker credibility.

Another way you can establish ethos in your informative speech is by giving source citations. A **source citation** is when you acknowledge the authenticity of your information by stating the author, name of publication, title, and date of the source for the audience. When you cite your sources in your speech you are verifying for the audience that your information is accurate and correct. Citing sources also illustrates that the speaker has done the proper research to become knowledgeable on the topic. The more knowledgeable you are on a topic, the more credible you will be perceived by the audience. Finally, citing sources enables you to use information from "experts" in the field to bolster your own credibility.

Pathos

The second artistic proof is pathos. **Pathos** refers to emotional appeals that are directed to deeply felt values, attitudes, and beliefs of the listeners. In addition, pathos also refers to the emotional intensity in which speakers deliver their message to an audience. Most of the time pathos is used primarily for persuasive presentations. However, with skill, an informative speaker should use pathos to elicit positive emotions such as excitement or intrigue to keep the audience's attention.

Also, informative speakers should deliver their speeches with pathos to avoid dull and monotone deliveries. You can't expect your listeners to be attentive and interested in your speech topic if you do not show any enthusiasm for the topic, as well as the audience. An energetic, animated speaker might even be able to turn a dull or mundane topic into an interesting, enthusiastic presentation. As we have mentioned under the guidelines for informative speaking, use colorful and rhythmic language to incorporate pathos into the delivery of your speech.

On the other hand, when a speaker attempts to move the emotions of an audience and appeals to patriotism, family values, and fairness, pathos is used to *persuade* the audience. Many of the speeches and protests of the 1960s anti-war and civil rights movements contained emotional appeals. Today we often see pathos in the speeches on either side of the abortion debate or in testimonial speeches by speakers representing such organizations as Mothers Against Drunk Driving (MADD) or Students Against Destructive Decisions (SADD). When the President of the United States appeals to our sense of patriotism in a time of national crises or tragedy, emotional appeals are often used. Interestingly, even television commercials for Coca-Cola or McDonald's during the Olympic Games integrated patriotic appeals to intensify the emotions of the audience to support America, drink Coke, and buy Happy Meals! However, as long as you are not intentionally trying to persuade an audience, use pathos in your informative speech to keep your audience's interest and attention.

Logos

The logical appeals in our speeches and presentations are called logos. **Logos** is a systematic pattern of thought based on reasoning and evidence. Logos includes the content or argument of the speech, as well as the considerations of structure and organization in the speech. Logos is an essential element in all speeches because a well-structured and organized speech containing a logical sequence of ideas or arguments will be much more effective than a speech with little or no structure. Logos is based on the premise that a speech has a definable logic. Also, logos assumes that your audience will come into any speaking situation with a set of needs and expectations. Logos meets the listener's expectations of a well-structured and organized speech, which is easy to follow and comprehend because it contains a logical flow of ideas and arguments.

ETHOS	PATHOS	LOGOS
ethical appeal	emotional appeal	logical appeal
image	values, beliefs	reasoning
reputation	primarily persuasive	structure
speaker credibility found in all speeches	speeches and presentations	organization found in all speeches

THE TYPES OF INFORMATIVE SPEECHES

When we share information with others we use a number of techniques to help the other person understand our ideas. Sometimes we have to define new, complex, or technological words for the other person to understand. Sometimes we have to provide a detailed description of an object, place, or person for the listener to understand. Other times, we actually show someone what we mean. Finally, we might have to take our time and explain elaborate events or processes for people to understand. All of these examples illustrate the four common types of informative speeches: the speech of definition, the speech of description, the speech of demonstration, and the speech of explanation. Each type will be further discussed.

The Speech of Definition

The primary function of the speech of definition is to define a perspective, an idea, or a concept. A **speech of definition** provides an "extended" definition of a perspective, idea, or concept for the audience's understanding. In essence, a speech of definition helps the audience understand the meaning of the perspective, idea, or concept. When a speaker wants to demystify a new phenomenon that is occurring in society or to clarify an idea or concept, the speaker should consider giving a speech of definition.

Often, the audience receives a clearer understanding of the perspective, idea, or concept when the speaker also clarifies the misconceptions and myths surrounding the concept. For example, when the AIDS epidemic was brought to the consciousness of the mainstream culture, there were a lot of misconceptions and myths about the disease. In this case, the speaker would provide an extended definition of the disease in addition to clarifying the misconceptions concerning this disease. Providing a definition and clarification of AIDS would lead to a better understanding of the disease for the audience.

The Speech of Description

When a speaker wants to describe a place, an event, or a person, this type of informative speech is classified as a speech of description. A **speech of description** attempts to provide a clear, vivid, and detailed "picture" of the place, event, or person. The more descriptive the speaker is (by using concrete and precise language) the more likely the audience will be able to understand the idea the speaker is attempting to describe.

There are two ways speakers can make their ideas more descriptive. First, speakers need to be very accurate with their language. A major problem with description speeches is that the speaker is too vague and the audience does not truly understand what the speaker is trying to describe. However, when colorful and rhythmic language is used, the speaker's ideas will be more vivid and memorable. A good example of the use of colorful and rhythmic language in a presentation was Martin Luther King's "I Have a Dream" speech. King was able to describe ideas like "freedom" and "liberty" solely through the use of words. King's speech also illustrates that speakers can make their ideas more vivid and memorable through the use of colorful and rhythmic language.

The second way speakers can make their ideas more descriptive is by using presentational aids. Showing a visual image is a very effective way to describe a place, an event, or a person. In fact, the visual image can show what might take you several minutes to explain. For example, a speaker who gave a speech on Mt. St. Helens greatly benefited from using presentational aids in his speech. He was able to describe the impact of the explosion by showing the before and after eruption images of the mountain with poster board size pictures. This example illustrates how presentational aids serve as a shorthand way of presenting concrete information.

The Speech of Demonstration

Sometimes a speaker wants to go beyond simply describing and instead teach the audience a process. The **speech of demonstration** is often called the "how to" speech because the speaker actually shows the audience how to do something or how a process works. Demonstration speeches make great informative speeches because the speaker can involve the audience in the process of what the speaker is demonstrating.

Whether speakers are demonstrating how to do something or how a process works, they must simplify the procedure for the audience's understanding. For example, if a speaker is demonstrating a self-defense move, the speaker needs to start at the beginning of the move and "break down" each move step-by-step. This way the audience will be able to follow and understand what they need to do to accomplish the movement step-by-step. At the end of the speech the audience should be able to demonstrate a process step-by-step or understand the process or procedure more clearly.

As for demonstrating how a process works, speakers must have their speech accompanied by a presentational aid; most commonly a model. The model will help the audience visualize and understand the process. For example, if a speaker is demonstrating the mechanics of aircraft flight, the speaker would need a model of a plane to demonstrate how such components as the engine and wings function for flight.

The Speech of Explanation

When a speaker discusses a complex, abstract, or unfamiliar event or process it is called a **speech of explanation**. A speech of explanation attempts to take an abstract concept and make it more concrete for the audience. Some examples of possible speech of explanation topics include: "How Hurricanes Form," "How the Internet Works," or "How Wine Is Fermented." Since the speech of explanation focuses on complex and abstract events or processes they are more difficult to present to an audience. For a speech of explanation to be successful the speaker has to be able to know and explain the event with clarity.

Whenever speakers are presenting a speech of explanation they should definitely incorporate colorful and descriptive language along with presentational aids into their speech. As we have mentioned, many times abstract ideas can be better explained for the audience through the use of a good analogy or metaphor. For this reason, make sure you review Chapter 11 for ideas on how to use these language devices in your speech. Also, review Chapter 14 on presentational aids to gain an understanding of how to incorporate presentational aids into your speech.

Although we presented the ideas of the speech of definition, description, demonstration, and explanation as separate entities, in reality you will probably use a combination of these types of information speeches within any informative speech. For example, in any informative speech you should define unfamiliar or new terms for your audience, you should describe ideas and concepts with colorful and precise language, you should demonstrate processes to clarify ideas, and you should use presentational aids to help you explain complex or abstract ideas. When you can demonstrate these techniques from the various types of informative speeches you will be able to express yourself in a clear and understandable way.

BASIC, SKELETAL, AND SAMPLE OUTLINES OF THE INFORMATIVE SPEECH

In this chapter, we have provided an overview of informative speaking. We have discussed the nature of informative speaking and we have explained the guidelines for informative speaking. We have also shown the relationship between the artistic proofs and informative speaking. Then, we illustrated the different types of informative speeches. In providing this information, you should have a better idea of what encompasses informative speaking and you should know how to present your informative speech in an interesting and vivid manner. We will close this chapter by illustrating three types of informative speech outlines to highlight what a completed outline looks like. For more specific information on how to develop and organize your speech see Chapters 8 and 9. Chapter 13 will examine the structure and organization of the persuasive speech.

IMFORMATIVE SPEECH BASIC OUTLINE

I. Introduction

    A. **Attention-Getter**: How many of you would like to reduce your risk of heart attack, lose weight, exercise two to three times a week, and meet new people?

    B. **Common Ground**: Jogging is an exercise that benefits everyone because jogging allows a person to stay in shape by keeping off any unecessary weight, decreasing the risk of heart attack, and lowering high blood pressure. In addition, jogging allows you to meet other people with similar interests.

    C. **Credibility**: I've been jogging for ten years now, ran on my track team in high school, and have run competitively in several 5 kilometer and 10 kilometer races. I am currently in training for my first "marathon" next year, a 26-mile race.

    D. **Thesis**: A person needs to take the proper steps in order to receive the benefits of jogging.

    E. **Preview**: You can enjoy the benefits of jogging by, first, selecting the proper type of running shoe to meet your needs as a runner; second, incorporating the proper warm-up and stretching exercises into your pre-jogging routine; and third, developing your own jogging program to chart your personal accomplishments as a runner.

II. Body

    A. Selecting the proper type of running shoe to meet your personal needs as a runner

        1. Short distance shoes

        2. Intermediate distance shoes

        3. Long distance shoes

    B. Incorporating the proper warm-up and stretching exericses into your pre-jogging routine

        1. Warm-up exercises

        2. Stretching exercises

    C. Developing your own jogging program to chart your personal accomplishments as a runner

        1. Assessing your needs

        2. Identifying goals

        3. Charting your personal accomplishments

12

III. Conclusion

A. **Thesis**: Today I have talked about how everyone can benefit from jogging when they prepare properly. **Review**: More specifically, I have discussed how to select the proper running shoe to meet your personal needs as a runner, the importance of warm-up and stretching exercises, and how to develop your own jogging program to help you chart your personal accomplishments as a runner.

B. **Reinforce Message**: When you follow the proper steps, you will receive all the benefits of jogging.

C. **Clincher**: Now that you know the proper steps involved in receiving all the benefits of jogging, I'll ask again, "How many of you would like to reduce your risk of heart attacks, lose weight, and meet new people?"

SKELETAL OUTLINE FOR THE IMFORMATIVE SPEECH

I. Introduction

    A. **Speaker introduction and audience salutation** (self introduction and audience greeting)

    B. **Attention-getter (attention-getting device)** to catch and maintain the audience's attention

        1. Refer directly to the topic or the occasion of the speech

        2. Use a personal story, experience, or reference

        3. Ask a "rhetorical question" to your audience

        4. Make a startling statement of fact or opinion

        5. Use a detailed example or illustration

        6. Ask for audience participation or feedback

        7. Use a direct quotation

        8. Tell a humorous story, joke, or anecdote

    C. **Credibility/ethos** (speaker qualifications, expertise, training, and experience with the topic)

    D. **Rationale/common ground** (reasons for listening and audience benefits or listener "payoff")

    E. **Thesis** (major point, idea, and assertion made by the speaker)

II. Body (discussion section)

    A. **Preview or initial summary** (preview major areas to be discussed)

    B. **Evidence and support material**

    C. **Definition of terms** (define all terminology, vocabulary, and jargon associated with the topic)

    D. **Evidence and support material**

    E. **Transition statement** (review of previously covered areas and preview of final area to be discussed)

III. Conclusion (summary statement)

    A. **Thesis** (reinforces major point, assertion, and idea made during the speech)

    B. **Review/summary statement** (briefly and concisely reviews or summarizes the major areas covered during the speech)

    C. **Final rationale/reinforce message** (the "bottom line"; audience "payoff" and benefits)

    D. **Clincher** (provides a memorable and fitting end to the speech; leaves the audience with a vivid and exciting image related to your topic)

12

SAMPLE OUTLINE FOR THE IMFORMATIVE SPEECH
"JOGGING FOR FITNESS AND FUN" BY JOE E. JOCK

I. Introduction

    A. **Speaker introduction and audience salutation**

        "Good morning. My name is Joe E. Jock and I want to welcome you today."

    B. **Attention-getter** (rhetorical question as **attention-getting device**)

        "How many of you would like to reduce your risk of heart attack, lose weight, exercise two to three times a week, and meet new people?"

    C. **Credibility/ethos** (speaker credibility)

        "I've been jogging for ten years now, ran on my track team in high school, and have run competitively in several 5 kilometer and 10 kilometer races. I am currently in training for my first 'marathon' next year, a 26-mile race."

    D. **Rationale/common ground** (benefits and significance of the topic for the audience)

        "I have found that jogging promotes a healthy lifestyle by maintaining a healthy weight. In addition, jogging decreases the risk of heart attack and high blood pressure. Moreover, jogging enables you to meet other people with similar interests and it gives you a sense of accomplishment."

    E. **Thesis** (major point, idea, and assertion made by the speaker)

        "While there are many benefits to jogging, several important steps need to be taken into consideration before you can receive the benefits of running. These crucial aspects will assure you that your jogging will be safe and effective."

II. Body (discussion section)

    A. **Preview or initial summary**

        "In discussing jogging as a popular form of aerobic exercise, there are three important considerations for the beginning runner. How to select the proper running shoe for your personal needs, the importance of stretching and 'warm-up' exercises to prevent leg cramps or damage to your muscles, and how to develop your own jogging program to chart your personal accomplishments as a runner, are all important considerations in discussing jogging as aerobic exercise."

    B. **Detailed discussion of the three major areas to be covered**

        1. Selecting the proper type of running shoe to meet your personal needs as a runner

        2. The importance of warm-up and stretching exercises

        3. How to develop your own jogging program and chart your personal accomplishments as a runner

    C. **Definition of terms**

        Make sure you define any terms or vocabulary and terminology associated with jogging or running:

1. "Runner's knee"
2. "Hitting the wall"
3. "Aerobic exercise"
4. "Cool-down period"

D. **Evidence and support material** (research and fact-finding)

The body of the speech should include any research, evidence, and support material (detailed example or illustration, expert testimony, personal testimony, statistics)

E. **Transition statement** (provides a review of points already made and preview of final area to be discussed)

"Now that I've discussed how to select the proper running shoe to meet your personal needs as a runner, and the importance of stretching or warm-up exercises to prevent leg cramps and damage to your muscles, I'd like to conclude today by talking about how you can develop your own jogging program and help chart your personal accomplishments as a runner."

III. Conclusion (summary statement)

A. **Thesis** (reinforces major point, assertion, and idea made during the speech)

"There are several important steps to take when considering jogging for fitness and fun."

B. **Review/summary statement** (provides a brief and concise review of the major areas covered during the speech)

"Today I have talked about jogging as a popular form of aerobic exercise. I have discussed how selecting the proper running shoe to meet your personal needs as a runner, the importance of stretching or warm-up exercises, and developing your own jogging program to help you chart your personal accomplishments as a runner, are all very important considerations for anyone interested in jogging for fitness and fun."

C. **Final rationale/reinforce message**

"I have found, and I know you will discover, that jogging makes me feel good about myself. It will allow you to look and feel better, and be a happier, healthier individual, while achieving a sense of personal accomplishment."

D. **Clincher** (leaves the audience with a vivid and memorable image and provides a fitting end to the speech)

"Now that you know all of the proper steps to take when considering jogging for fitness and fun, let me ask you again. How many of you would like to reduce your risk of heart attack, lose weight, and meet new people?"

"Thank you. Do you have any comments or questions?"

VOCABULARY

Call to action — a speaker's specific appeal to the audience to respond to the speaker's persuasive goal.

Common ground — when the speaker explains to the audience how a topic relates to the audience to establish a common interest between speaker and audience (similar to the concept of rationale).

Ethos — the audience's perception of the speaker's credibility which includes the speaker's integrity, honesty, knowledge, and competence.

Information overload — when the audience receives too much information or is presented with too much technical language or jargon for the audience to understand.

Informative speaking — when a speaker attempts to increase the audience's understanding or knowledge on a given topic.

Information underload — when a speaker underestimates what the audience knows and presents basic information that the audience already knows.

Logos — a systematic pattern of thought based on reasoning and evidence.

Pathos — emotional appeals.

Persuasive speaking — when a speaker attempts to shape, reinforce, or change the audience's feelings, attitudes, beliefs, or behaviors.

Presentational aid — any physical device or material that speakers use in a speech to enhance, clarify, and/or reinforce the verbal message.

Rationale — the benefits and significance of the topic to the audience (similar to the concept of common ground).

Speech of definition — provides an "extended" definition of a perspective, idea, or concept for the audience's understanding.

Speech of demonstration — is often called the "how to" speech because the speaker actually shows the audience how to do something or how a process works.

Speech of description — attempts to provide a clear, vivid, and detailed "picture" of the place, event, or person.

Speech of explanation — when a speaker discusses a complex, abstract, or unfamiliar event or process.

Support material — the specific descriptions such as examples, facts, statistics, testimony, narratives, and anecdotes that verify information.

REFERENCES

[1] Teri Kwal Gamble and Michael Gamble, *Communication Works*, 11th edition (Boston: McGraw-Hill, 2013) 393.

12

213

PERSUASIVE SPEAKING 13

"There are two levers for moving men—interest and fear."
-*Napoleon*

"Whatever words we utter should be chosen with care, for people will hear them and be influenced by them for good or ill."
-*Siddhartha Gautama Buddha*

"I've never failed to convince an audience that the best thing they could do was to go away."
-*Thomas Love Peacock*

This Chapter Examines:

+ the nature of persuasive speaking

+ the importance of the artistic proofs

+ the types of persuasive speech structures

+ debate propositions

+ logical fallacies

+ ethics and persuasive speaking

+ the principles of persuasive speaking

For, while this year it may be a Catholic against whom the finger of suspicions is pointed, in other years it has been, and may someday be again, a Jew—or a Quaker—or a Unitarian—or a Baptist. It was Virginia's harassment of Baptist preachers, for example, that led to Jefferson's statue of religious freedom. Today, I may be the victim—but tomorrow it may be you—until the whole fabric of our harmonious society is ripped apart at a time of great national peril.

These words spoken by John F. Kennedy during his campaign for President in 1960 illustrate how a speaker can use reasoning to persuade an audience. Unlike the informative speaker, the persuasive speaker tries to influence the audience's feelings, attitudes, beliefs, or behaviors. In Kennedy's case, he was trying to change the audience's attitudes and beliefs toward Catholic candidates. He wanted people to accept him not as a Catholic candidate for President, but as a candidate for President. Although persuasive speaking is more challenging than other forms of speaking, we are all familiar with persuasion because we are saturated with persuasive messages every day. In fact, one estimate states that we are exposed to 5,000 persuasive messages a day from sources such as interpersonal interactions, social media, the Internet, and television.[1]

In this chapter, we will begin our discussion of the persuasive speech by providing an overview of the nature of persuasive speaking. Then, we will discuss the importance of the artistic proofs in persuasive speaking. Next, we will identify three types of persuasive speech structures. We will also clarify the three types of debate propositions. After the discussion of debate propositions, we will identify and explain certain logical fallacies that you want to avoid when making an argument. Finally, we will end the chapter by discussing ethics and persuasive speaking along with the principles of persuasion.

THE NATURE OF PERSUASIVE SPEAKING

Persuasive speaking occurs every day in many different contexts. Whether we are pressuring a friend to lend us money or we are talking ourselves into buying new clothes (or not buying ourselves new clothes!), persuasive speaking is a daily part of our lives. In this first section we will explain the nature of persuasive speaking by providing a definition of persuasive speaking, by discussing audience motivations, and by explaining three purposes of persuasive speaking.

Figure 13-1. Persuasive

What Is Persuasive Speaking?

Persuasive speaking is when a speaker attempts to shape, reinforce, or change the audience's feelings, attitudes, beliefs, or behaviors. Unlike informative speaking, persuasive speaking involves constructing speeches that are more emotional, argumentative, and supported with evidence to verify the speaker's message. A brief comparison illustrates the differences between informative and persuasive speaking.

INFORMATIVE SPEAKING	PERSUASIVE SPEAKING
General Purpose: To provide understanding or to increase knowledge	General Purpose: To shape, reinforce, or change the audience's feelings, attitudes, beliefs, or behaviors
Speaker's Role: To be objective	Speaker's Role: To be an advocate
Audience Role: To learn new information	Audience Role: To evaluate evidence to either accept or reject the speaker's message

The comparison between informative and persuasive speaking illustrates that persuasive speaking uses evidence to influence an audience. A persuasive speaker's job is difficult because a public speech represents a one-time event, while persuasion is a gradual process between a speaker and an audience. For instance, an audience member might not change his/her mind until later that day, later that week, later that month, or later that year (or years). Since public speakers only have one chance to influence the audience, speakers must make their message as persuasive as possible. This is why persuasive speakers need to have near perfect delivery, infallible evidence, sound reasoning, and an organized message. We will further break down this process of persuasion into two parts: the motivations of an audience and the purposes of persuasive speaking. A speaker needs to address both parts in order for persuasion to be successful.

Audience Motivations

As we discussed in Chapter 4, audience analysis is important in understanding the characteristics of an audience. These characteristics can help a speaker adapt a message to the audience. Not only is it important to know the audience's characteristics, but it is also important to understand their **motivations** or **needs**—in other words, what makes the audience "tick." In persuasive speaking, you want to target these motivations with logical and emotional appeals. We will identify four different audience motivations speakers can target in their persuasive speech.

The first level of motivation is feelings. **Feelings** are our emotions. Usually, feelings are best expressed by our nonverbal communication, especially our faces. When we use the face to express feelings, it is called affect displays. Common affect displays we demonstrate would be looking happy when we receive some good news, looking sad when we are feeling down, and looking angry when someone frustrates us. These are all ways we show our feelings. These examples also indicate that our nonverbal communication can communicate our feelings more accurately than our verbal communication. We call feelings the first level of motivation because feelings are constantly changing. One type of persuasive speech, which targets the emotions, is the speech of inspiration, which we discuss in the next section.

The second level of motivation is attitudes. **Attitudes** are our likes and dislikes. Everyone has attitudes toward persons, places, and ideas. Attitudes can be positive and negative. Regardless of what type of attitude we hold, our attitudes are learned through our experiences, from observation, from other people, and from our own reasoning. Attitudes are also relatively enduring. They allow us to perceive the world and interpret information in a consistent way in order to build solid beliefs and values. If we did not have cognitive consistency with our attitudes, we would have to laboriously assess each new situation we encounter. It would be very hard to interpret the world. Without careful thought, we would not know what we liked and disliked, and not knowing our likes and dislikes would make it difficult for us to establish stronger motivations such as beliefs and values. On the other hand, enduring attitudes, beliefs, and values, allow us to quickly evaluate each new person, place, or idea. A speaker can then target these attitudes by using reasoning and pathos appeals in the effort to shape, reinforce, or change attitudes.

The third level of motivation is beliefs. **Beliefs** are what we accept to be true. Do not confuse belief with truth. A belief does not necessarily have to be true, it only has to be accepted as true. For example, most children believe in Santa Claus. While most adults know that Santa Claus is not a real person, nevertheless, children *believe* he is a real person. This example also points out how beliefs are a powerful motivation. If the belief is strong enough, it will influence thoughts and actions. As a speaker, if you can successfully appeal to beliefs, your persuasive message will most likely have a long-lasting effect, because most people are reluctant to change their beliefs. As a caveat, however, be aware that changing people's beliefs, especially religious beliefs, is not easily done in a one-time speaking situation.

The fourth level of motivation is values. **Values** are deeply ingrained morals that are shaped by culture. Our values determine what we consider to be appropriate behavior and conduct for ourselves, and they form the inner core of the self. Values are very resistant to change and many people hold the same values for a lifetime. For example, most Americans hold the value of free speech. We value the right of free expression even to the point of allowing expression that is considered hateful, such as "hate speech." If any change occurs to values, it usually happens over a gradual period of time. However, values can sometimes change quickly in life-threatening events. Usually in the public speaking situation values are not changed. Therefore, it is best to incorporate common values such as liberty, freedom, and patriotism into your own persuasive messages because most people hold these values. If the audience agrees with the value, most likely they will agree with your speech.

Although behavior does not constitute a motivation, we included behavior because it is often the target of persuasive speakers. A speaker has successfully gained an audience behavioral response when the audience acts on the persuasive message. Most of the time a speaker wants to not only shape, reinforce, or change audience motivation, but also wants the audience to act on the persuasive message. For example, if a salesperson is selling a product, the salesperson is not only working to change your attitude toward the product, the salesperson wants a behavioral response; the salesperson wants you to buy the product! A behavioral response can be as simple as the audience raising their hands in agreement or as involved as buying a new car.

Three Purposes of Persuasive Speaking

Identifying the motivations of an audience helps the persuasive speaker adapt a message. Speakers can determine what audience motivation they want to persuade and then start to develop a strategy to influence that audience motivation. Developing a strategy begins with deciding what purpose the persuasive speech will accomplish. The three purposes of persuasive speaking, which are to inspire, to convince, and to actuate, will be discussed next. In reality, all three purposes can be present in any one persuasive speech, but usually one purpose is primary.

Sometimes the goal of the speaker is simply to encourage an audience. Whenever a speaker attempts to shape an audience's feelings, this is called a **speech to inspire**. Sometimes the speech to inspire is called the "feel good" speech because the main point of the speech is to encourage the audience to be determined in pursuing their dreams and goals. The overall goal of the inspiration speech is to make the audience feel good about themselves. Speeches to inspire are largely ceremonial speeches, such as the presidential inaugural, the pep talk, and the graduation speech.

Another purpose of persuasive speaking is to influence an audience's thinking. The **speech to convince** is when the speaker attempts to shape, reinforce, or change the audience's beliefs and attitudes. This persuasive speech does not require audience action; it only attempts to change the audience's current thinking or position. For example, one student gave a speech to convince in which he attempted to persuade the audience that leasing a car is better than buying one. He didn't ask the audience to go out and lease a car; he only wanted to persuade the audience to accept the idea that leasing a car is better than buying a car.

Sometimes a speaker wants to go beyond convincing an audience's thinking and call for a behavioral response to the persuasive speech. When a speaker attempts to influence the audience's beliefs and attitudes by requesting a behavioral response, the speaker has used the speech to actuate. The **speech to actuate** is common among salespersons who not only attempt to convince you that their product is great but give you many reasons why you should buy it. Being a salesperson is difficult because you can often convince people that your product or service is valuable, but unless you receive a change in behavior that leads to action, the persuasion is deemed unsuccessful. Usually in the speech to actuate, the speaker ends the speech by making a call to action. The **call to action** is a speaker's specific appeal to the audience to respond to the speaker's persuasive goal. It could be as simple as signing a petition or as involved as changing a personal behavior.

THE IMPORTANCE OF THE ARTISTIC PROOFS

As we briefly mentioned in the opening of this chapter, one difference with persuasive speaking is how the speaker incorporates more evidence and emotion into the speech to shape, reinforce, or change the audience's feelings, attitudes, beliefs, or behaviors. As mentioned in Chapter 12, the artistic proofs of ethos (credibility), logos (logic), and pathos (emotion) are key ingredients a speaker needs to demonstrate in order to effectively persuade the audience. In fact, dynamic speakers such as Martin Luther King, Jr., John F. Kennedy, and Ronald Reagan have demonstrated how to incorporate these three artistic proofs into moving speeches that represent ideal models of persuasive speaking.

Ethos

In the public speaking situation, the speaker should never overlook ethos. **Ethos**, also known as credibility, is the audience's perception of the speaker's integrity, honesty, knowledge, and competence. Credibility is even more important in the persuasive speech because the speaker is attempting to elicit some change in the audience. In order to do this, the audience has to be able to trust and respect the speaker. If the audience cannot trust the speaker, this greatly diminishes the speaker's ability to persuade regardless of the speaker's logical and emotional appeals. Plus, as we discussed in Chapter 10, appearance can greatly affect a speaker's credibility. If the speaker's appearance is contrary to the audience's expectations, this can cause a poor first impression and undermine the speaker's credibility.

How do speakers improve their credibility? We have identified four factors that speakers should strive to demonstrate in a speech to maintain high credibility. A speaker should demonstrate competence. **Competence** is the audience's perception of the speaker's intelligence, expertise, and knowledge of a topic. Demonstrating competence in a speech involves speakers being thoroughly prepared and well researched (by citing sources), in addition to being able to adapt their message to their audience.

A speaker should also demonstrate composure. **Composure** is the audience's perception of the speaker's poise. To demonstrate composure, speakers need to show a natural and relaxed delivery style in which they look relaxed, calm, and poised. Composed speakers never seem to lose their cool. Practicing nonverbal delivery such as eye contact, gestures, and movement will help the speaker appear to be very poised and in control.

Another factor a speaker should strive to demonstrate is character. **Character** is the audience's perception of the speaker's integrity, honesty, and trustworthiness. Character is not demonstrated in the public speaking situation, but it is created, maintained, and/or lost in the more public roles of the person. How do people conduct themselves in the public sphere? Are the speakers decent and respectful of others or are they self-serving and know how to put on a good "face"? The public persona (and increasingly one's private life) can influence an audience before they even hear the speech.

13

Finally, a speaker should foster sociability. **Sociability** is the audience's perception of the speaker's friendliness, warmth, and amiability. Sociability is directly related to a speaker's personality. Some speakers have very jovial personalities that can light up a room and make everyone feel as if they are best friends. The more sociable the person seems, the more comfortable and relaxed the audience can be with the speaker.

Logos

Logical appeals are how the speaker uses reasoning and evidence to construct a persuasive message. In order to persuade an audience, a speaker needs to be able to use reasoning. **Reasoning** is making conclusions based on evidence. When we use reasoning, we are using a systematic pattern of thought in which one idea is directly related to another. The key with using logos is to make sure you have accurate facts, sound evidence, and clear examples so the audience can see the "logical connection" of the reasoning. Using both reasoning and evidence help the speaker verify claims and persuade the audience. We will look at four different types of reasoning (deductive, inductive, analogy, and casual) and briefly discuss evidence.

Deductive Reasoning

When a speaker starts with a socially accepted general rule, principle, or belief and then moves to a more specific conclusion, the speaker has used **deductive reasoning**. In other words, the speaker is starting from an established position and then making a conclusion from a logical deduction of facts. Deductive reasoning can be illustrated by the syllogism. A **syllogism** is a deductive reasoning pattern in which there is a major premise, a minor premise, and a conclusion. The **major premise** is the generally accepted principle, the **minor premise** is the specific application of the accepted principle, and the **conclusion** is the idea that is produced by accepting the major and minor premise. For example, consider this well-known syllogism:

Major Premise: All human beings are mortal

Minor Premise: Socrates is a human being

Conclusion: Therefore, Socrates is mortal

What the example illustrates is if you accept the major and minor premise, then you have to accept the conclusion. As you can see, it is important for the speaker to start with a generally accepted principle. If not, the audience can reject the major premise and the reasoning concluded from the general principle. If done correctly, a syllogism can lead the audience exactly to where the speaker wants the audience to make the "logical connection."

Another deductive reasoning pattern that is related to the syllogism is the **enthymeme**. The enthymeme is a deductive reasoning pattern that has no explicit conclusion. In other words, the enthymeme is a truncated syllogism, because it only has a major premise and minor premise.

For example, an enthymeme would look like:

> Major Premise: All human beings are mortal
>
> Minor Premise: Socrates is a human being
>
> Conclusion: Therefore…

As the example illustrates, by omitting the conclusion, the audience is able to make the logical deduction of the conclusion in their own mind. The speaker uses reasoning and evidence to lead the audience to the speaker's implicit conclusion. The speaker attempts to paint a clear picture for the audience so the audience will naturally "see" the painting without having to be told to "see" the picture. When the audience can make up their own minds, they have more ownership of the persuasion, because they have made the "logical connection" as a result of accepting the major and minor premises. The key is to make sure you establish enough reasoning and evidence so the audience will make the conclusion you want them to make!

Inductive Reasoning

While deductive reasoning moves from general to specific, **inductive reasoning** uses reasoning that moves from specific facts to a specific conclusion. Another way to distinguish between deductive and inductive reasoning is that deductive reasoning is like subtraction, where you are reducing from a general principle to a conclusion. On the other hand, inductive reasoning is like addition where you add up facts to a specific conclusion. With inductive reasoning, you start from no preconceived principles; instead you are adding up the facts to illustrate the conclusion you will make. For example:

> Fact 1: Mr. Mehta comes late to work.
>
> Fact 2: Mr. Mehta has used six sick days this month.
>
> Fact 3: Mr. Mehta has complained about taking inventory.
>
> Fact 4: Mr. Mehta refuses to work overtime.
>
> Conclusion: Mr. Mehta does not like his job.

As this example illustrates, this person was led to the conclusion that "Mr. Mehta does not like his job" by adding up the preceding four facts. Using inductive reasoning is a common practice that we use every day to understand events and

13

behaviors. However, similar to deductive reasoning, we have to be careful with inductive reasoning. We can easily make inductions that are wrong. For example, Mr. Mehta's behavior might be explained in a different way; he likes his job, but his mother is very ill, and he is the only person available to visit her in the hospital and discuss her prognosis with the doctors. These errors in inductive reasoning are called **hasty generalizations**, which will be defined in the logical fallacies section of this chapter. Whenever you use inductive reasoning, make sure your facts are accurate and your conclusions are representative of the situation.

Analogy Reasoning

Another type of reasoning uses the audience's imagination and ability to draw conclusions from comparisons. **Analogy reasoning** is when you make a figurative comparison between two or more cases to infer that what applies in one case can also apply to the other. When you make an analogy, this allows the audience to make a creative comparison that they might not have considered. The strength of an analogy is you can take a case that is not well known and compare it to a more familiar case to make a logical point. Consider the following analogy:

> In preparing for retirement, you can think of the classic story of the grasshopper and the ant. We can be complacent like the grasshopper and assume that everything will be fine when we reach retirement. Or we can be diligent like the ant and make sure we invest in the best retirement plans so we can be financially prepared for retirement. It is our choice. What will yours be?

Whenever you use an analogy, you must make sure the analogy is reasonable enough for the audience to accept the figurative comparison. In the previous example, it would be reasonable for the audience to accept the figurative comparison the speaker was attempting to make, which was the idea of being prepared. A figurative comparison that appears to be reasonable is referred to as a parallel case. Only when you have parallel cases can you draw similar conclusions from the figurative comparison. If you make a figurative comparison that is not reasonable or too extreme, the audience will reject your argument. This is called an **invalid analogy**, a concept we will define in the logical fallacies section.

Causal Reasoning

The final type of reasoning we will examine is causal reasoning. **Causal reasoning** is when the speaker attempts to establish a direct link between causes and effects. When you are using causal reasoning, you are making a prediction that one outcome will occur based on past events. Two primary ways speakers use causal reasoning are by establishing cause and effect relationships and effect to cause relationships.

Cause and effect reasoning is when the speaker makes an argument based on past experience that a cause has led to a certain effect. In this case the speaker is predicting the same outcome will occur in the future. A cause and effect argument could be, "*The faster you drive, the more severe your accident will be.*" In this example the speaker is identifying a cause (fast driving) and then linking it to the effect (severe accidents). The speaker is able to make this claim based upon accidents in which speed directly affected the severity of the accident. In the persuasive speech, the speaker needs to cite evidence to verify that the cause and effect reasoning is accurate.

Meanwhile, **effect to cause reasoning** is when the speaker makes an argument that the same effect was produced by a certain cause in the past. In this case, the speaker is making an inference that the effect has the same cause. An effect to cause argument could be, "*The roof is leaking, therefore the workers must not have done a good job.*" In this example, the speaker is identifying an effect (a leaking roof) and then linking it to the cause (a poor job). The speaker is able to make this claim based upon what seems like a logical association between the effect and the cause in order to verify the facts that establish that the workers did a poor job which caused the effect.

Evidence

In a persuasive speech, speakers need to incorporate evidence to verify their claims, to make their ideas more descriptive, to clarify their reasoning, and to enhance their credibility. In Chapter 7, we clearly explained the types of support material you can use as evidence. These types include examples, facts, statistics, testimony, narratives, and anecdotes. When speakers use these types of support material, it is a way for them to establish logic for their case. If you are unsure about how to incorporate support material as evidence in your speech, see Chapter 7.

Pathos

For any persuasive speech to be a success, it needs to have pathos. **Pathos** means emotional appeals. Speakers should strive to incorporate emotional appeals into their speech by appealing to the feelings of the audience and by demonstrating emotion in their delivery. When a speech demonstrates pathos, the message comes alive; it is more vivid, and it has more impact. We will further describe emotional appeals and nonverbal delivery.

There are endless emotional appeals a speaker can use to touch the inner feelings of audience members to motivate them to action. While emotional appeals are great for persuasive speaking, you never want to use emotional appeals in an unethical way. Rather, ethical persuaders use emotional appeals that target positive emotions that people like to experience such as compassion, idealism, pride, joy, and security. These are all positive appeals because these feelings tend to reinforce positive human behavior.

On the other hand, emotional appeals that elicit fear, anger, and guilt tend to motivate individuals by making people experience feelings they do not usually enjoy. While fear, anger, and guilt appeals can work effectively and quickly to motivate people, these appeals are not as long lasting. If you do choose to use fear appeals (such as explaining the health effects the audience is exposed to), anger appeals (such as demonstrating how the audience is getting ripped off), or guilt appeals (such as telling the audience how they are morally bankrupt) make sure you give the audience an immediate and positive action they can take to relieve the fear, anger, or guilt you are intensifying. This way you are giving the audience an "outlet" for releasing the negative emotion you have intensified in them.

One way you can effectively communicate emotional appeals is by using colorful language that creates images, makes creative associations, and maintains your audience's interests (see Chapter 11 for a complete discussion of colorful language). Colorful language can be incorporated into a speech by using metaphors and similes that help enhance the delivery styles of your persuasive message. Colorful language brings facts, examples, and appeals to life to motivate audience members to action.

A third component that will help your emotional appeals is your verbal and nonverbal delivery (see Chapter 10 for a more detailed discussion of verbal delivery). Your vocal delivery consists of the vocal qualities of volume, pitch, rate, pauses, and enunciation that help you present your message in an interesting, fluent, and vivid manner. When you can perfect a conversational delivery, it allows your audience to focus on your message and not on how you are saying your message. Plus, you want to demonstrate conviction in your delivery. **Conviction** is a deep feeling of certainty that your cause is righteous and truthful. When you deliver your speech with conviction, you sound confident, and you are bold because you truly believe in your topic.

Nonverbal delivery includes your appearance, breathing, eye contact, facial expressions, gestures, and movement (see Chapter 10 for a more detailed discussion of nonverbal delivery). In a persuasion speech you want to match your vocal intensity with your nonverbal intensity. Your appearance, breathing, eye contact, facial expressions, gestures, and movement must be well polished to engage the audience. Not only do you want to demonstrate a dynamic delivery, but you will want to demonstrate charisma, a speaker characteristic which appeals to an audience. An audience is more likely to be motivated by a charismatic speaker than a speaker who is dull and timid.

THE TYPES OF PERSUASIVE SPEECH STRUCTURES

When developing a persuasive speech, speakers need to consider questions such as what type of message they want to construct, where they want to put their evidence, and what type of reasoning they want to incorporate into the speech. Persuasive speaking requires more organization, evidence, and reasoning in order to build a convincing case that can influence an audience. We will describe and provide a sample outline for three different types of persuasive speech structures: the problem solution, the motivated sequence, and the position, option, proposal.

The Problem-Solution Structure

The problem-solution organizational structure is when a speaker identifies a problem and then offers a solution to solve the problem. The persuasive message is accomplished in two steps. First, speakers convince the audience through evidence that there is a particular problem that is affecting the audience. Second, speakers try to convince the audience of what they think is the best solution(s) to the problem.

Figure 13-2. Persuasive

PROBLEM-SOLUTION SAMPLE OUTLINE

(This outline is based on hypothetical evidence.)

I. Introduction

    A. **Attention-Getter**: Tell the devastating story of "Jill," who attributes her unemployment, drug problem, loss of children to foster homes, and divorce to her abuse as a child. According to the February 9, 2014 issue of *Time* magazine, "Jill" represents one of the two million victims a year who are or were abused as children.

    B. **Common Ground**: We might not be the victims of child abuse, and we might not know anyone who was abused as a child, but child abuse is not only a family problem, it is a national problem. It could happen to your children. It could happen to your nieces and nephews. It could have happened to you.

    C. **Preview**: In order to understand the prevalence of child abuse, I will, first, discuss the problems associated with child abuse, and second, I will offer some solutions to the problem.

    Signpost—When we analyze the problem of child abuse, three significant types of problems are evident: physical, emotional, and judicial.

II. Body

    A. **Problems**

        1. The first problem associated with child abuse is physical harm.

            a. Most commonly associated form of child abuse

            b. 1/8 cases results in serious injury or death

            c. Explain "John's" story

        2. The second problem associated with child abuse is psychological harm.

            a. Words can hurt as much as a physical blow

            b. 50% of child abusers were abused as a child

            c. Refer to "Jill's" story

        3. The third problem associated with child abuse is judicial.

            a. Lack of enforcement of Child Protection Laws

            b. Some cases are hard to legally prove

            c. Parents' rights

Transition—Now that I have provided you with three problems associated with child abuse, I will offer some solutions that we as a society and individuals can take.

Signpost—Two societal solutions to the problem include more federal enforcement and to maintain current child abuse programs.

B. **Solutions**

1. Societal #1: The first societal solution is to provide more federal enforcement.

   a. Need to hire more child welfare workers to uphold children's rights

   b. Give child welfare workers more authority in cases

2. Societal #2: The second societal solution is to maintain current child abuse programs.

   a. Congress threatening to cut programs

   b. Mobilize communities

   c. Write members of congress

Signpost—In addition to the societal solutions, I propose three steps we as individuals can take to help solve the problem, these include: getting involved in Child Abuse Prevention Programs, recognizing the signs of child abuse, and informing the proper authorities if you suspect child abuse.

3. Individual #1: The first individual solution we can take is to get involved in Child Abuse Prevention Programs.

   a. Most communities have some type of program

   b. Contact local group in your community

   c. National Hotline number

4. Individual #2: The second individual solution we can take is to recognize the signs of child abuse.

   a. Give the warning signs

   b. Related missed signs in "Jill" example

5. Individual #3: The third individual solution we can take is to alert the proper authorities.

   a. Contact local group or police

   b. National Hotline number

13

III. Conclusion

    A. **Review**: Now that you have heard the facts concerning the problems and solutions associated with child abuse, can we as a society and as individuals afford not to act against this problem?

    B. **Reinforce Message**: If we are going to stop the wave of abuse against children, child abuse will have to be everyone's problem.

    C. **Clincher**: Refer back to "Jill" story and tell how anyone in the audience, male or female, could have been "Jill." Would you like to be "Jill" knowing that someone could have helped you as a child, instead of living a life of pain? It might take a whole community to raise a child, but it only takes one person to stop child abuse.

An advantage of this type of organization is that it allows speakers to develop the speech into two parts. Speakers will have to determine how much time they should spend on each part. If the problem is well known, the speaker might want to spend more time on the solution. If the problem is not well known, the speaker might want to spend equal time on the problem and the solution.

Monroe's Motivated Sequence

The motivated sequence, developed by Alan Monroe, is a five-step sequential method for motivating an audience to a specific action.[2] The five steps of the motivated sequence represent a logical pattern of arranging information. This pattern has been an effective way to organize information because it follows a predictable pattern of thinking. The motivated sequence involves five steps: attention, need, satisfaction, visualization, and action.

The **attention step** is where the speaker gains the audience's attention and establishes the importance/relevance of the topic to the audience. Since the purpose of the motivated sequence is to motivate the audience to action, the speaker not only needs to start with a creative introduction, but also, the speaker's vocal and nonverbal delivery needs to match the level of intensity the speaker establishes in the introduction. There are plenty of ways to gain your audience's attention (see Chapter 9 for a discussion on attention-getters) such as a story, a quotation, or a striking statistic.

The **need step** is where the speaker articulates how the audience is affected by a problem so the audience feels a need for change. To convince the audience there is a need for change, the speaker must show and describe a problem facing the audience. In addition, speakers must show the extent or degree of the problem by incorporating evidence and support material, while documenting their evidence and citing their sources. For the need step to be successful, the speaker must link the speech to the interests, attitudes, and beliefs of the audience. When this link is successfully done, the audience should be motivated to hear what the solution will be.

The **satisfaction step** is where the speaker shows the audience how they can resolve the problem. In this step, speakers convince the audience that their proposed solution will bring the most satisfaction. Solutions should contain ample detail and show reasonable thought. Moreover, speakers should offer solutions that are logical and that are documented from their research. The speaker must also decide whether the speech will be "problem oriented" or "solution oriented" in terms of form and content, or if equal time will be devoted to discussing the problem and solutions.

The **visualization step** is where the speaker gives the audience an image of how the solution solves the problem. In this step the speaker is looking "into the future" with the audience. Here the speaker must try to intensify the audience's feelings or beliefs. The speaker might also warn or advise the audience about the problem. Visualization can be accomplished by the positive method, negative method, or by contrast.

The positive method is when the speaker explains the benefits the audience will receive by taking action such as: "The death penalty in New York State will help reduce violent crime and solve the problem of overcrowding in our prisons." The negative method is when the speaker explains the consequences the audience will experience if they do not take action such as: "If parents are not better informed about the serious nature of eating disorders such as anorexia nervosa and bulimia, the proportion of those afflicted by these disorders will rise significantly."

Meanwhile, the method of contrast is when speakers combine both the positive and negative method to show the benefits and the consequences of their plan such as: "Without DWI laws, the number of deaths and injuries will rise. If we do enforce tougher laws and raise the drinking age nationally, we will assure a decrease in alcohol-related accidents throughout the country."

The **action step** is where the speaker makes a persuasive appeal for the audience to act on the request. The action step should specify how the need will be satisfied. The speaker wants the audience to make a commitment and asks the audience to act on the request. Be specific in what you want the audience to do. This final appeal is often referred to as the **call to action** because the speaker personally asks audience members to take some desired action in relation to the problem and solutions generated. The speaker can use an emotional appeal, a logical appeal, and/ or the speaker can tell the audience a future action they should take.

13

MONROE'S MOTIVATED SEQUENCE SAMPLE OUTLINE

(This outline is based on hypothetical evidence.)

I. **Attention:** Tell the story of John who was a Magna Cum Laude senior about to graduate from college. However, John's life was snuffed out prematurely due to a drunk driver who lost control of his car and crossed the sidewalk where John was walking. According to March 3, 2012a *The New York Times*, despite the educational campaigns and DWI laws, there were 300,000 drunk driving fatalities last year.

II. **Need:** Drunk driving is a problem that affects us all.

   A. Increased fatalities

      1. Give facts and statistics

      2. Brian's story

   B. Increased driving dangers

      1. Robert Chapman, State Trooper's testimony

      2. DWI example

   C. Increased car insurance

III. **Satisfaction:** Despite these problems there are some solutions.

   A. Increased fatalities

      1. Have a designated driver

      2. Call a cab

      3. Call a friend

   B. Social solutions

      1. Mandatory college DWI course

      2. Support and join organizations such as SADD and MADD

      3. Tougher DWI laws

IV. **Visualization:** Imagine that everyone who drank was responsible for their actions and didn't drive while under the influence of alcohol. There would be less drinking-related accidents which would save thousands of lives each year, and this would help lower the costs of insurance for all drivers.

Transition—Now that I have discussed the problem of DWI in this country, explained the solutions to help alleviate the problem, and stated the positive effects of taking individual responsibility, there is something I would like to ask you.

V. **Action**: Stopping DWI requires a simple but important step that you as audience members can take. All it requires is for you to act responsibly when you go out and drink. The next time you go out, and you have had too much to drink, think about the information I have told you today. Do you want to take a chance? I am asking you, each and every one of you, be responsible. Stop drinking and driving!

The Position-Option-Proposal Structure

The position-option-proposal organizational structure is similar to the motivated sequence except the speaker provides the audience with several options. Then, the speaker persuades the audience to adopt one particular option. The first step is to establish the current position or current state of affairs. When speakers describe the current condition or current state, they expose the problems of the current condition and/or provide the causes of the current condition. The second step is to give the audience options. The speaker articulates several options that the audience could take to solve the current problem. The final step is to persuade the audience to adopt one proposal by explaining how the proposal has more strengths and less weaknesses than the other options, so the audience can see why they should support the speaker's proposal.

POSITION-OPTION-PROPOSAL SAMPLE OUTLINE

(This outline is based on hypothetical evidence.)

I. Introduction

   A. **Attention-Getter**: Tell the story of how the Clarrow Company went bankrupt because the organization could not increase productivity in its old, cramped building. We face the same problem.

   B. **Common Ground**: Since we all work in this company, we should all have an interest in how we are going to resolve this problem to ensure our company's future.

   C. **Preview**: I will discuss our company's dilemma by first, describing our current position; second, I will state our options; and third, I will discuss our proposal.

II. Body
  A. **Position**: We have outgrown our current facility.
    1. Our facility and equipment need to be modernized
    2. Our current facility hampers our productivity
    3. Our current facility does not have enough storage space
    4. Our current facility does not have enough parking space
  B. **Options**: We have three options that could be implemented within two years.
    1. Build an addition onto the current facility
      a. Positives
        1) Would be done within a year
        2) The cost to build an addition would be only $1 million
      b. Negatives
        1) The rest of the facility would still need to be modernized
        2) Would still need parking space
        3) Parking space would be reduced
    2. Buy and renovate the old McGregor Building
      a. Positives
        1) Would have enough storage space
        2) Would have enough parking space
      b. Negatives
        1) The cost to renovate would be over $500 million
        2) The project would probably take more than two years
    3. Build a new building in Westfield
      a. Positives
        1) The cost would be under $80 million
        2) Would have a modernized facility
        3) Would have enough storage space
        4) Would have enough parking space
      b. Negatives
        1) It is located 20 miles east of our current building
  C. **Proposal**: Proposal: Build the new building in Westfield.
    1. We will be able to increase productivity
    2. We will be able to build exercise and recreational facilities
    3. Restate positives

III. Conclusion

    A. **Review**: Now that I have presented you with our position, our options, and our proposal, you know that building a new facility in Westfield is our best opportunity to ensure the future of this company.

    B. **Reinforce Message**: Unlike the Clarrow Company we have a chance to ensure our future by voting for a new facility in Westfield.

    C. **Clincher**: Decisions are not easy, especially those that involve your employment. However, if you do not vote for the Westfield facility, we might not have any employment to worry about.

DEBATE PROPOSITIONS

Sometimes persuasive speaking occurs not in single-speaker performances but in debates that have two opposing sides arguing a position using evidence, reasoning, and emotion to persuade an audience. The audience evaluates the evidence to decide which side was more persuasive. Debates are great opportunities for persuasive speaking because there is an element of friendly competition between the two opposing sides that motivates the debaters to develop sound persuasive speeches.

The two opposing teams in a debate are called the affirmative and the negative. The **affirmative team** is for change in the status quo. The status quo is the nature of how reality currently exists. In other words, the status quo is the current state of affairs. The affirmative side identifies some societal problem that needs to be changed. The affirmative side

Figure 13-3. Debate

uses evidence, reasoning, and emotion to make a persuasive speech for change. Meanwhile, the **negative team** is against change in the status quo. They argue that change is not needed because there are options already available in the status quo to fix the problem. The negative side also uses evidence, reasoning, and emotion to make a persuasive speech against change. In a debate, the affirmative side has the **burden of proof**, which means they have the obligation to prove beyond a doubt that change is needed in the status quo.

What forms the basis of the debate is the proposition. The **proposition** is a resolution that is phrased in the form of a statement of opinion rather than as a question. The proposition is always written in favor of the affirmative side. For example:

Resolved: Women should be allowed in combat.

The proposition defines the nature of the debate, and it is the focus to which all evidence, reasoning, and emotion should be directed. The affirmative side wants to prove the resolution (that change should occur), while the negative side wants to disprove the resolution (that change should not occur). Debate propositions can be of three varieties: fact, value, and policy.

Proposition of Fact

Propositions of fact involve debates that argue over the truth or falsity of a claim. The purpose of the debate is to try and persuade the audience whether the perceived fact is correct. Some examples of proposition of facts include:

Resolved: "Electronic money" will replace paper money by the year 2020.

Resolved: Making tougher laws against violent offenders will decrease violent crime.

As these examples point out, proposition of fact debates deal with issues that are not certain facts. It is up to the debates to try and prove or disprove the claim.

Proposition of Value

Propositions of value are debates that evaluate or judge the worth, righteousness, or morality of an issue. In essence, a value debate is a judgement of an issue. For example:

Resolved: Protecting American jobs is more important than protecting endangered species.

Resolved: Maintaining a strong military is more important than increasing spending on social programs.

Value debates do not call for specific action from the audience. Instead, the debaters are trying to persuade the audience to accept or reject a moral standard.

Proposition of Policy

Propositions of policy are debates that argue whether a specific action should or should not be taken. The debate centers on a societal program that needs to be addressed. Policy debates are the most common debates because they provide the debaters with a concrete policy that is more tangible for the speakers to debate. For example:

> Resolved: A nationwide curfew should be implemented to reduce juvenile crime.

> Resolved: Companies that pollute the environment should be financially responsible for cleaning up their damage to the environment.

Propositions of policy can involve facts or values, but they always go beyond fact and value debates by specifically arguing what should or should not be done. Both sides attempt to persuade the audience that action either should (the affirmative team) or should not (the negative team) be taken.

LOGICAL FALLACIES

Whenever you are dealing with evidence, reasoning, arguments, and support material you must make sure your evidence is sound so you are not making any logical fallacies. A **logical fallacy** is simply an error in reasoning. Any time speakers make a logical fallacy, their argument will lead to faulty assumptions and faulty conclusions. We will briefly identify some common logical fallacies that you want to avoid.

Hasty Generalization

We briefly mentioned this logical fallacy in the inductive reasoning section. This error in reasoning is when a speaker makes a wrong conclusion based on a wrong interpretation of facts or from insufficient evidence. In the example we provided, the person made an inaccurate conclusion about Mr. Mehta from the four facts known about Mr. Mehta.

False Cause

This is when a speaker makes an error in causal reasoning. Specifically, it is when a speaker makes an assumption between cause and effect or effect to cause that is not true. The speaker is assuming the causal relationship is true because one event follows another, but in reality, the relationship is not causal. For example, a speaker can say the setting sun results in sleep. Most people do go to sleep at night, but the setting sun does not cause sleep. This fallacy is also known as the *post hoc* fallacy (short for *post hoc ergo propter hoc,* which translated from Latin means "after this, therefore because of this").

Invalid Analogy

This is when the speaker makes an analogy that is not reasonable, too extreme, or not parallel. The speaker assumes just because two cases can be compared, the same conclusions can be made for both. However, a closer look at the analogy reveals different circumstances surrounding the two cases. When this occurs the speaker's comparison is invalid, which also makes the speaker's argument invalid.

Ad Hominem

This error in reasoning is when a speaker attacks the person instead of addressing the issue. Modern politics are an example of how candidates often attack the other candidate's character rather than debating the issues. Ad hominems are "cheap shots" at a person's character that add no insight into a debate of the issues. They are nothing more than "name-calling" and personal attacks. Instead of debating the topic, this logical fallacy detracts attention away from the real issues.

Either-Or

This is when the speaker forces the listeners to choose between two alternatives when more than two alternatives exist. This strategy is a clever way to "pin down" the opponent into two narrow choices that do not help the opponent's cause. However, it is an error in reasoning because rarely are there ever just two choices for an issue. Sometimes either-or arguments are a way for a speaker to use fear appeals in an unethical way.

Bandwagon

We are all familiar with the phrase, "jumping on the bandwagon." This is when the speaker uses the general claim that what is popular is right. We know from experience that what everyone else thinks, believes, does, supports, or wants does not make it right. Always be wary of these general claims. When faced with a bandwagon argument consider who is the "everyone" the person is referring to? Who is benefiting from the general claim? Why do I have to follow the crowd?

Slippery Slope

This is the argument that if a person takes one step, it will lead to another and eventually it will lead to severe negative consequences. Be careful not to make slippery slope arguments unless you can prove with evidence that some type of negative spiral is possible. If you cannot establish a negative spiral based on direct cause, you will appear to be an overreactive speaker.

Loaded Question

This is when a question places the respondent in a no-win situation. For example, if one speaker said to another, "Are you still beating your wife?" If the speaker responded by saying yes, he is obviously admitting guilt. However, responding *no* still reveals that he is guilty. Loaded questions have the effect of undermining the other speaker's credibility regardless of whether the claim is true or not.

ETHICS AND PERSUASIVE SPEAKING

We felt it appropriate to mention the ethical standards of a persuasive speaker. Never underestimate the power of the spoken word in motivating people to action. Words can be just as comforting as a hug, as inspirational as a pat on the back, and also just as hurtful as a physical blow. To ensure a high ethical standard, make sure you do not mislead your audience, that you do not make logical fallacies, and that you do not try to twist facts and evidence just to influence your audience to accept your persuasive message. When you can present an ethical message, you will not only be respected by your audience and maintain credibility, but you will be able to evaluate what strategies worked and what strategies did not work. It might be easier to twist your evidence or make ad hominem attacks, but true persuasive speakers use evidence, reasoning, and emotional appeals ethically to motivate an audience to action. Ethical persuasive speaking demonstrates your intellectual development and understanding in the use of "all the available means" of persuasion.

THE PRINCIPLES OF PERSUASIVE SPEAKING

As we close this chapter, we will list the principles of persuasive speaking that you should remember as you prepare your persuasive speech.

Principle 1: You are more likely to persuade an audience when your proposition/thesis/argument is clear, reasonable, and supportable.

Principle 2: You are more likely to persuade an audience when you give them logical reasons and good evidence.

Principle 3: You are more likely to persuade an audience when you organize your material according to expected audience reaction.

Principle 4: You are more likely to persuade an audience when your language motivates them.

Principle 5: You are more likely to persuade an audience when they like, trust, and have confidence in you.

Principle 6: You are more likely to persuade an audience if your delivery is convincing.

After reading this chapter, you should understand the complexity and the necessary ingredients for persuasive speaking. To increase your understanding of persuasive speaking, we began this chapter by addressing the nature of persuasive speaking, which included defining persuasive speaking, the motivations of the audience, and the three purposes of persuasive speaking. This was followed by an explanation of the three artistic proofs a persuasive speaker should demonstrate, which are ethos, logos, and pathos. Then, we illustrated how a speaker can organize a persuasive speech by highlighting the three different types of persuasive speech structures.

After discussing persuasive speech structures, we talked about the debate propositions of fact, value, and policy and then discussed the nature of debate. Next, we explained the importance of identifying and eliminating logical fallacies from the process of reasoning. We have explained your responsibility as a speaker to present your persuasive speech in an ethical manner. Finally, we listed the persuasive principles that you should keep in mind as you prepare your persuasive speech. When you follow these suggestions we explain in this chapter, you will be able to construct an effective and ethical persuasive speech.

VOCABULARY

Action step — the fifth step in Monroe's motivated sequence where the speaker makes a persuasive appeal for the audience to act on the request.

Ad hominem — a logical fallacy in which the speaker attacks the person instead of addressing the issue.

Affirmative team — one opposing side in a debate that advocates change in the status quo.

Analogy reasoning — a figurative comparison between two or more cases to infer that what applies in one case can also apply to the other.

Attention step — the first step in Monroe's motivated sequence where the speaker tries to gain the audience's attention and establish the importance/relevance of the topic to the audience.

Attitudes — our likes and dislikes.

Bandwagon — a logical fallacy in which the speaker uses the general claim that what is popular is right.

Behavioral response — when the audience acts or responds to a persuasive message.

Beliefs — what we accept to be true.

Burden of proof — affirmative side's obligation to prove beyond a doubt that change is needed in the status quo.

Call to action — a speaker's specific appeal to the audience to respond to the speaker's persuasive goal.

Causal reasoning — when the speaker attempts to establish a direct link between a cause and an effect.

Cause and effect reasoning — when the speaker makes an argument based on past experience that a cause has led to a certain effect.

Character — the audience's perception of the speaker's integrity, honesty, and trustworthiness.

Competence — the audience's perception of the speaker's intelligence, expertise, and knowledge of a topic.

Composure — the audience's perception of the speaker's poise.

Conclusion — the third step in deductive reasoning. It is the idea that is produced from accepting the major and minor premise.

Conviction — a deep feeling of certainty that your cause is righteous and truthful.

Deductive reasoning — when a speaker starts with a socially accepted general rule, principle, or belief and then moves to a more specific conclusion.

Effect to cause reasoning — when the speaker makes an argument that the same effect was produced by a certain cause in the past.

Enthymeme — a type of deductive reasoning pattern that is a truncated syllogism, because it only has a major premise and minor premise, but no explicit conclusion.

Either-or — a logical fallacy in which the speaker forces the listeners to choose between two alternatives when more than two alternatives exist.

Ethos — the audience's perception of the speaker's credibility which includes the speaker's integrity, honesty, knowledge, and competence.

False cause — a logical fallacy in which the speaker makes an assumption between cause and effect or effect to cause that is not true.

Feelings — our emotions.

Hasty generalization — a logical fallacy in which the speaker makes a wrong conclusion based on a wrong interpretation of the facts or from insufficient evidence.

Inductive reasoning — using reasoning to move from specific facts to a specific conclusion.

Invalid analogy — a logical fallacy in which the speaker makes an analogy that is not similar or parallel.

Loaded question — a logical fallacy in which the speaker asks a question that places the respondent into a no-win situation.

Logical fallacy — an error in reasoning.

Logos — a systematic pattern of thought based on reasoning and evidence.

Major premise — the first step of deductive reasoning. It is the generally accepted principle.

Metaphors — an implied comparison that does not use the word "like" or "as" (see Chapter 11).

Minor premise — the second step of deductive reasoning. It is the specific application of the accepted principle.

Monroe's motivated sequence — a persuasive organizational pattern that involves five steps: attention, need, satisfaction, visualization, and action.

Motivation — an internal drive that explains why people behave and act (or react) in a certain way when engaged in human communication (see Chapter 4).

Need — physical and psychological desires and wants (see Chapter 4).

Need step — the second step of Monroe's motivated sequence where the speaker articulates how the audience is affected by a problem so the audience feels a need for change.

Negative team — one opposing side in a debate that is against change in the status quo.

Pathos — emotional appeals.

Position-option-proposal — a persuasive organizational pattern that involves three steps: acknowledge the current situation (position), express options that can improve the situation (options), and offer one option as the best (proposal).

Problem-solution — organizational pattern that organizes information by first identifying a problem and second by offering a solution to the problem.

Proposition — a resolution that is phrased in the form of a statement of opinion rather than as a question.

Proposition of fact — a statement that defines a debate as being an evaluation over the truth or falsity of a claim.

Proposition of policy — a statement that defines a debate as whether or not a specific action should or should not be taken.

Proposition of value — a statement that defines a debate as an evaluation or judgment of the worth, righteousness, or morality of an issue.

Reasoning — making conclusions based on evidence.

Satisfaction step — the third step in Monroe's motivated sequence where the speaker shows the audience how they can resolve the problem.

Similes — a direct comparison between two concepts, objects, or ideas that uses the words "as" or "like" (see Chapter 11).

Slippery slope — a logical fallacy in which the speaker argues that if a person takes one step, it will lead to another, and eventually it will lead to severe negative consequences.

Sociability — the audience's perception of the speaker's friendliness, warmth, and amiability.

Speech to actuate — one of three purposes of persuasive speaking where a speaker attempts to influence the audience's beliefs and attitudes by requesting a behavioral response from the audience.

Speech to convince — one of three purposes of persuasive speaking where the speaker attempts to shape, reinforce, or change the audience's beliefs and attitudes.

Speech to inspire — one of three purposes of persuasive speaking where the speaker attempts to encourage and uplift the audience.

Values — deeply ingrained morals that are shaped by culture.

Visualization step — the fourth step in Monroe's motivated sequence where the speaker gives the audience an image of how the solution solves the problem.

REFERENCES

[1] Larson, Charles, *Persuasion: Reception and Responsibility*, 12th edition (Belmont, CA: Wadsworth, 2010), 11.

[2] Douglas Ehninger, Bruce E. Gronbeck, and Alan H. Monroe, *Principles of Speech Communication*, 9th brief edition (Glenview, Illinois: Scott, Foresman, and Co., 1984), 249.

PRESENTATIONAL AIDS 14

reative minds have always been known to survive any kind of bad training."
Anna Freud

iss principle: Keep it simple, stupid."
Anonymous

ur life is frittered away by detail… Simplify, simplify."
Henry David Thoreau

This Chapter Examines:

+ the purpose, rules, and functions of presentational aids

+ the types and kinds of presentational aids

+ the "dos" and "don'ts" of using presentational aids

As Mariana was preparing for her informative speech on identity theft she began to contemplate what type of presentational aid she should use for her speech. Her first thought was to provide a handout that lists ways for the audience to lower their risks of having their identity stolen. However, Mariana decided she would rather state this information herself instead of including it on a handout. She also considered showing information from a Web site that tracks identity theft. However, she was unsure if she would have Internet access in her presentation. She also thought of constructing a PowerPoint presentation but she did not know where to begin with constructing her slides. Although she had many options, Mariana was unsure what type of presentational aid to use for her presentation.

Far too many speakers face the same dilemma as Mariana—trying to decide what type of presentational aid they should use in their presentation. The wide range of presentational aids that speakers can use for a presentation can make the choice of one a little overwhelming. However, speakers can make their choice of a presentational aid more clear when they can identify specific concepts or ideas that would be enhanced by a presentational aid. In this chapter, we will discuss the purpose of presentational aids, the types of presentational aids, and some guidelines for using presentational aids.

Figure 14-1. Presentational Aid

THE PURPOSE, RULES, AND FUNCTIONS OF PRESENTATIONAL AIDS

It might be useful to understand public speaking as a series of decisions made by the speaker. Topic selection, how to narrow or focus the speech, selecting examples appropriate for your audience, and even the decision to use presentational aids, are all considerations for any speaker. A **presentational aid** is any physical device or material that speakers use in a speech to enhance, clarify, and/or reinforce the verbal message. This chapter will examine the use of presentational aids in speeches and presentations.

Many people feel a compulsion to use presentational aids in their speeches. These speakers might reason that if they don't have presentational aids their speeches will not be as effective or interesting. This might or might not be true. There are some speeches or presentations where presentational aids are not appropriate, or even worse, they can actually distract the audience. Therefore, we stress that presentational aids must be chosen carefully by the speaker and should not be "forced" on the audience just for the sake of having them as part of your individual or group presentation. Instead, determine if a presentational aid will enhance or clarify your message before you commit yourself to incorporating one into your presentation.

There is really a very simple "rule of thumb" in using presentational aids in your speech. If you can't imagine giving the speech *without* the presentational aid, or if you are convinced the speech will not be as effective without them, then by all means, incorporate them into the planning of the speech. Remember that the purpose of presentational aids is to enhance, clarify, and/or reinforce your information for the audience. This means the presentational aid should complement your information and make your ideas more concrete for the audience to understand. If you have complex or difficult ideas or concepts to discuss then it would be helpful to use a presentational aid. However, if the presentational aids under consideration really have no purpose or don't enhance your presentation, you might want to consider not including them as part of your individual or group presentation.

Once you have decided to incorporate presentational aids into your presentation, you should follow the rules of appropriateness, simplicity, size, and neatness. The rule of **appropriateness** refers to making sure the presentational aid is relevant for the presentation. The presentational aid should be relevant and directly relate to your topic. The rule of **simplicity** means the presentational aid should make an idea more understandable. The presentational aid should clarify and not confuse the audience. The rule of **size** refers to the dimensions of the presentational aid.

The presentational aid should be large enough for everyone to see while not over-powering the message. Meanwhile, the rule of **neatness** relates to the aesthetics of the presentational aid. The presentational aid should be use sharp and contrasting colors, easy to read text, charts, or graphs, and vivid photos or images

Presentational aids serve a number of useful functions. First, presentational aids can make the speech more vibrant, memorable, and easier to comprehend for the audience. Second, they can serve to make speeches more interesting and enter-taining. Third, presentational aids can function to enhance the speaker's credibil-ity by serving as a secondary form of evidence and support material. Fourth, they can also enhance a speaker's verbal delivery by taking pressure off the speaker and reducing speech anxiety, as we indicated earlier in Chapter 2.

THE TYPES AND KINDS OF PRESENTATIONAL AIDS

The use of presentational aids as support material should be a major consider-ation for all public speakers. Keep in mind, however, the presentational aids you use in your speeches or group projects should never be a substitute for genuine evidence or research. They should also not dominate the speech or become the primary focus of the presentation. There are endless possibilities for the speaker interested in using presentational aids. The examples we list here are not limited to the following:

Presentation	PowerPoint, Prezi, Keynote
The Internet	Web sites
Media	Digital video Audio clips
Two-Dimensional	Handouts Charts/diagrams Graphs Pictures and photographs
Three-Dimensional	Demonstration Actual object Models

Presentation Software

We begin our discussion of presentational aids by discussing presentation software such as PowerPoint, Prezi, and Keynote. Presentation software programs enable speakers to create professional-looking slides, handouts, and outlines for the audience. Depending on the needs of the audience and the ability of the speaker, presentation software programs can also incorporate audio and video clips. A great advantage of using a presentation software program like PowerPoint is the information on the slides is easy to see by large audiences because the graphics and text on the slides are projected onto a screen. Given this advantage, the use of PowerPoint has transformed the use of presentational aids in the classroom, workplace, and professional conferences of all disciplines.

Creating slides for a PowerPoint presentation is very simple as the software includes an easy-to-follow tutorial that helps speakers select a background, text, and content layout. Speakers also can insert pictures, video, sound, and images onto their slides. Since there are so many options (from backgrounds to animation) that are available through PowerPoint, sometimes speakers can go overboard by including too many features, causing the slide show itself to overshadow the actual content of the speech. Therefore, speakers need to be aware that PowerPoint, like any other presentational aid, should follow the four rules for presentational aids: appropriateness, simplicity, size, and neatness. When a PowerPoint presentation violates these rules, the result is poorly constructed slides that support the argument that PowerPoint presentations place style over substance.[1] In fact, some argue that PowerPoint is evil and should not be used for presentations.[2]

What are some of the problems associated with PowerPoint presentations? One of the most common is providing too many unclear content slides per presentation. When speakers are clicking through slide after slide of content, the attention of the audience is focused on keeping up with the text and images on the slide and not on the speaker's message. Likewise, speakers should avoid including too much text on a single slide. Again, the audience will focus more on the text than on what is being said by the speaker.

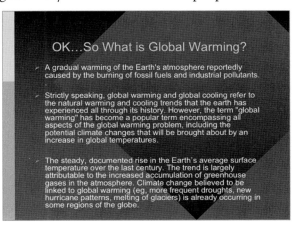

Figure 14-2. Poorly Constructed Slide

The idea with PowerPoint is to highlight ideas and concepts—not to provide paragraphs of text. Other problems include speakers reading word for word from the PowerPoint slide or talking to the slides instead of the audience, and not testing Internet links, media clips, or other aspects associated with the PowerPoint presentation *before* the actual speech. Therefore, we believe that simplicity (especially for beginning speakers) is the key when using PowerPoint. For example, a common practice when using PowerPoint is to use bulleted lists that highlight ideas or concepts as opposed to using complete sentences.

Figure 14-3. Well-Constructed Slide

Although we point out many problems associated with using PowerPoint, when used correctly PowerPoint can greatly enhance a presentation. The effectiveness of a PowerPoint presentation begins with the construction of the slides. The PowerPoint slides should be simple and uniform. In other words, if the speaker has six slides for a presentation, all the backgrounds, headers, fonts, and styles should be generally consistent for each template.

For example, if a speaker is using a bulleted list for a slide, then there should be a bulleted list throughout the presentation; if the speaker is using roman numerals, then roman numerals should be used throughout. Furthermore, we suggest that speakers include a title page as the first and last slide of the presentation. The title page signals to the audience the introduction and conclusion of the speech.

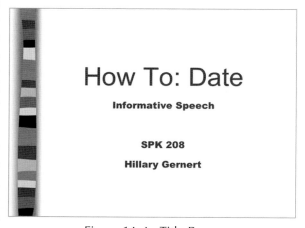

Figure 14-4. Title Pages

Sometimes the introductory title page is followed by a preview of the main points of the speech and the same slide of the main points is repeated as a review before ending with the concluding title page.

An additional consideration when constructing PowerPoint slides is the type of font that is used. **Sans serif fonts** such as Arial, Helvetica, and Avant Garde are commonly used because it is easier and quicker for audiences to read these font types as opposed to **serif fonts** such as Times New Roman, Courier, and Palatino (for example, street signs all use san serif fonts). These two types of fonts can be identified by whether there are (or are not) any small decorative lines at the end of each letter. Serif fonts have the small decorative lines and sans serif fonts do not (see Figure 14-5).

E E

Serif Font   Sans Serif Font
(Times New Roman)   (Arial)

Figure 14-5. Font Types

Furthermore, the type of font used should be consistent for each slide. A common rule is to use a 44-point font for titles, a 32-point font type for subtitles, and a 28-point font size for text. However, if there are no subtitles in the PowerPoint presentation, a 32-point font can be used for text (see Figure 14-6 for additional tips on how to construct PowerPoint slides). These guidelines will help you to create effective PowerPoint slides. When PowerPoint slides are constructed properly, their use as a presentational aid can greatly enhance presentations, especially for visual learners and individuals for whom English is a second language.[3]

POWERPOINT: BASIC SLIDE CONSTRUCTION TIPS

- Keep the design simple—check out the PowerPoint templates.

- Give a strong title to the first slide.

- No more than six words per line and no more than six lines (including the title).

- Use adequate margins and be consistent in listing information (bullets or numbers, etc.).

- Make sure there is a dynamic contrast between your background and your text. AVOID ALL CAPS.

- No more than three type sizes (minimum 28-point font) and no more than three font styles (that are sans serif fonts such as Arial, Helvetica, Avant Garde, etc.).

- Check spelling and numbering. Avoid acronyms or abbreviations that may confuse the audience.

Figure 14-6.

All of these suggestions will help speakers create well-constructed PowerPoint presentations. The underlining principle is consistency. When each PowerPoint slide follows the same format, it helps make the slide show more coherent.

The construction of the PowerPoint slides is not the only aspect speakers should consider when using PowerPoint as a presentational aid. Speakers also need to be very mindful of the additional preparation that is necessary *before* the actual presentation in order to make an effective PowerPoint presentation. First, speakers need to practice setting up their equipment in advance in order to eliminate any problems. This is especially true if speakers have saved their PowerPoint slides on a "thumb drive" or disk and they plan on using a different computer or laptop than their own for the actual presentation. Also, speakers will have to find out what capabilities they have in the presentation room. Is a laptop or computer available? Does the computer in the presentation room have a USB port or disk drive? Is there a wireless connection to the Internet in the presentation? Will the PowerPoint slides be projected through a ceiling projector or a portable projector on a chart? Will the speaker have a remote clicker to advance the PowerPoint slides or will the speaker have to manually advance the slides from the computer or laptop? Speakers will need to know this information in advance and not leave it up to chance or assume that the presentation room will have exactly what they need. Many speakers' best plans are ruined when they assume that the presentation room has exactly what they need when in fact, it does not.

Second, speakers need to practice with their PowerPoint slides well in advance so they can direct their vocal and nonverbal delivery to the audience and not to their slides. Again, all effective presentations require a polished delivery that conveys the information in a conversational tone. An effective delivery cannot be accomplished when the speaker is looking at the slides instead of the audience.

Third, keep the information and images on the slides simple. Speakers do not want to draw the audience's attention away from the presentation with too much text, too many slides, or cluttered images. Remember that the content of the speech is more important than the presentational aid. The PowerPoint presentation only clarifies and reinforces the content of the speech.

Fourth, make sure that the PowerPoint presentation enhances your presentation and is not *the* presentation. Without interesting, relevant, and important information to present (and the proper delivery) a PowerPoint presentation by itself cannot accomplish your goal as a speaker. Any successful presentation needs content and delivery to be successful. PowerPoint is only a means to help you present your content.

The Internet

The Internet enables speakers to show specific types of information for presentations. Sometimes speakers are not interested in creating a complete PowerPoint presentation. Instead, speakers simply want to show information from a specific Web site. For example, a presentation on a political candidate's message might show media clips from the campaign's official Web site. In this case, the Web site contains the various television commercials that were broadcast on television during the campaign. Showing the actual commercials reinforces for the audience the information the speaker was conveying about the campaign.

When using media clips or information from Web sites, follow the same guidelines for using media, which we discuss next. In addition, speakers need to make sure the room has the capability to access the Internet and they need to plan when in the presentation the audience should view the Web site.

Media

The use of media, whether it is from a **DVD** or the Internet, has also contributed greatly to the quality of our speeches and presentations. Like presentation software and the Internet, media clips underscore the "visual" culture that we live in. Using media clips as a presentational aid allows the speaker to gain the audience's attention; it provides a concrete experience for the audience to observe; and it illustrates complex ideas, concepts, procedures, or situations more clearly to the audience. Likewise, audio files can significantly enhance a speech or group presentation. For example, a speech on the history of "blues" music would be more effective if the audience is actually able to hear the music. Similarly, audio files of diverse sounds such as birdcalls, dolphins, whale "communication," or a famous historical speech can all contribute to the effectiveness of the presentation.

Regardless of the type of media used, speakers should keep the following guidelines in mind if they are going to use media as a presentational aid. Make sure that the media clip is appropriate for your presentation and know the length of the segment. Never show a media clip before *you have personally* viewed it yourself. Before your presentation, make sure your presentation room has the capability to show the media clip. Test out the equipment to make sure it works and to become familiar with the controls. Make sure your media clip is cued to the scene you want to show. If you do show a media clip, it is always a good idea to follow the segment with discussion to link the media clip to the presentation.

Two-Dimensional

PowerPoint makes the use of most two-dimensional presentational aids such as poster board obsolete. Any information a speaker could place on a poster board such as maps, diagrams, charts, and photos can be greatly enhanced and more effectively presented through PowerPoint. When displaying a map, diagram, or chart through PowerPoint, the speaker should follow the general guidelines for using a presentational aid (appropriateness, simplicity, size, and neatness). Furthermore, the speaker can decide whether to import the map, diagram, or chart into the PowerPoint slide or to re-create the map, diagram, or chart on the slide.

There are some instances, however, in which speakers might want to display an enlarged map, diagram, chart, or photo on a **poster board** instead of using PowerPoint. We have seen students use poster boards very effectively in ceremonial speeches, especially in after-dinner speeches (see Chapter 15). In an after-dinner speech, the two-dimensional presentational aid becomes part of and adds to the humor of the speech. For example, a student who gave an after-dinner speech on the quality of the food in the various eating locations on campus used a poster board to display the eating locations on campus. The speaker placed cut out faces with various expressions (that attached with Velcro to the poster board) to indicate the degree to which the food was satisfactory or not. The less than perfect poster board and drawings of the faces was intentional and added to the humor of the speech.

Meanwhile, **flipcharts** represent another two-dimensional presentational aid that speakers use for speeches and group presentations. Flipcharts are commonly used by consultants and focus groups, and at conference meetings. Using a flipchart in these contexts enables the facilitator to interact and record group feedback as the group discusses an issue (see Figure 14-7 for additional tips for how to use flipcharts).

FLIPCHART: BASIC TIPS

- Print—Make lettering large and simple. Title and number each page.

- Keep to ten lines or less of information per sheet.

- Step away from flipchart after writing.

- Reveal sheets when discussed. When not using marker, put it down.

- Pre-tear masking tape strips for posting sheets.

- Write on every other page to avoid marker spotting. (Use a piece of tape to tape pages together.)

- Check writing tools/markers before using; make sure they have sufficient ink.

- Use dark-colored markers for main points, use light colors to underline, circle, etc.

- Use red markers only to emphasize.

Figure 14-7.

As a two-dimensional presentational aid, **handouts** continue to be one of the easiest, yet most effective types of presentational aids. While the speaker is delivering the speech, the audience can listen to what is being said, while also simultaneously following the handout. When used this way, handouts can provide a double reinforcement for the audience. For example, a speaker who is giving a speech on the lunar cycles of the moon could provide the audience with a handout that shows the various phases of the moon in relation to its orbit around the Earth. Much like PowerPoint, handouts can include a combination of images, photos, and text.

When using handouts, speakers should follow the four general rules for presentational aids that are discussed at the beginning of this chapter. In addition, it is strongly recommended that the handouts be in color to enhance the appearance of the information. Finally, the handout should be simple and easy to read. If you want the audience to follow your ideas, the handout should be given out prior to your speech. However, if the handout is only supplementary material for your speech, it should be given out at the end of your speech (see Figure 14-8 for additional tips for using handouts).

HANDOUT: BASIC TIPS

+ Determine the best time to distribute a handout (outlines and material essential to discussion distribute at the beginning of the session—summary and supplemental information distribute at the end of the session).

+ Highlight special instructions, issues, etc.

+ Keep to ten words per sentence. Also, don't overdo volume of handouts.

+ Keep them simple, colorful, vivid, varied, and visual.

Figure 14-8.

Three-Dimensional

Over the years, we have listened to hundreds of speeches and continue to be impressed with the novelty and imagination of speakers who incorporate presentational aids into their presentations. One way to present innovative and interesting support materials is through a **demonstration**. A very popular topic for a standard informative classroom speech has been, "How to Perform CPR" (cardiopulmonary resuscitation). Some speakers have "gone the extra mile" by visiting the local Red Cross Center to borrow a lifelike demonstration mannequin named "Annie." The "dummy" is an excellent piece of equipment for demonstrating the proper technique for administering "CPR" to a victim. Rather than simply discussing the technique, the speaker is able to demonstrate and illustrate for the audience.

The demonstration should never stand on its own in any speech, but it can be a useful component for speeches covering a variety of topics. Speeches on "Self-Defense Moves," "How to Play the Guitar," "How to Plan a Home Fire Escape," "How to Read a Nutrition Label," and "How to Splint a Broken Leg or Ankle" represent only a few possibilities. And that's just the tip of the iceberg! It is important to note, however, that the demonstration itself is only part of any informative or persuasive speech. Unless your purpose is to actually deliver a speech about "demonstrating" some process or technique, the demonstration should not become the speech itself.

Other three-dimensional objects include actual objects and models. Actual objects enable the audience to see the real object. When using an actual object such as a boxing glove, a guitar, or a wood carving, make sure the object is large enough for the audience to see. Also, do not pass the object around if possible; it's too distracting. Meanwhile, models are often of exact replicas or scaled replicas of real objects; often larger (an atom) or smaller (space shuttle) than the real object. Often, models are more durable and lightweight than actual objects. Using a model as a presentational aid is an excellent way to show an audience what you are talking about, especially abstract concepts, without having the actual object. However, as with actual objects, make sure the model is large enough for all to see.

THE "DOS" AND "DON'TS" OF USING PRESENTATIONAL AIDS

The final part of this chapter will present several guidelines for using presentational aids in your speeches and group presentations. While these "dos" and "don'ts" to using presentational aids seem quite logical and simple, they do represent the most commonly observed problems and mistakes made by speakers who incorporate presentational aids into their speeches and presentations.

Use Only Those Presentational Aids That Are Necessary to Your Speech Topic

Speakers will often use presentational aids although they contribute very little to the speech. The reasoning here is that anything at all will "spice up" the presentation, even if it doesn't really enhance, clarify, or reinforce the verbal message of the speech. In fact, sometimes the presentational aids speakers use in speeches and presentations actually make the message more confusing or complicated. This is obviously the inverse of how presentational aids should function. Try to overcome your compulsion to "force" presentational aids into your presentations by incorporating them only if they really clarify, enhance, and reinforce the message.

Make Sure That All Equipment and Materials Related to Your Presentational Aids Are in Proper Working Condition before Your Speech

There really is no excuse for showing a media clip that is not cued to the exact starting point you want your audience to see or PowerPoint slides that are constructed poorly (such as providing too much text or text that is difficult to read due to the chosen background). In addition, distributing a crudely photocopied black and white handout with handwritten notes on it, not knowing where to stand when giving your PowerPoint presentation, or any other problem with equipment or setup are not acceptable. This only serves to hurt the image or credibility of the speaker in the eyes of the audience and shows a lack of preparation and concern on behalf of the speaker. Don't assume that your presentational aid will function properly because it has worked for previous presentations. If you decide to incorporate presentational aids in your speeches, it is imperative that all equipment and materials function properly *before* the speech. It is much too late to think about this during the speech or regret that it happened *after* the fact.

Do Not Block or Obstruct Your Presentational Aids

It is important not to obstruct or block your presentations aids with your body or any equipment you might be using during your speech. This will require some additional planning on your behalf before you begin the speech. Put yourself in the shoes of the audience and imagine how difficult it might be if the podium or even the speaker is blocking part of the projected image on a screen. Where should you place your working models, objects, equipment, and other materials you will be using in the speech? If possible, arrive early for your speech using presentational aids to set up the equipment before the presentation is scheduled to begin.

Make Sure That the Timing Is Correct and Appropriate for Your Presentational Aids

Timing is everything when using presentational aids in your speeches and presentations. When should you distribute handouts or other materials you want your audience to have during the speech? When do you show a specific PowerPoint slide or media clip you have planned for the audience? At what point in the speech do you go over the charts or diagrams you have prepared for your listeners? These are all questions worthy of consideration for the speaker and add to the decision-making process.

When is the ideal time for the demonstration you have planned? It's a tough call for many speakers. Do you want to show the materials or present the demonstration early on in the speech to set the tone for your speech? Do you want to provide a context for the materials before the demonstration for the audience? Conversely, do you want to save the presentational aids for the end of the speech so that they have a "recency" effect? In other words, the last idea exposed to the audience will be the first idea they think about or remember. Again, these are all decisions the speaker needs to make.

The use of presentational aids will truly enhance your speeches and presentations, while serving as a secondary form of evidence. Moreover, presentational aids psychologically take the pressure off the speaker. There are a variety of presentational aids available to the speaker, especially with the advances in technology we enjoy today. Following the "do's" and "don'ts" we discussed earlier in this chapter, you will be able to construct more effective and interesting presentational aids for your speech or panel presentation. Presentational aids can enhance any speech or group presentation.

VOCABULARY

Appropriateness — one of four rules to follow when using a presentational aid that states the presentational aid should be relevant and directly relate to your topic.

Demonstration — when the speaker actually shows the audience a process.

Digital versatile disk (DVD) — an optical disk that is similar to a CD-ROM but it has a much greater storage capacity.

Handouts — a presentational aid that is printed on paper.

Neatness — one of four rules to follow when using a presentational aid that states the presentational aid should be clear, colorful, and pleasing to the eye.

PowerPoint — a presentation software program that enables speakers to create professional-looking slides, images, handouts, and outlines for the audience.

Presentational aid — any physical device or material that speakers use in a speech to enhance, clarify, and/or reinforce their message.

Sans serif font — a category of typefaces that do not use serifs (small decorative lines) at the ends of characters. Examples of sans serif fonts include: Arial, Helvetica, Avant Garde, and Century Gothic.

Serif font — a category of typefaces that use small decorative lines (which are called serifs) at the end of characters. Examples of serif fonts include: Times New Roman, Courier, Palatino, and Garamond.

Simplicity — one of four rules to follow when using a presentational aid that states the presentational aid should make an idea more understandable; it should clarify and not confuse the audience.

Size — one of four rules to follow when using a presentational aid that states the presentational aid should be large enough for everyone to see.

14

REFERENCES

[1] Buss, C.W. (2006). Stop death by PowerPoint. *T+D*, *60(3)*, 20–22.

[2] Tuffe, E. (2003). *The cognitive style of PowerPoint*. Cheshire, CT: Graphics Press.

[3] Daniels, L. (1999). Introducing technology into the classroom: PowerPoint as a first step. *Journal of Computing in Higher Education*, *10*, 42–56.

CEREMONIAL SPEAKING 15

"The more you praise and celebrate life, the more there is in life to celebrate."
-Oprah Winfrey

"We are nothing but ceremony; ceremony carries us always, and we leave the substance of things; we hang on the branches and abandon the trunk and body."
-Michael de Montaigne

"Audiences are the same all over the world, and if you entertain them, they'll respond."
-Liza Minnelli

"Talk low, talk slow, and don't say too much."
-John Wayne

"Every ceremony or rite has a value if it is performed without alteration. A ceremony is a book in which a great deal is written. Anyone who understands it can read it."
-George Gurdjieff

This Chapter Examines:

+ the nature of ceremonial speaking

+ the types of ceremonial speeches

+ presenting the ceremonial speech

The big day has finally arrived. Up until now, James has not felt nervous at all and why should he? After all, it is his best friend Craig who is getting married, not him. The planning, the rehearsals, and even the ceremony did not make James feel uneasy. It is not until the reception, where James will give the toast, that he begins to feel nervous. Normally, James does not get nervous in front of an audience. But this time is different. James's speech is part of a larger ceremony. He has prepared some thoughts, but he hopes his ideas convey his genuine feelings for his best friend and the new bride. The wedding party is now situated around the table and James is given the cue to stand to make his toast. Will his remarks be fitting for the situation?

This is just one example of the opportunities we are given to make public presentations during special ceremonies and events. Weddings, graduations, award ceremonies, funerals, and orientations are some of the special events where we might be asked to make a presentation. We refer to these types of speeches as ceremonial speeches. **Ceremonial speeches** are presentations that are given as part of a special occasion or social event. The opening example is an example of a ceremonial speech called a toast, which is often given at weddings.

The opening example also illustrates the unique nature of a ceremonial speech since the speech is given extra importance due to the context of the special occasion or social event. Special occasions such as weddings are joyful events where family and friends, along with all the rituals associated with the event (such as the ceremony, the music, the food, and the dancing) create the contextual importance of the speech. The importance of the context that surrounds a ceremonial speech is illustrated by rhetorical scholar Lloyd Bitzer, who argued that "a speech is given *rhetorical* significance by the situation" and that "the situation controls the rhetorical response."[1] Bitzer's perspective is true for ceremonial speeches for clearly the speech is given more importance due to the context of the special occasion. Furthermore, the context influences the speaker's presentation because the speaker's remarks are guided by tradition and precedent that have been set by previous speakers. Therefore, the speaker must meet the expectations of both the audience and of the event. These two expectations illustrate, one, the uniqueness of ceremonial speaking, and two, they highlight the challenge of ceremonial speaking.

Understanding the context and expectations of ceremonial speeches will help speakers make effective presentations. Therefore, in this chapter, we will discuss how to present a ceremonial speech. Specifically, we will explain the special nature of ceremonial speaking, the types of ceremonial speeches, and guidelines for presenting the ceremonial speech. We believe this information will help speakers apply the principles we have discussed in previous chapters to the ceremonial speech.

THE NATURE OF CEREMONIAL SPEAKING

Ceremonial speeches represent an intersection of tradition, expectations, and public celebration on one hand and the principles of public speaking such as preparation, organization, delivery, and support material on the other. What makes ceremonial speeches challenging are the preconceived ideas the audience has about the content of the speech before the speech is even given. Audiences have preconceived ideas, because they have attended many ceremonies and have heard many speeches, which can result in audience members believing they have heard it all before. Therefore, speakers who make ceremonial speeches have to be creative in the topics they address and the information they convey. Speakers also have to demonstrate even better organization and delivery when making a ceremonial speech. Developing an effective ceremonial speech, however, begins with identifying the purpose, context, and audience for the ceremonial speech along with perfecting the presentation of the speech. Each of these ideas will be further explained.

Purpose

Although there are many different types of ceremonial speeches, we have categorized them into one of three general purposes: to motivate, to give public recognition, and to entertain and inform. Keep in mind that three general purposes of ceremonial speaking while identified separately are not mutually exclusive. Any ceremonial speech might have elements that relate to each general purpose. The key is, however, the overall general purpose the speaker wants to accomplish. As we will discuss further in the next section, **motivational speeches** operate primarily to uplift, energize, and persuade individuals to some type of action or change in attitude, belief, or behavior. **Public recognition speeches** are characterized by acknowledging to the public an individual's or group's contribution to society. Finally, **entertaining and informative speeches** use all the means of rhetoric (such as the voice, gestures, humor, etc.) to provide insight, to increase our knowledge, and to challenge our way of thinking.

Context

The purpose of any ceremonial speech is directly related to the traditions associated with the special occasion or event the speech is a part of. When a speech is given over and over again on a periodic basis, certain guidelines emerge for the speech which become a tradition. When the guidelines become a tradition, it means the culture in which the practice emerged becomes the "common sense" way for individuals to enact the practice. As Bitzer explained, it is the context that sets up the guidelines and the audience's expectations for what a speech should cover in a ceremonial speech. For example, audiences have come to expect that graduation speeches usually cover certain themes such as overcoming challenges and having the motivation to succeed. The specific facts, examples, and stories will vary from speaker to speaker, but audiences anticipate these general themes based upon tradition.

Given the importance of the context, speakers should be aware of the traditions and rituals that accompany any ceremonial speech. Violating them not only impacts the effectiveness of the speech, but it can ruin the credibility of the speaker. For example, a ceremony was scheduled a few years ago at the White House for poets to celebrate the achievements of various American writers. When the poets wanted to not only commemorate the accomplishments of American writers, but to also speak out against specific political policies, the event was cancelled because it did not fit the context of a celebratory ceremony for American writers.[2]

Audience

Another challenge for ceremonial speakers is the audience. As we have already mentioned, audiences that gather for ceremonial speeches are difficult to address because they have expectations of what the speaker should say and whether the speech is exemplary and worthy of the event (which is often based upon comparisons to past speakers). In addition, we live in a multicultural society where it is critical for speakers to address the various needs of diverse audiences (see Chapter 4). Speakers need to be aware of cultural differences represented in an audience. This is especially true if the speaker is presenting a ceremonial speech to a specific cultural group such as speaking to an African American congregation during a Martin Luther King Jr. Day celebration. Speakers need to be aware of different cultural norms and avoid language that can be interpreted as offensive by an audience (see Chapter 11).

In order to include diverse populations, ceremonial speakers can capitalize on addressing themes that transcend various demographics such as culture, gender, and political affiliation by appealing to cultural values (such as liberty, freedom, equality), cultural beliefs (such as the possibility of success, the value of challenge, the value of humbleness, and the eternal return), and needs (safety, security, belonging, esteem, and self-actualization). Ceremonial speeches that can transcend the general purpose of the speech to more universal values are more likely to unify diverse audiences and influence them to identify with the goodwill and positive feelings that accompany the ceremony or event (see Chapter 4).

Presentation

Speakers who incorporate universal values into their speeches must do so with a strong extemporaneous (and often impromptu) delivery. Speakers who lack a well-prepared, effectively delivered speech will fail to achieve any of the three general purposes of the ceremonial speech. Therefore, speakers presenting a ceremonial speech have to demonstrate a command of the organizational and delivery principles we have discussed in Chapters 7, 8, 9, and 10. The ceremonial speech must be presented in a confident, engaging, and flawless manner that gains the appreciation and support of the audience. For this reason, we will discuss some additional guidelines in the last section of this chapter that will help you present a ceremonial speech. In the meantime, we will discuss more specifically the types of ceremonial speeches.

THE TYPES OF CEREMONIAL SPEECHES

There are many types of ceremonial speeches. The types we discuss in this chapter are not an exhaustive list. Rather they represent some of the most frequent types of ceremonial speeches that are given. For convenience, we have organized the types of ceremonial speeches by the three general purposes we have already defined: motivational speeches, public recognition speeches, and entertaining and informative speeches.

Motivational Speeches

The first type of ceremonial speeches we discuss are those that we have identified as motivational speeches. **Motivational speeches** operate primarily to uplift, energize, and persuade individuals to some type of action or change in attitude, belief, or behavior. Ceremonial speeches that are motivational include introduction, welcome, and inspirational speeches.

Introduction Speeches

Ceremonial speeches that introduce or present a speaker to the audience are called **introduction speeches**. Introduction speeches are usually given by someone of significance within an organization (often of a leadership position) who is familiar with the guest speaker or who is directly responsible for bringing the speaker to the organization for the special occasion. Guest speakers are chosen because they represent some idea/value that is consistent with the organization or group having the special occasion.

In an introduction speech, the person introducing the guest speaker wants to motivate the audience by: 1) creating interest in the anticipated speech by discussing the guest speaker's background, qualifications, career highlights, and significant accomplishments; 2) building up the speaker in order to stimulate the audience's interest in the speech; and 3) to encourage the speaker so he/she can engage the audience with a dynamic delivery. When these three goals are met the person giving the introduction is able to create common ground between the speaker and audience, which sets up a positive tone and mood for the occasion. Successful introductions energize the guest speaker and help the audience receive the guest speaker with the proper respect.

When giving an introduction speech, it is important to follow these guidelines:

Provide Information about the Speaker

Introduction speeches summarize the most important aspects about the guest speaker's life that are relevant to the topic the guest speaker is presenting. Basic information such as the speaker's origins (hometown, parents, siblings, etc.), basic facts (when graduated from high school, college, along with any awards won/honors earned), career facts (positions, responsibilities, accomplishments). Depending on the guest, sometimes this information is provided by a speaker's agent or publicist, and sometimes it has to be researched.

Discuss the Significance of the Speaker's Work/Career

When highlighting the guest speaker's career accomplishments and accolades, it is important to convey to the audience how they are significant. Significance might be illustrated by awards or promotions the guest speaker has earned that are associated with the accomplishment. If, for example, the guest speaker is an author, maybe the speaker's book has been on the *New York Times* top ten list. The purpose is to show the audience that the speaker's work has made a significant impact on society.

Discuss the Importance of the Speaker and Topic

Effective introductions also link the speaker to the topic the speaker will be addressing at the special occasion. Once this link has been made, the person giving the introduction is ready to introduce the guest speaker to the podium.

Additional Guidelines to Follow

Use personal examples, stories, and quotes to bring the guest speaker's background and accomplishments to life. In this way, audiences will be able to identify more readily with the speaker. Also, always make sure you know how to correctly pronounce the speaker's name and know the speaker's title/position.

When organizing speeches of introduction, the length of the introduction depends on the context, the occasion, and how much discussion pertaining to the speaker's background and accomplishments is necessary. We stress that introductions, like any other speech, should have a general introduction, body, and conclusion. Speakers giving a speech of introduction might consider starting with an interesting example, quote, or story as an attention-getter, then link to the topic/occasion. Based upon the nature of the introduction, the person giving the introduction can provide background that links to accomplishments that lead up to the topic of the special occasion.

Welcome Speeches

A second type of motivational speech is the welcome speech. **Welcome speeches** are ceremonial speeches that offer sincere comments of appreciation to a group of individuals for joining or visiting a particular organization or event. The welcome speech serves as a common greeting to a group of individuals such as new employees attending an orientation, an audience gathered to hear a keynote speaker, a group of students visiting a television or radio station, or vacationers touring a significant cultural or historic site.

Unlike introduction speeches where the speaker is motivating the audience to listen to a guest speaker, welcome speeches are almost always presented to a group. Welcome speeches serve to spark the group's interest in the organization by reinforcing the group's central attitudes and beliefs and reminding the group of why they joined the organization. The overall goal is to provide a genuine and warm welcome to the group. Depending on the nature of the special occasion, the welcome address speaker can vary. If the event is some type of orientation, someone of significance will give welcoming remarks to the group (to illustrate the value of the new employees, for example), whereas tours usually designate someone specifically trained to communicate with and inform the group.

15

The wide-ranging nature of welcome speeches can be illustrated in sports by the familiar "tours" taken by free agents who are welcomed by the organization's leadership. In this era of multimillion dollar contracts and signing bonuses which team the free agent decides to play for is often determined by the warmest welcome (and the most money!).

When giving a welcome speech, you should adhere to the following guidelines:

A Genuine and Warm Welcome to the Group

Welcome speeches begin with sincere comments that welcome the group to the organization. Speakers should be enthusiastic and make effective eye contact with the group.

Acknowledge the General Background and Accomplishments of the Group

Depending on the type of welcome, the speaker might state some general facts about the group to create a common ground and to illustrate the qualities that make the incoming group valued. For example, it is not uncommon for universities to mention basic facts about its incoming freshmen such as average SAT score, number of states represented, etc.

Link the Group to the Purpose, Goals of the Organization

Linking the group to the purpose and goals of the organization is a way to illustrate how the group fits into the organization. Effective welcomes stress the "team" aspect of organizations; when individuals accomplish their tasks, the whole team is successful.

Repeat a Genuine and Warm Welcome to the Group

The welcome speech should close with sincere comments of appreciation and welcome to the group.

Inspirational Speeches

The third type of motivational speech we will discuss is the inspirational speech. **Inspirational speeches** are ceremonial speeches that help individuals feel enthusiastic, empowered, and encouraged. In general, inspiration speeches uplift individuals by creating hope and a sense of purpose in achieving and overcoming obstacles. Typically, graduation speeches and pep talks are inspirational speeches.

Since the individual giving an inspiration speech is attempting to motivate the audience, the speaker is targeting their attitudes, beliefs, and values. Therefore, the cultural values and beliefs that we mention in Chapter 4 should be used by speakers who want to motivate a diverse audience. Regardless of the culture, individuals share cultural beliefs such as the possibility of success and the value of challenge, which all people can identify with.

Since inspiration speeches deal with emotional appeals, it is important for speakers to deliver their ideas with passion in order to motivate the audience. Speakers have to have as much passion and conviction in their delivery as they want the audience to possess. Speakers, however, should always motivate their audiences ethically with positive emotional appeals and specific positive actions they can take. Positive emotional appeals target emotions that make the audience feel good about themselves, others, and their environment. Positive emotional appeals include idealism, encouragement, and happiness. Negative appeals, however, target feelings that make the audience feel bad about themselves, others, and their environment. Negative appeals include guilt, hate, and fear. We argue that negative appeals should be avoided in inspirational speeches because: 1) the goal of the speech is to build individuals up, not tear others down; 2) negative appeals manipulate individuals into action, and we consider manipulation to be unethical; 3) negative appeals might influence individuals to act in negative ways.

Here are some guidelines to consider when giving an inspiration speech:

Appeal to a Cultural Value or Belief that Unites Diverse Audiences

When speakers appeal to a cultural value or belief (see Chapter 4), speakers will be able to transcend different cultural norms, needs, and expectations to values and beliefs that are held by a wide range of individuals regardless of their culture.

Link the Cultural Value or Belief to a Specific Theme

Once particular values and beliefs are enacted, the speaker should link the values and beliefs to the theme of the speech. This way everyone can identify with the theme that is being used by the speaker to inspire the audience.

Be Clear in What You Want the Audience to Accomplish

A criticism of inspirational speeches is they sound good but do not offer specific or concrete actions for the audience to take. We recommend that after speakers have motivated audiences to particular themes, they should offer specific actions the audiences can take to enact the theme. For example, instead of simply inspiring college graduates to work hard to achieve success, tell college graduates they are a success if they volunteer to help another person learn to read, if they register and vote, etc.

15

Use Emotional Appeals Ethically

We believe public speakers have the responsibility to make ethical appeals when addressing an audience. Speakers should use positive emotional appeals and give audiences specific actions they can take.

Public Recognition Speeches

A second category of ceremonial speeches we refer to as **public recognition speeches**. Public recognition speeches are characterized by acknowledging to the public an individual's or group's contributions to society. Normally, these speeches are positive and convey sincere sentiments about the individual or group that is being honored. We will discuss four types of public recognition speeches: the tribute speech, the farewell speech, the eulogy, and the acceptance speech.

The Tribute Speech

Ceremonial speeches that give public recognition and express appreciation to an individual, a group, an institution, or event are called **tribute speeches**. In essence, tribute speeches honor individuals or groups who have made some type of significant contribution to society. Tribute speeches can honor individuals who have acted bravely in the line of duty such as firefighters or officers or who have served the public such as teachers. Sometimes during national disasters or tragedies entire groups can be honored such as the public memorial services that honored firefighters and officers who died during the terrorist attacks on 9/11.

Tribute speeches are often given during memorial services, public ceremonies, and special national recognition days where an individual or group is honored publicly. For example, Memorial Day is often marked by communities who pay tribute to those who served and died for our county. Furthermore, tribute speeches are often given by someone who is in public or private leadership such as a mayor or a CEO. When giving a tribute speech, you should follow the following guidelines:

Express Genuine Praise for the Individual or Group

Tribute speeches begin with sincere praise for the individual or group. Speakers should be enthusiastic and make effective eye contact with the individual or group.

Identify the Individual's or Group's Accomplishment to Society

Speakers should discuss how the individual or group have made or continue to make a significant contribution to society. Sometimes the contribution is already well known so include little-known facts or examples that provide additional insight into the work ethic, unselfishness, and dedication of the individual or group.

Incorporate Personal Examples about the Individual or Group into the Speech

Including personal examples and stories in the speech personalizes the speech for the audience and builds identification. Also, it makes the individual or group more human to the audience.

Appeal to Emotions

Another function of using personal examples and stories is they appeal to the emotions of the audience. When audiences are made aware of the struggles and sacrifices made by the individual or group, the audience develops an emotional bond with the individual or group.

The Farewell Speech

Ceremonial speeches that give public recognition to a person who is retiring from an organization, leaving an organization, or leaving a community are called **farewell speeches**. Either the person who is retiring or leaving can give the speech or the speech might be given by someone else who speaks on behalf of the person who is retiring or leaving. Farewell speeches provide a fitting closure for an individual who has made a significant contribution to an organization or community.

When individuals who are leaving are the speakers, they should express their appreciation for their colleagues or individuals from the community. Speakers should be humble and should acknowledge those who helped them with their accomplishments and contributions. When individuals are referred to, the comments should be positive, highlighting personal achievements and the impact they have made to the organization or community.

General guidelines for the farewell speech include:

Express Genuine and Sincere Appreciation of the Individual(s) Who Are Leaving (or who are remaining)

When making a farewell address on behalf of someone else, it is important to thank the person for his/her work and the contribution he/she made to the organization or community. When giving a farewell address, you should acknowledge those individuals who helped you achieve success in the organization or community.

Comment on the Importance of the Special Occasion and Discuss What You Will Miss about the Individual(s) Leaving (or the individuals remaining)

Farewells are nostalgic affairs where the person giving the farewell on behalf of someone else or the person giving his/her own farewell should reflect upon the occasion, the past, and what will be missed when the person leaves. The key is to create positive emotions that help everyone reflect upon the "good times" shared with the individual.

Provide Personal Stories and/or Personal Reflections Concerning Significant Career Highlights or Low Lights (which you learned from)

Personal stories and memories create nostalgic emotions for everyone gathered for the farewell address. They also help provide personal reflections upon achievements, events, and milestones that were accomplished.

Sometimes, depending on the tone and nature of the farewell, the departing person might want to challenge audience members to continue the practices, programs, and/or ideas he/she created as a way to maintain legacy and legitimacy of his/her policies.

Convey Heartfelt and Sincere Feelings for the Future Success of Those Leaving (or remaining)

The farewell should end positively by expressing sincere comments of happiness and success for the individual who is moving on or for the individuals who are staying behind.

The Eulogy

Sometimes ceremonial speeches honor those who are no longer living. **Eulogies** are ceremonial speeches that give public honor and praise to someone who is deceased. Regardless of the circumstances of how the person lived his/her life, eulogies are primarily positive and concentrate on the person's accomplishments and the impact he/she had on his/her family, friends, colleagues, and community.

Eulogies are commonly delivered at funerals and memorial services by someone who has known the individual very well and can comment on his/her character, accomplishments, and impact on society. Sometimes the eulogy might involve one speaker or it can involve more than one speaker who is able to comment on the various aspects of the person's character. The nature and tone for the eulogy can differ depending on the culture. For example, in African American culture, the eulogy typically takes place during a religious funeral that is often called a "going home" ceremony. Instead of a funeral being a somber occasion, guests celebrate, through song and music, the individual's life. Because of the upbeat nature of the service, the eulogy is expected to match the intensity of the celebration.

While eulogies can include many different content areas, speakers should not follow a simple chronological order. A speaker might want to gain attention, develop themes with personal examples, and highlight important accomplishments in the person's life. Furthermore, speakers might want to include stories that illustrate the person's humanity and character. Also, it is appropriate to include humor and to address any issues/ideas the person espoused or followed.

Eulogies can be guided by the following questions:

Why was the deceased a great human being?

What did this individual accomplish?

What unusual difficulties did this person overcome?

What admirable qualities did this individual possess?

To what agencies or sources did the subject owe his or her success?

What dramatic or interesting life incidents best reveal this person's personality and character?

What did the individual's contemporaries think of him or her?

What benefits do we reap from this special person's manner of living?

What should be our final judgement of this human being?[3]

The Acceptance Speech

Although it might seem as if acceptance speeches are self-serving addresses for award winners, in reality, effective acceptance speeches reflect the spotlight away from the winner to those who have most significantly supported the award winner. **Acceptance speeches** are ceremonial speeches that express appreciation for an award or gift. These speeches usually take place during or after an award ceremony.

There are two goals for the acceptance speech: 1) to express sincere appreciation to the individual or organization presenting the award and 2) to acknowledge the individuals who helped the winner achieve the award.

15

Although not a specific goal, tact is something award winners always want to demonstrate when giving an acceptance speech. The award winner should be prepared (this should be easy, since individuals are usually notified in advance that they have been nominated for an award). Therefore, even if it is the first time, the award winner should conduct themselves with tact (showing that they have "been here before") and have a prepared, concise statement that demonstrates forethought. Long rambling statements or ego-driven statements can turn off an audience and damage the goodwill between speaker and audience, which can make the speaker appear to be insincere.

Figure 15-1. Acceptance Speech

Sometimes the emotions are so monumental given the historical significance of the award that it is difficult for winners to maintain composure. An example is Halle Berry when she became the first African American woman in the history of the Academy Awards to win the Oscar for best actress. Given the context and history of the event, it is understandable that Berry was overwhelmed by her emotions.

For acceptance speeches, keep these guidelines in mind:

Give a Concise Statement

Acceptance speeches should begin with a specific remark thanking the individual or organization for the award.

Express Genuine Appreciation

Speakers should follow up their concise statement with sincere comments of appreciation for winning such an award and an explanation of how much the award means to them.

Identify Individuals Who Helped

Effective acceptance speeches acknowledge the individuals who were most vital to their success. The key is to thank only the most vital individuals. When a speaker thanks each and every person they know, audiences tend to become impatient. Instead speakers should choose three to four individuals who were the most significant in helping them win the award.

Express Sincere Gratitude

Speakers should conclude their speech by expressing genuine feelings of gratitude.

Entertaining and Informative Speeches

The final category of ceremonial speeches we will discuss are entertaining and informative speeches. **Entertaining and informative speeches** use all the means of rhetoric (such as the voice, gestures, humor, etc.) to provide insight, to increase our knowledge, and to challenge our way of thinking. We have identified three types of entertaining and informative speeches: the after-dinner speech, the keynote speech, and the reception speech.

The After-Dinner Speech

Sometimes when a ceremony includes a luncheon or dinner, it is accompanied by an after-dinner speech. **After-dinner speeches** are ceremonial speeches that use humor to illustrate the irony and satire of everyday life. Since individuals have had a meal, they simply want to relax and enjoy themselves. After-dinner speeches fulfill this role. Therefore, the speech itself should be uncomplicated but deal with subjects the audience is intimately familiar with.

Since the after-dinner speech deals with humor, speakers have to demonstrate effective delivery (voice variety, gestures, eye contact, rhythm, colorful language). In addition, successful after-dinner speeches use a variety of "humor support material" such as anecdotes, exaggeration, puns, irony, indirection, satire, and jokes to elicit humor. Although the speech should be funny, it is not a monologue of one-liners. Just like any other speech, the after-dinner speech should have an introduction, body, and conclusion.

Here are some guidelines to keep in mind for the after-dinner speech:

Discuss a Familiar Topic

Since the after-dinner speech is light-hearted, it should cover a topic the audience is familiar with. For example, a sports team celebrating the end of a season might enjoy an after-dinner speech that highlights the humorous aspects of the completed season. Being familiar with the topic enables the audience to understand the context and nuances of the speech.

Use Humor Ethically

When giving an after-dinner speech, it is important to use humor that is ethical. Ethical humor does not include personal cheap shots that specifically demean a person in order to create laughter. Rather, effective after-dinner speeches focus on the circumstances and common experiences that everyone can identify with and laugh at. The difference is the skill of the speaker to draw everyone into the topic in a humorous way instead of singling out someone to belittle.

15

Demonstrate a Friendly Tone

How the after-dinner speech is presented is critical to the success of the speech. Speakers, in addition to having a flawless delivery, need to demonstrate a friendly tone that audiences feel comfortable with. When the audience is comfortable with the speaker, they are more likely to respond to the speaker's humor.

Be Concise

Effective after-dinner speeches are focused on a specific topic and organized (this is what separates it from the monologue, which can shift from topic to topic without a specific thesis that links all the topics together). The speech should follow the basic speech structure (introduction, body, and conclusion) that includes a thesis in the introduction and support material in the body.

The Keynote Speech

At first glance it might seem odd to categorize a keynote speech as an entertaining and informative speech, but we believe keynote speakers need to be entertaining in how they present their speech to the audience. Being entertaining is necessary due to the oversaturation of speeches audiences hear, and the influence of the media age where individuals are bombarded with all types of video images. Audiences' attention spans are short, so the speaker has to demonstrate excellent delivery and be entertaining to be successful.

A **keynote speech** is a ceremonial speech that takes place during a conference or meeting that addresses issues, ideas, and themes that are consistent with the general philosophy of the organization holding the conference or meeting. Usually, keynote speakers are individuals of national recognition and they are chosen to speak based upon their expertise, knowledge, accomplishments, and experiences in a particular field or career.

Keynote speeches take place at all types of national conferences and special public events that are held by various organizations (such as political parties, professional/academic organizations, protest movements, etc). The keynote is to help attract organizational members and to address important organizational or public issues.

Here are some guidelines to follow when giving a keynote speech:

Acknowledge Individuals and Express Gratitude

It is an honor for a speaker to be chosen as a keynote speaker. To show their gratitude, speakers normally begin their speech by thanking the most significant individuals responsible for choosing them to speak and by expressing sincere gratitude to those individuals and the audience.

Gain Attention

As with any speech, it is important to gain the attention of the audience in a creative and memorable way (see Chapter 9). A story, a fact, or personal testimony that is linked to the keynote topic are all ways speakers might begin their speech.

Identify Issues/Ideas and Relate to the Group

When giving a keynote speech, speakers should address issues or ideas that are linked to the topic and then relate the issues/ideas to the group. Sometimes within keynote speeches a theme emerges that links the various issues/ideas. Whether a keynote address has a theme or not is up to the speaker, the nature of the event, and the topic the speaker was asked to address.

Challenge the Group (audience)

Effective keynote speeches not only highlight issues/ideas for the audience to think about, but they challenge the group to address certain practices or circumstances. The audience who gathered for the keynote speech is in a unique situation since they are part of the organization or group that has the ability to address the issues raised by the speaker. Effective keynote speakers challenge the audience to change/address certain issues to better society.

The Reception Speech

The final type of entertaining and informative ceremonial speech we will discuss is the reception speech. **Reception speeches** take place during an "informal" gathering where light refreshments are served. Reception ceremonies often take place either before a special ceremony (like a keynote speech) or after (like a graduation). The key with reception speeches is that they should provide information that reinforces the themes and tone of the special ceremony it is linked to.

The length and content of the reception speech varies with the purpose, length, and content of the reception itself. Usually reception speeches are followed by mingling so the remarks should be brief.

Here are some guidelines for the reception speech:

Acknowledge Individuals and Express Gratitude

Like the keynote address, the speaker should thank the most significant individuals responsible for choosing them to speak and express sincere gratitude to those individuals and the audience. Unlike the keynote address, however, the speaker's remarks can be more personalized since the gathering is smaller and more intimate.

Be Sincere

Since receptions are small gatherings, speakers have to be aware that their every move and action is being watched. Audiences can tell whether speakers are sincere or not when making their comments. Speakers should be sincere in their comments and show gratitude during the mingling.

Identify Theme and Relate to the Group

When making reception remarks, speakers should address a theme and link the theme to the group, the occasion, or the event. The key is to be brief and concise.

PRESENTING THE CEREMONIAL SPEECH

This chapter has identified several types of ceremonial speeches and it has provided some guidelines for speakers to prepare for these types of speeches. At this point, we would like to briefly discuss how speakers should present their ceremonial speech because how it is presented is just as important as the content. How can a speaker inspire if they are monotone? How can a speaker give a welcome when they are not enthusiastic? How can speakers give a proper tribute if the audience can't follow their ideas? Therefore, we emphasize how all ceremonial speeches must be accompanied by a flawless presentation which includes delivery and organization.

Delivery

We discussed, in Chapter 10, the importance of delivery (vocal aspects, nonverbal aspects). In ceremonial speeches, audiences expect that speakers will have flawless delivery. Therefore, preparation and practice are essential in making an effective ceremonial speech. The key is to start with audience analysis (Chapter 4) to identify the purpose and context of your speech. For example, with a toast, it might be short enough that the speaker can practice with notecards until they are familiar enough that they can give it effectively from memory. Meanwhile keynote speeches will take a great deal of time practicing to perfect an extemporaneous speaking style. Regardless of the delivery style, all the elements of effective delivery such as eye contact, conversational delivery, and gestures need to be perfect. Remember your presentation is part of the larger ceremony, you want to match (or in some cases exceed) the level of the ceremony. You never want to detract from a ceremony due to poor delivery.

Organization

In Chapter 8, we discussed the importance of organization when making a presentation. We also acknowledge how this textbook follows the Western tradition of linear logic, where ideas are linked sequentially in a straight line. As we discussed in Chapter 8, mainstream American culture is based upon linear logic; it is the philosophy that drives political, economic, and social structures. That is why we have stressed throughout this book the importance of learning and using linear logic when organizing a speech because it is the organizational structure that is the norm of the larger dominant culture. Ceremonial speeches, however, depart from linear logic as speakers do not have to adhere to the Western tradition. Again, speakers need to consider audience analysis, but for the most part strict adherence to an organization pattern is a rarity in ceremonial speaking. Therefore, a speaker can be more creative in how they present their ideas. We still advocate that the ceremonial speech should have a general introduction, body, and conclusion, but it does not have to strictly adhere to it. This allows for more creativity and creativity is needed with ceremonial speeches, since audiences have been oversaturated with special occasion presentations, which might influence them into believing that they have "already heard it all" before the speech even begins. As you practice the speech, have others critique how your ideas are presented. You want to make sure that they can follow the progression of your ideas. If they think ideas are missing, then you can adjust your speech accordingly.

In this chapter, we have discussed the presentations that take place during special events and occasions called ceremonial speeches. We have explained the nature of ceremonial speaking, we identified the different types, and we mentioned the importance of how to present the ceremonial speech. We believe the ideas presented in this chapter will help any speaker prepare for a ceremonial speech.

VOCABULARY

Acceptance speech — a public recognition ceremonial speech that expresses appreciation for an award or gift.

After-dinner speech — an entertaining and informative ceremonial speech that uses humor to illustrate the irony and satire in everyday life.

Ceremonial speeches — presentations that are given as part of a special occasion or social event.

Entertaining and informative speeches — a category of ceremonial speeches that use all the means of rhetoric (such as the voice, gestures, humor, etc.) to provide insight, to increase our knowledge, and to challenge our way of thinking.

Eulogy — a public recognition ceremonial speech that gives public honor and praise to someone who is deceased.

Farewell speech — a public recognition ceremonial speech that honors a person who is retiring from an organization, leaving an organization, or leaving a community.

Inspirational speech — a motivational ceremonial speech that helps individuals feel enthusiastic, empowered, and encouraged.

Introduction speech — a motivational ceremonial speech that introduces or presents a speaker to the audience.

Keynote speech — an entertaining and informative ceremonial speech that takes place during a conference or meeting that addresses issues, ideas, and themes that are consistent with the general philosophy of the organization that held the conference or meeting.

Motivational speeches — a category of ceremonial speeches that operate primarily to uplift, energize, and persuade individuals to some type of action or change in attitude, belief, or behavior.

Public recognition speeches — a category of ceremonial speeches that are characterized by acknowledging to the public an individual's or group's contribution to society.

Reception speech — an entertaining and informative speech that takes place during an "informal" gathering where light refreshments are served.

Tribute speech — a public recognition ceremonial speech that expresses appreciation to an individual, a group, an institution, or event.

Welcome speech — a motivational ceremonial speech that offers sincere comments of appreciation to a group of individuals for joining or visiting a particular organization or event.

REFERENCES

[1] Bitzer, L. (1968). The rhetorical situation. *Philosophy and Rhetoric, 1,* 6–7.

[2] Katha Pollitt, "Poetry Makes Nothing Happen? Ask Laura Bush" *Nation* (24 February 2003), 9.

[3] R. T. Oliver and R.L. Cortright, *Effective Speech*, 4th edition (New York: Rinehart and Winston). 1961.

"Never doubt that a small group of thoughtful, committed citizens can change the world."
–Margaret Mead

"Individual commitment to a group effort—that is what makes team work, company work, society work, a civilization work."
–Vince Lombardi

"We all know we are unique individuals, but we tend to see others as representatives of groups."
–Deborah Tannen

This Chapter Examines:

+ the nature and role of group communication

+ the types of groups

+ group dynamics

+ culture and group dynamics

Five weeks ago Todd, Serena, Sanjay, April, and Brent were assigned the task of forming a group for the end of the semester project. Although their goal seemed simple, the group made little progress in creating their presentation. In fact, the group lacked cohesiveness and conflict was a common occurrence as some members were responsible in completing tasks while others were not. One of the difficulties with the group was their assumption that everyone would work together and understand their role in creating an effective group presentation. However, with their group presentation scheduled for next week, the tension in the group increased. Will the group be able to perform the necessary roles and manage their differences in order to create a successful group presentation?

The opening example illustrates a common misconception about groups and group communication—that individuals can be placed into a group and they will work together effectively to reach a goal. The truth is, effective groups are not simply assembled; they must be nurtured and developed into an organized unit. The cohesiveness of the group is dependent on individuals demonstrating specific behavioral roles within the group. Therefore, in this chapter we will discuss several concepts that are vital for effective group communication beginning with an explanation of the nature and role of group communication.

THE NATURE AND ROLE OF GROUP COMMUNICATION

We have discussed at length how a speaker should prepare for a speech for a public presentation. Up until this point, we have concentrated on public speaking from a speaker/audience perspective. However, not all public speaking occurs in this setting. Another context for public speaking involves group communication. Group communication plays an integral role in society today, from business to education to government. The formation of work groups, task forces, blue-ribbon panels, Senate investigating committees, and community forums or debates are all examples of how prevalent group communication has become in our democratic society.

We define **group communication** as three to nine persons engaged in discussion or purposeful talk in an attempt to make decisions, solve problems, and recommend policy. We use the arbitrary cut-off of nine persons because once a group becomes larger than nine persons, it is difficult for each member to communicate face-to-face with each person every time the group meets. The dynamics of group communication are interesting because of the role that interpersonal communication or face-to-face interaction plays in all group situations or contexts.

Furthermore, group communication takes on different qualities than interpersonal or public communication because of the following factors. First, each group member is united by a common goal. In group communication, individuals often have to forgo their own individual goals and embrace the goal of the group. For a group to be successful, it takes great skill, leadership, communication, sensitivity, and all members working towards the same goal.

Figure 16-1. Group Communication

16

Second, group members must interact with one another. Without interaction among group members, the group would not be able to achieve its goal. It is through interaction that ideas are exchanged, issues discussed, and solutions created. Groups are at their best when each member is communicating his or her ideas to help the group reach the best possible outcome.

Third, the size of the group affects the type of communication. Unlike interpersonal communication where individuals control the nature and type of communication, group communication requires individuals to work with others to reach agreement, to persuade others, and to resolve conflict. The size of the group changes the nature of communication from solely focusing on oneself to working with others.

Fourth, group dynamics and communication are shaped over time. If a group only meets once, it is not a very good example of group communication because it takes time for aspects such as leadership, rules, and norms to develop. However, over time, these group dynamics emerge that help the group accomplish its task. All these dynamics (and more) must be addressed correctly in order for the group to function properly.

It is these four factors, a common goal, interaction, the size of the group, and meeting periodically, that create the unique characteristics of group communication. We will continue our discussion of these unique characteristics by first exploring the different types of groups that are part of our daily experiences.

THE TYPES OF GROUPS

Most of the time when we think of groups, we think of the ones we are assigned to in class or in the workplace—a forced coalition of individuals who are united by a common goal to complete their assigned tasks. However, this type of group represents only one kind of group that we might experience. Whether we realize it or not, we belong to many groups and the groups we are a part of underline our need for being connected to others. Our need to be connected to or belong with others illustrates one of Maslow's hierarchy of needs (see Chapter 4). Furthermore, the groups we belong to can be defined by their general goal or purpose. We will briefly discuss some of the most common types of groups that we are a part of: family, study, therapy, problem-solving, focus, and social.

Family

One of the most important groups we belong to is the family. A **family** is a primary social group that lives together. Oftentimes, a family is linked through descent from a common ancestor, marriage, or adoption. The family is the building block of society where we learn our morals, values, and ethics. In addition, we develop important skills such as interpersonal sensitivity, leadership, and cooperation within the family. Families create long-term "permanent relationships" that directly affect how we communicate and interact with other individuals in our family. The family is such an important social group that even if we don't get along with our biological families we seek others who we can bond with in order to create "family"—whether it is other relatives or close friends.

Study Groups

A **study group** is defined as individuals who meet on a regular basis to learn new information. Most commonly, we think of the study groups that college students form when they are preparing for a test. This type of group illustrates one type of informal group that works together to achieve their goals. Other times formal groups are convened, such as a research group that is created to study a certain problem. When the group is finished with its study, the information is then presented to the organization that created the study group such as a government body, medical center, or community group. The research from the study helps the organization to understand the problem more clearly in order to address the issue better.

Therapy Groups

Sometimes individuals are in crisis and they need to be part of a group in order to deal with their difficulties more effectively. **Therapy groups** are groups that meet regularly to help individuals manage their problems. One of the strengths of therapy groups is they enable those who face a particular dilemma to know that they are not alone with their problem and there is a support system available to help them. Therapy groups underline the concept of **identification** that we discuss in Chapter 4; that individuals are able to connect with one another because they share similar experiences. One of the most well-known therapy groups is Alcoholics Anonymous, where alcoholics help one another to stop drinking and deal with issues related to their drinking.

Problem-Solving Groups

Meanwhile, a **problem-solving group** is formed to study an issue and to offer either recommendations or a solution to the problem. It is the task of making recommendations or creating solutions that separates a problem-solving group from a study group. Also, given the nature of the dilemma often there is much more pressure on a problem-solving group than a study group. For example, one of the most recent and prominent problem-solving groups that was convened was the 9/11 Commission. The 9/11 Commission was created to study why the government was inadequate in responding to the terrorist attacks on 9/11 and to offer recommendations to help the government to avoid future attacks. When the 9/11 Commission was an active committee it faced overwhelming pressure from the public, the families of victims, and the political parties to create an objective and fair assessment of 9/11. The hearings held by the Commission and its eventual report, illustrate the importance of group discussion and problem-solving. We address both of these concepts in more detail in Chapter 17.

16

Focus Groups

A **focus group** brings together a group of people to listen to and respond to a particular topic in order for researchers to understand how a group of people think, respond, or perceive an issue or topic. Marketing companies spend a great deal of time identifying certain demographic groups and holding focus groups in order to learn how to market products to individuals from a specific demographic group. Another related example are the town hall meetings that take place during the Presidential campaign. Average citizens from a "typical" American town are convened to listen to the candidates then give their opinions of what they liked or disliked about the candidate or the candidate's message.

Social Groups

The groups that we are a part of, however, do not always have a formal goal. **Social groups** are formed because of our need to be with others. Therefore, the purpose of a social group is to socialize and enjoy the friendship of others. Social groups can vary from more formalized ones such as a reading group, to informal ones like getting together with friends. Regardless of what we do when we are with a group of friends, it fulfills the basic need of being connected to and interacting with others.

GROUP DYNAMICS

As we mentioned at the beginning of the chapter, there are many concepts and characteristics of group communication. The following group concepts provide a better understanding of how group communication is distinguished from the other kinds of oral communication.

Functional Group Characteristics

The first set of characteristics that are central to group communication we define as functional group characteristics, because these concepts help the group to achieve its goal. Whether the group is formal or informal, these characteristics must be present in order for the group to function properly.

One of the most implicit but critical elements that is necessary for effective group communication are the roles group members take on to help the group achieve its goal. A **role** is a specific behavior of an individual that is consistently communicated to other group members. Researchers Benne and Sheats are acknowledged as identifying the general types of roles that individuals can demonstrate in a group. These roles are commonly defined as task roles, social roles, and individual roles.[1] **Task roles** help the group to accomplish its goal. **Social roles** help the group maintain positive relationships. However, **individual roles** are dysfunctional roles that emphasize the individual instead of the group, thus hindering the group from achieving its goal. Figure 16-2 lists each general role and specific behavioral roles for each.[2]

TASK-ORIENTED ROLES

These roles help the group to accomplish its goal:

+ Initiator-contributor: Generates new ideas.
+ Information-seeker: Asks for information about the task.
+ Opinion-seeker: Asks for input from the group about its values.
+ Information-giver: Offers facts or generalizations to the group.
+ Opinion-giver: States his or her beliefs about a group issue.
+ Elaborator: Explains ideas within the group, offers examples to clarify ideas.
+ Coordinator: Shows the relationships between ideas.
+ Orienter: Shifts the direction of the group's discussion.
+ Evaluator-critic: Measures group's actions against some objective standard.
+ Energizer: Stimulates the group to a higher level of activity.
+ Procedural-technician: Performs logistical functions for the group.
+ Recorder: Keeps a record of group actions.

SOCIAL ROLES

These roles help the group to maintain positive relationships:

+ Encourager: Praises the ideas of others.
+ Harmonizer: Mediates differences between group members.
+ Compromiser: Moves group to another position that is favored by all group members.
+ Gatekeeper/expediter: Keeps communication channels open.
+ Standard-setter: Suggests standards or criteria for the group to achieve.
+ Group-observer: Keeps records of group activities and uses this information to offer feedback to the group.
+ Follower: Goes along with the group and accepts the group's ideas.

INDIVIDUALISTIC ROLES

These are dysfunctional roles that emphasize the individual instead of the group, and thus hinder the group from accomplishing its goal:

+ Aggressor: Attacks other group members, deflates the status of others, and other aggressive behaviors.
+ Blocker: Resists movement by the group.
+ Recognition-seeker: Calls attention to himself or herself.
+ Self-confessor: Seeks to disclose nongroup related feelings or opinions.
+ Dominator: Asserts control over the group by manipulating the other group members.
+ Help-seeker: Tries to gain the sympathy of the group.
+ Special interest-pleader: Uses stereotypes to assert his or her own prejudices.

Figure 16-2.

Implicit in the roles that individuals enact to help the group achieve its goal is that group members will demonstrate rhetorical sensitivity when communicating in the group. **Rhetorical sensitivity** means group members will show respect and collegiality when interacting with each other. This concept can be further understood as a strategy that combines common courtesy and persuasive tactics. For example, it is human nature for people to disagree with each other. However, when voicing those differences of opinion, it is crucial to do so in a professional and respectful manner. How would you respond if somebody attacked a comment that you made by saying, "That's crazy. It will never work. That's the dumbest thing I've ever heard anybody say!" Surely, this is not being very sensitive to the feelings and ideas of others. A far better and more rhetorically sensitive response would be, "I understand where you are coming from and your idea does have some merit, but when we tried that five years ago, we lost money." It doesn't really take that much more effort to show respect and sensitivity when responding to and interacting with others in a group setting.

In addition to the roles that are demonstrated in groups are rules that govern group behavior. **Rules** are laws, guidelines, and regulations that are written down in a handbook or manual, which define group procedure and group conduct. All organizations or groups have official rules that explicitly state how the group is to function. For example, most groups have rules for a variety of group functions such as how to conduct meetings, how to handle conflict, and how to hold elections. Another example of rules held by groups is "Robert's Rules of Order," where only one person speaks at a time, and no one can be interrupted while speaking. Robert's Rules of Order helps the group proceed during its meetings in an "official" way. All relevant information is usually recorded by the secretary who later types up the information into another official document, the group minutes.

While rules are explicit guidelines that are found in written form, norms are implicit guidelines that stipulate how group members ought to behave (or not behave) in groups. **Norms** refer to the unwritten and unspoken rules that define acceptable behavior for group members. They constitute the regularities of behavior in groups. Since norms are implicit, they might not even be noticed until they are violated or broken. Norms also include the attitudes, beliefs, and values of the individuals in the group. Many departments, committees, and groups share an unwritten or unspoken rule against the use of profanity by its members, although it is often violated. Other group members who show their displeasure to the violators often confront those who break the norms with negative body language and nonverbal cues.

Rules and norms are present in any group. In fact, some researchers of group communication argue that without rules and norms a group can not function properly—they are critical to the success of the group. One example of how rules and norms work in tandem would be a company dress code. In many larger companies and organizations, there is an "official policy" (a rule) in the company's manual for the proper dress code. There are also many "norms" for the proper dress code. However, an employee often will come to work dressed in jeans, a sweatshirt, and without socks only to be reprimanded by the boss. The jeans and sweatshirt would violate the company's rule, while the lack of socks would violate a company norm.

Moreover, **cohesiveness** means group unity. It can be best described as an "us against the world" attitude taken by a group as they face outside pressures and criticism. The concept of cohesiveness should also be thought of as group "togetherness" with group members supporting each other and "bonding" with one another as they are attacked by others from outside the group. Many professional sport teams who are criticized by the media and their fans become more cohesive and use their bond to become even stronger when faced with adversity and criticism.

On the surface, it might seem odd to follow the discussion of cohesiveness with conflict or to include conflict as a functional group characteristic. However, conflict is a necessary component of group communication, as all groups will have conflict. **Conflict** is the disagreement that emerges in groups with people who hold diverse and contrary opinions, attitudes, beliefs, and values. Sometimes conflict is the "creative tension" that moves the group towards a recommendation or solution. Therefore, conflict is actually a neutral concept. What makes conflict positive or negative is how the group attempts to manage it. **Negative conflict** is when people engage in name-calling, personal clashes, and ridicule; this is surely something all groups want to avoid because it hinders effective discussion and genuine communication, while increasing tension and bitterness in the group. In contrast, **positive conflict** is when people "agree to disagree" in a respectful way. Individuals might have a difference of opinion but their disagreement does not get personal. It would be dull and boring, as well as unrealistic, if all group members agreed on every single issue being discussed or debated. When people have a genuine disagreement but use lively and respectful discussion to express such differences, they are engaged in positive conflict.

Dysfunctional Group Characteristics

Unfortunately, as our opening example references, not all group experiences are positive or productive. Groups can fail to achieve their goal or they can create animosity among group members (and sometimes they do both). The following concepts explain some of the dysfunctional group characteristics that can be part of groups.

Group hate is a perception or tendency by people to avoid, be reluctant, or even despise working in groups. It is exactly what the term seems to imply; most people don't like to work in groups and some even hate the thought of doing so! There are some very legitimate reasons why people despise groups. First, many people feel that they will lose their "individuality" once they are put into any group setting or situation. Second, they feel they could do better and be more efficient if they are allowed to work alone and not with others. In addition, many people have had negative experiences in groups and come into a group with preconceived notions of what might happen. Also, some people have very little trust or confidence in other group members to achieve their goals and objectives in the group. In other words, many people feel intimidated by groups. Perhaps they have been ridiculed or laughed at by others while participating in group interactions. While your authors recognize these perceptions of group communication, we would assert that group communication and discussion, if done properly, could be far more effective and productive than individual effort.

Baggage is something all groups must cope with. **Baggage** represents the opinions, attitudes, beliefs, and values held by each group member. Baggage is "carried" into each group we join. When those attitudes, beliefs, and values emerge in a group, there is often potential for conflict, bias, and stereotyping. In the film classic *12 Angry Men*, several members of the jury voice racist and prejudiced comments about minorities during their deliberations in a trial where a Latino youth is charged with murdering his father. These racist attitudes are eventually attacked by the rest of the jury members and rebuked. In real life it is quite common for biases, stereotypes, and prejudices to emerge during group interaction. It is important that the group not allow these perceptions to negatively affect the group in achieving its goals and objectives.

Groupthink is a phenomenon that is always negative and harmful for effective group interaction and productivity. **Groupthink** is the suppression of critical thought or simply going along with the rest of the group even when you don't agree with them. A group member who is simply anxious to end a meeting and go home might do anything to bring the meeting to a close. By going along with the majority of the group just to end the meeting, this group member is contributing to one of the most potentially dangerous situations a group can experience. Groupthink usually comes back to hurt or haunt a group because the true beliefs and feelings of those engaging in this sort of behavior might never be known. As is often the case, the member who does use groupthink could later have a change of heart. "I really didn't want to do this in the first place," or "I never wanted to do this topic for our presentation; I just wanted to get on with the project" are the sort of comments we often hear from a group member who has engaged in groupthink.

One way to prevent groupthink from occurring is to engage in the practice of playing **devil's advocate**. A devil's advocate is a group member who discusses alternative ideas or opinions in a group in order to prevent groupthink. Playing devil's advocate is also an excellent way to demonstrate your leadership in a group situation. The group member who takes on the role of devil's advocate might say something like, "Well, I know where you are coming from, but have you considered what can happen if we do make this recommendation?" Or, the devil's advocate could state, "Let me explain to you why an alternative to your solution might be more effective in solving our problem." The person who does engage in the role of devil's advocate might not even disagree with what is being said, but is simply raising an alternative perspective to encourage the group to discuss or debate the issues.

CULTURE AND GROUP DYNAMICS

No discussion of the types of groups and the roles of group members would be complete without discussing how culture is an important factor in understanding group dynamics. The cultural values and beliefs that individuals from different cultures and co-cultures hold impact group communication. In review, a person's **culture** includes the traditions, customs, beliefs, values, norms, and perspectives that are learned through shared behavior patterns and cultural practices that are passed down from generation to generation. A **co-culture** can be defined by one's nationality, ethnicity, or religion. In essence, we use culture to define those individuals who do not live in the United States and co-cultures for those minority groups who live in the United States (see Chapter 4).

The importance of understanding cultural values and beliefs (regardless of whether the person is from another culture or co-culture) is illustrated by the example of what is considered a norm for communicating a task between an authority figure and a group member. How the authority figure and group member communicate in one culture can have a totally different meaning (or approach) in another culture because norms and rules vary from culture to culture. The challenge of understanding cultural values and beliefs in a group context leads to both advantages and disadvantages. The advantages of having a variety of cultural values in a group is it will bring a greater diversity of ideas, perspectives, and approaches, while the disadvantage is bridging cultural differences, which tends to make group development slow.[3] However, with society becoming more and more multicultural, researchers are studying how culturally diverse groups can be successful groups.[4]

Therefore, we return to the idea of building **identification** with a multicultural audience that we discussed in Chapter 4. The more individuals understand the cultural composition of their group and the varying cultural values and beliefs

16

that are commonly held by individuals from a different culture or co-culture, the more likely the group will develop ways to relate to (and understand) the different approaches to communication. We believe that groups can demonstrate effective rhetorical sensitivity and role enactment (and leadership) by understanding one of the central concepts of intercultural communication—the difference between low-context and high-context cultures.

LOW-CONTEXT CULTURE	HIGH-CONTEXT CULTURE
1. Overly displays meanings through direct communication forms	1. Implicitly embeds meanings at different levels of the sociocultural context
2. Values individualism	2. Values collectivism
3. Emphasizes linear logic	3. Emphasizes spiral logic
4. Values direct verbal interaction and is less able to read nonverbal expressions	4. Values indirect verbal interaction and is more able to read nonverbal expressions
5. Tends to use "logic" to present ideas	5. Tends to use more "feeling" in expression
6. Tends to emphasize highly structured messages, give details, and place great stress on words and technical signs	6. Tends to give simple, ambiguous, noncontexting messages

Figure 16-3.

We reintroduce the concept of low-context and high-context cultures, because it has a great impact on how individuals from different cultures communicate (see Chapter 4).[6] Specifically, we will explain how low-context/high-context affects the perception and communication within a group. We will identify how culture affects the group dynamics of tasks, conflict, and roles, and then discuss ways in which to manage these challenges.

Culture and Task Completion

In review, in **low-context cultures** such as mainstream American society, the meanings of a communication message are directly communicated by individuals through verbal expressions of intention, opinion, and thought. On the other hand, in **high-context cultures**, such as Eastern cultures like China or Japan, the meanings of a communication message are imbedded in the situation, the relationship of the individuals, and the implicit norms, beliefs, and values of the culture.

These two orientations can cause some challenges when it comes to the group attempting to complete tasks. For example, low-context cultures are defined by **individualism** where individuals are responsible for their efforts and the assumption is if someone is given a task, the person is responsible for completing the task on his/her own and then bringing the finished task to the group. Meanwhile, high-context cultures value the concept of **collectivism** where everyone in the group contributes to the task. With collectivism, individuals work together on tasks, from the planning, to the discussion, to the implementation.

The different orientations towards tasks can lead to misunderstanding and possibly conflict. For example, a high-context individual placed within an individualist group could feel "left out" when not assigned to work with a specific team. In addition, the high-context individual might feel unimportant and isolated if given an assignment to complete on his/her own. Meanwhile, the low-context individual placed within a collectivistic group might become frustrated because it takes too long to accomplish each task by the group. In addition, underlying these ideas of individualism and collectivism in task completion is the different emphasis on competition versus cooperation. Individualism assumes that there should be some competition between group members and that some competition is healthy in motivating others in the group. Collectivism downplays competition and places emphasis on cooperation and group recognition instead of individual recognition.

Culture and Conflict

Not only can a low-context/high-context culture illustrate various orientations toward task completion, but also, it highlights the different perspectives towards conflict. High-context cultures tend to emphasize spiral or **configural** logic, where being indirect and talking around a point is an important aspect of maintaining the other person's face. **Face** is the public self-image that a person wants to maintain in a specific social context (see Chapter 4). For example, if a supervisor was disappointed in his employee, Charlie's, work, the supervisor would say it in an indirect way (which saves face). The supervisor might say, "I must have misread the figures because we have always produced reliable results. I must do a better job in reviewing the data and sharing the data with the rest of the team." Notice how the supervisor's message was not direct; it did not mention Charlie by name, and it did not place blame on Charlie. The only way Charlie knows he messed up is by understanding the embedded meaning of what his supervisor is saying. Charlie would know the embedded meaning (which is learned in the culture) from the nature of his relationship with his supervisor, each person's status, and from the traditions/customs of the culture. Charlie would understand that since his supervisor is discussing the mistake (which came from Charlie), Charlie needs to go

16

back and review his work to correct the mistake. While this is an indirect means of communication, it illustrates how high-context cultures place the value of saving face over creating conflict.

Since both individuals are from the same culture, the message and meaning was understood and conflict was avoided. However, if someone from a low-context culture was given this message, the person would probably miss the meaning of the message and assume that he/she did not make a mistake (or worst yet, assume that the supervisor made the mistake). This misinterpretation would most likely take place because in low-context cultures, individuals value the direct communication of thoughts, feelings, and ideas. In a low-context culture, if someone does not address us directly, then we assume the person is not talking to us. You can see how these two different orientations can (and do) lead to conflict.

Perceptions towards conflict can also vary within a culture. For example, researcher Thomas Kochman has spent years understanding cultural differences and explains that conflict is communicated differently in African American culture as opposed to the mainstream dominant culture.[7] Kochman explains that within African American culture, conflict between individuals might appear to be very argumentative and verbally aggressive (with name-calling and put downs) as part of the exchange. In African American culture, expressing one's ideas is more important than the other person's feelings. This type of conflict is perceived to be positive because individuals are expressing their true feelings. Meanwhile, in the dominant culture it is the opposite, as positive conflict is when individuals engage in "discussion" and attempt to maintain composure. It is better to keep the discussion civil than to lose one's composure. Conflict can arise between these two perspectives because the African American individual might perceive the person from the dominant culture as not being true to his/her feelings and thus untrustworthy in what the person has to say. Meanwhile, the person from the dominant culture might perceive the African American as being too emotional to discuss the issue.

These cultural examples also point out that cultures have different perceptions of positive and negative conflict. In high-context cultures, it is better to maintain someone's face than to engage in conflict. In low-context cultures, we attempt to resolve the issue or manage the conflict. Persons from these two different perspectives could actually "go around in circles" or be perceived as avoiding the problem because they do not want to address the issue. Meanwhile, other cultures welcome conflict and anything less than direct expression is not viewed as trustworthy or being honest. All these perspectives have to be dealt with in a multicultural society.

Culture and Role Enactment

Another area that is very salient with culturally diverse groups is the types of roles group members demonstrate when interacting with one another. As we have mentioned, in high-context cultures, concern for an individual's face is more important than the task. Therefore, in high-context groups it is important for group members to enact social roles such as *encourager, harmonizer,* and *compromiser* to maintain the positive relationships of the group members (see Figure 16-2). From a high-context perspective, achieving a goal is worthless if the relationships in the group were destroyed in the process. The emphasis on face underlies the principle that to accomplish a task or goal, individuals need to work with the entire group.

Meanwhile, in a low-context culture, the task is more important than an individual's face. As a result, low-context cultures tend to emphasize task-oriented roles such as *initiator-contributor, opinion-giver,* and *energizer* (see Figure 16-2). From a low-context perspective, creating "warm and fuzzy" positive relationships among group members is meaningless if the group does not achieve its goal. The emphasis on the task underscores the principle that to accomplish a task or goal, the group must work through individuals.

Identifying the cultural values of a high-context and low-context culture highlights the tension between these two perspectives in regards to role enactment in a group. An individual from a low-context culture could be disenchanted with a high-context group if the group spent too much time on relating and supporting one another as opposed to focusing on the task. Likewise, an individual from a high-context culture might perceive the low-context group as unfriendly and "cold," because the group spent most of their time focusing on the task. Varying cultural values like these make group communication within culturally diverse groups a challenge.

Strategies for Managing Diverse Groups

Despite the numerous challenges facing culturally diverse groups, effective group dynamics can take place with enough understanding, rhetorical sensitivity, leadership, and relationship building. Charles Bantz explains that the only constant in managing diverse groups is to realize that each situation will not be handled consistently.[8] Since cultural values, beliefs, and norms vary from situation to situation, so should the approaches that groups use to address and manage group dynamics. Therefore, groups are in a perpetual learning environment of integrating and coordinating cultural differences within a group. Bantz summarizes that managing culturally diverse groups involves four general principles: 1) acquiring information on different cultural values and beliefs, 2) adapting to various situations, issues, and needs, 3) creating social and task cohesion, and 4) identifying specific and mutual long-term goals. When groups are able to incorporate these four general principles they are engaging in **third-culture building** where different cultural norms and rules are integrated into a group to create effective group communication. The benefits will bring a greater diversity of ideas, perspectives, and approaches.

This chapter has discussed the nature and role of group communication within a culturally diverse society. We have explained the different types of groups that individuals are commonly a part of along with discussing the characteristics of functional and dysfunctional group dynamics. Then, we concluded the chapter by illustrating how culture impacts group dynamics. In the next chapter, we focus more specifically on how groups engage in discussion and problem-solving.

VOCABULARY

Baggage — opinions, attitudes, beliefs, and values held by group members and "carried" into group settings or situations.

Co-culture — cultural values held by a group of individuals who exist within a larger dominant culture. A co-culture can be defined by one's nationality, ethnicity, or religion, such as Japanese culture, African American culture, or Jewish culture.

Cohesiveness — group unity and togetherness; a sense of "us-against-the-world" mentality experienced by groups.

Collectivism — cultural value that emphasizes the importance of the group instead of the individual (see Chapter 4).

Configural logic — based upon presenting information in a spiral or cyclical pattern where information jumps from idea to idea with content, evidence, and arguments used as needed (see Chapter 8).

Conflict — disagreement that may emerge in groups with people who hold diverse and contrary opinions, attitudes, beliefs, and values. Conflict may be either positive or negative.

Culture — the traditions, customs, beliefs, values, norms, and perspectives that are learned through shared behavioral patterns and cultural practices that are passed down from generation to generation (see Chapter 4).

Devil's advocate — discussing alternative ideas or opinions in a group in order to prevent groupthink.

Face — the public self-image that a person wants to present in a specific social context (see Chapter 4).

Family — a primary social group that lives together. Oftentimes, a family is linked through descent from a common ancestor, marriage, or adoption.

Focus group — brings together a group of people to listen to and respond to a particular topic in order for researchers to understand how a group of people think, respond, or perceive an issue or topic.

Group communication — three or more persons engaged in discussion or purposeful talk in an attempt to make decisions, solve problems, and recommend policy.

Group hate — a perception or tendency by people to avoid, be reluctant, or even despise working in groups.

Groupthink — the suppression of critical thought; going along with the rest of the members of the group even though you don't agree with them.

High-context culture — the meanings of a communication message are embedded in the situation, the relationship of the individuals, and the implicit norms, beliefs, and values of the culture (see Chapter 4).

Identification — is any attempt by the speaker (or group member) to establish some sort of common ground on an issue or problem (with other group members) (see Chapter 4).

Individual roles — specific behaviors that emphasize the individual instead of the group, which hinders the group from achieving its goal.

Individualism — cultural value that emphasizes the importance of the individual more than the group (see Chapter 4).

Low-context culture — the meanings of a communication message are directly communicated by individuals through the verbal expression of intentions, opinions, and thoughts (see Chapter 4).

Negative conflict — when people engage in name-calling, personality clashes, and ridicule.

Norms — the unwritten and unspoken rules that define acceptable behavior for group members.

Positive conflict — when people "agree to disagree" in a respectful way. Individuals might have a difference of opinion but their disagreement does not get personal.

Problem-solving group — a group that is formed to study a problem and to offer either recommendations or a solution to the problem.

Rhetorical sensitivity — mutual respect and collegiality between group members.

16

Role — a specific behavior of an individual that is consistently communicated to other group members.

Rules — laws, guidelines, and regulations that are written down in a handbook or manual which define group procedures and group conduct.

Social roles — specific behaviors that help the group maintain positive relationships.

Study group — a group of individuals who meet on a regular basis to learn new information.

Task roles — specific behaviors that help the group to accomplish its goal.

Therapy groups — a group of individuals who meet regularly to manage their problems.

Third-culture building — involves a speaker identifying common universal values that help the speaker and the multicultural audience (or an individual and group) create a new culture that draws from and extends the norms and values from the independent cultures.

REFERENCES

[1] Benne, Kenneth, & Sheats, Paul. "Functional roles of group members." *Journal of Social Issues 4* (1948): 41–49.

[2] Benne & Sheats, 41–49.

[3] Charles Bantz, "Cultural diversity and cross-cultural team research." *Journal of Applied Communication Research, 21.*1 (1993): 1–20.

[4] Ann Rosegrant Alvarez and Lila M. Cabbil. "The MELT program: promoting personal change and social justice through a year-long multicultural group experience." *Social Work with Groups 24.*1 (2001): 3–20. Katherine W. Phillips and Denise Lewin Loyd. "When surface and deep-level diversity collide: The effects on dissenting group members." *Organizational Behavior and Human Decision Processes 99.*2 (2006): 154–160.

[5] Guo-Ming Chen and William J. Starosta, *Foundations of Intercultural Communication* (Needham Heights, MA: Allyn and Bacon, 2001), 51.

[6] Chen and Starosta, 7.

[7] Thomas Kochman, "Black and White cultural styles in pluristic perspective," *Culture Communication and Conflict.* Ed. Gary R. Weaver. 2nd Ed. Needham Heights, MA: Simon & Schuster, 1998. 293–308.

[8] Bantz 14.

GROUP DISCUSSION AND PROBLEM-SOLVING 17

"A camel is a horse designed by a committee."
-Anonymous

"If Columbus had had an advisory committee he would probably still be at the dock."
-Justice Arthur Goldberg

"The ideal committee is one with me as chairman, and two other members in bed with the flu."
-Lord Milverton

"What is a committee? A group of the unwilling, picked from the unfit, to do the unnecessary."
-Richard Harkness

This Chapter Examines:

+ leadership in groups

+ the role of power in group communication

+ discussion as a group technique

+ types of group formats

+ group problem-solving techniques

After a series of meetings, the committee started deliberating as to what should be their plan of action. However, their discussion tended to get "sidetracked" and bogged down in unrelated issues or personal concerns. The chair of the committee did not seem interested in keeping the group on its task and it was unclear how the committee should make its decision. With the lack of leadership and an unclear problem-solving format, it seemed unlikely that the committee would develop an effective plan.

One of the challenges of working in groups is being able to have each group member committed to the group goal and working together in reaching it. When groups struggle as a cohesive unit, any attempt at making a decision, solving a problem, or offering a recommendation is difficult. Just putting a group together and having individuals perform specific behavioral roles is not enough to have an effective group. Successful groups need effective leadership, discussion, and a clear problem-solving format. We will expand upon each of these ideas in this chapter.

LEADERSHIP IN GROUPS

Leadership is perhaps the most essential element in group communication and discussion. Without solid leadership, groups would experience lack of organization and structure, as well as potential chaos and strife. The following types of leadership will provide a basic understanding and appreciation for the role of leadership in group contexts and situations.

Leadership Styles

Kurt Lewin is credited with what is commonly referred to as the "styles" approach to leadership. He believed that there are distinct types of styles of leadership exhibited in group settings or contexts. The situation or context, as well as the composition of the group, will determine which of the three types of leadership might be most effective. Democratic, autocratic, and laissez faire represent a diverse approach to leadership styles and characteristics, each having its strengths and limitations.

An ideal form of leadership, and one that all groups strive for, is **democratic leadership**; it is, by far, the most effective and equitable type of leadership style. This type of leadership is characterized by two-way communication between the group leader and the members constituting the group. A leader who demonstrates democratic leadership is open to feedback from the group members and is receptive to criticism and opposing points of view or contrary opinions. Each group member has a say in decision-making, problem-solving, and policy recommendation with this type of leadership. This will oftentimes result in a more open form of communication and will enhance the overall effectiveness or cohesiveness of a group.

Figure 17-1. Group Communication

Autocratic leadership (also called **authoritarian**) is the inverse of democratic leadership. The autocratic leader is not receptive or open to the opinions and ideas of others in the group. This leader is best personified by the popular expression, "it's my way or the highway" and engages in one-way communication only. This is not a very effective form of leadership because of the propensity to stifle feedback and interaction or discussion by the group members. Moreover, most individuals who participate in authoritarian groups become uninterested and show a lack of commitment or involvement with the group. Autocratic leadership when applied to forms of government is often classified as "dictatorships," "monarchies," and "oligarchies."

Laissez faire is a "hands-off" approach to leadership. In fact, it is often characterized by a lack of leadership in which the "leader" (boss, manager, supervisor, chair, president) demonstrates very little, if any, leadership initiative. It is then up to the group members to take leadership roles and make sure the group runs smoothly in meeting its goals. Usually this type of leadership is effective with highly motivated groups that have a long history together and do not need to be constantly "directed" by a leader. In these cases the leader can simply allow the group members to do their jobs.

17

Qualities of Leadership

Leadership in groups is a very complex and intricate phenomenon. There are several traits, qualities, and characteristics of leadership worthy of our consideration and discussion to provide us with a better understanding and appreciation for the complexities of effective leadership.

Task-oriented leadership is reflected in a regimented leader who is very concerned with structure, organization, and deadlines. This type of leader usually follows a strict agenda and will very seldom deviate from it, while also being very concerned with meeting deadlines and assigning specific tasks to the group members. The task-oriented leader is important in any group to see that progress is being made and that deadlines will be met.

Socio-emotional leadership addresses the social and psychological dimensions of group interaction. The socio-emotional leader is often described as "a people person" who is very interested in the psychological and emotional well-being of the group members. While it is possible for the same person in a group to demonstrate both task-oriented and socio-emotional leadership traits, it is usually two different people who represent these leadership styles because they are very different approaches to leadership and group interaction.

Single-leader leadership stresses the importance of a "single" leader managing a group, as opposed to "multiple" leaders, such as "co-chairs" on a committee or community task force. Your authors support the single-leader approach to leadership because it often prevents what we call "faction forming" in groups. If there is more than one leader in charge, there is too much potential for conflict and "power" struggles in groups with more than one dominant leader.

Theories of Leadership

Many scholars, sociologists, and researchers of group dynamics have written about the different "schools" or approaches to leadership inherent in group settings or contexts. These theoretical approaches to leadership effectiveness help provide us with a better perspective on what actually constitutes leadership and the pros and cons surrounding the different types of leadership we experience in groups.

Designated leadership is any leadership where the leader achieves the role of "leader" through rank, status, position, or title. The military is based on this type of leadership, where rank determines the status, power, and authority of a leader. In any courtroom, the judge becomes the designated leader who rules and presides over the court because of position, status, and role. Positions and titles such as "chair," "CEO," "boss," "president," "supervisor," "principal," and "captain" are all examples of designated or appointed leaders in society.

Emerging leadership is a very real and complicated phenomenon in group communication. In many instances, although a group has a designated or appointed leader, that person might begin to lose the respect of the group members. Also, it is not uncommon for other persons in a group to attempt to take control of the group. If this is successful, those persons become known as "emerging leaders" and they can actually become the "real" leader in the group, while the designated leader simply becomes a "figurehead" who is the leader by position, name, or status only. This can potentially lead to many problems in a group, especially if group members tend to split their loyalty and allegiance to two or more different "leaders" because factions may begin to form and split the group apart.

The **situational-contingency approach** to leadership says that for leaders to be truly effective they must incorporate different leadership styles to adapt to a particular situation or different group scenarios. Your authors believe that there are certain times when democratic leadership is called for, but autocratic, and even laissez faire leadership styles, are sometimes more appropriate or desired, depending on the group member and overall context of the group. Let's examine the typical college classroom as an example of how this leadership style might work.

If we assume that the professor is the "leader" in the group and the students are the group "members," the professor would probably be wise to incorporate all three styles throughout the semester. This would include being very receptive to feedback, student opinions, and allowing debate or discussion during class sessions (democratic leader). Similarly, the brilliant and kind professor might allow the students to select their own speech topics and choose their own groups for panel/group presentations (democratic leader). However, it would be unwise for the professor to allow the students to decide whether or not they should actually "do" the speeches or decide to abolish the course syllabus and substitute it for one they would devise. Therefore, the professor would need to become somewhat autocratic (authoritarian leader) in terms of leadership style. Finally, there are times when the professor may allow the students to work in class on their group presentations, or even leave to go to the library to conduct research (laissez faire leader).

The **life-cycle theory of leadership** is a contemporary approach to leadership based on two key variables: maturity and responsibility. The leader must determine the level of maturity or responsibility of the group members since this will determine which of four distinct leadership behaviors (telling, selling, participating, and delegating) will be most appropriate in managing a particular group.

For example, in a group that demonstrates both a low maturity level and a lack of responsibility, the group leader might need to engage in "telling" behavior. A little league coach or Boy Scout leader is often forced to tell the team or pack leaders what to do in order to reach goals and accomplish tasks. However, as the maturity and responsibility of the group members grows, the leader might be-ing using "selling" behavior (see, persuade, and convince), "participating" behavior (allow the group to take part in the decision-making), and "delegating behavior" (select group members to share in the group leadership). For example, the little league coach might appoint "team captains," and the Boy Scout leader might pick a "pack leader" from group members who demonstrate the highest levels of matu-rity and responsibility.

Empowerment has become a very popular idea in leadership and one of the most contemporary approaches utilized today. Empowerment is "transferred" leader-ship and is based more on a "transformational" approach than the traditional "transaction" approach to group interaction between the group leader and the group members. While the transaction approach entails a group member (em-ployee) performing a task or job for some reward (paycheck), this is very mechani-cal and often not very fulfilling for group members. On the other hand, the "trans-formation" approach of the empowerment style of leadership stresses that a leader can "empower" a group member through such factors as "intellectual stimulation" by providing knowledge or training to a group member.

Other ways to empower group members include "charisma," "inspiration," and "individual consideration." For example, a speech professor can "empower" stu-dents by teaching them public speaking skills, making students more effective communicators and more productive members of our democratic society. The little league coach who teaches the team such principles as "teamwork," "sports-manship," and "a strong work ethic" is hopefully "empowering" the little leaguers with these positive values. In turn, the little leaguers will become "transformed" from their experience.

THE ROLE OF POWER IN GROUP COMMUNICATION

It is impossible to discuss the role of leadership in group communication without considering the concept of **power**. Power in groups is achieved in a number of ways. The title, position, rank, or status held by the leader (usually a "designated" leader) is often inherent in the position itself. Power is a crucial element in group interaction because it establishes and controls relationships between the leader and group members. Moreover, it shapes the group interaction and communica-tion pattern within the group structure. The following types of power demon-strate the role that power plays in group interaction.

Reward Power

Reward power is the ability of a leader to provide monetary, status, and personal reward to group members. It recognizes the ability of those who possess power in groups and organizations to meet the needs of the group members, or control them, by providing rewards and benefits. Pay raises and promotions are two classic examples of reward power.

Coercive Power

Often the person possessing reward power also controls **coercive** or **punishment power**. Coercive power is when a leader intentionally inflicts "pain" or "punishment" on a group member in order to achieve a desirable behavioral response. Firing, ridiculing, and disciplining are the most common examples of coercive power. This type of power is often based on manipulation, which forces a group member to comply to the demand and wishes of the leader. A parent disciplining a child, or a football coach "benching" a star player because of poor grades, would be examples of coercive power.

Expert Power

Expert power is based on a person's expertise, specialization, or technical skill. While these people might not have rank, status, or position in a group, institution, or company, their particular skill or expertise makes them very valuable. In fact, expert power can directly or indirectly grant them leadership status. Knowledge of the Internet, computers, legal matters, and communication skills are all examples of expert power. Individuals who have expert power can gain high status in the group.

Referent Power

Referent power is very difficult to explain or conceptualize. It is a type of power people hold because of being liked or trusted. This type of leader is often said to have "charisma" and warrants respect from others in a group. Since this person has either expertise or "likeability," they often have the power to validate or endorse others. An example of this would be when a student asks a professor to write a letter of recommendation. This example illustrates how the student is relying on the professor's referent power to validate the student to a prospective employer.

17

In politics, President John F. Kennedy and his brother, Robert Kennedy, were said to possess referent power. Leaders with this sort of appeal are often approached by others in the group and confided in, a sure sign of respect and trust in any group situation. Interestingly, individuals holding referent power are often sought after in groups because many group members prefer not to go to a boss, manager, chair, or supervisor (designated leader); they feel safer seeking advice from those holding referent power.

Legitimate Power

Legitimate power is control or influence that is exerted by virtue of a person holding a particular position in a group. The power is inherent in the rights and responsibilities of the position, rank, or status. Legitimate power is held by a judge in a courtroom, a bishop in the Catholic church, the CEO of Microsoft, and the owner of the New York Yankees. This is often considered genuine or "real" power because people possessing legitimate power tend to control the interaction of the group and the organization.

Discretionary Power

Discretionary power is held by those who recognize the opportunity to become self-directed in the organization or group, as well as those who possess an awareness of their freedom to choose, the power to act, and the courage to make decisions. It also includes personal accountability and responsibility for one's own part in influencing the success of the group and the organizational process.

Information Power

Information power lies in a person's possession of data, knowledge, and information that allows others to make decisions, understand issues, and perform their jobs or duties. The prototype of information power, for example, would be a secretary or office clerk. Many times these individuals hold the "real" power in a group because they have an ability to locate materials and documents, simplify a complicated process by cutting through the "red tape," or by simply knowing "where the bodies are buried." Information power is essential to any successful group because the person holding information power often saves time, energy, and money for the group, company, or institution.

DISCUSSION AS A GROUP TECHNIQUE

Most effective groups have one characteristic in common: they are all able to engage in effective communication skills to make decisions, solve problems, and recommend policy—the three functions of groups. These functions are achieved through verbal communication, in general, and the technique of **discussion**, specifically. Group discussion is a necessary and viable technique that groups engage in to achieve their goal and objectives. However, discussion is much more than simple talk or idle conversation. For group discussion to be effective there are certain guidelines and characteristics group members must follow.[1]

Effective Discussion Is Goal Directed

When we say that effective discussion is goal directed, this means it must be purposeful and focused on the tasks and objectives confronting the group. Groups waste a great deal of time when they interact and this is usually caused by group members who are talking about personal matters or topics unrelated to the group's goals. It is imperative, therefore, to make sure that all discussion is focused and goal directed so that group participants will not "stray" from the topic. This might require the leader of the group to constantly monitor the flow and content of the discussion to make sure the discussion does not get "off-track."

Effective Discussion Is Regulated by a Public and Group Agenda

In order to maintain effective discussion, many groups incorporate a public/group agenda. This usually provides the necessary structure and organization in any meeting or group session to assure that all discussion will be directed and focused on the group's tasks and objectives. Group members must stay within the parameters of the agenda and not stray or get "side-tracked" during group deliberations. Once again, it is the responsibility of the group leader to make sure all group members are addressing the items on the group's agenda and maintaining a focused discussion.

17

Effective Discussion Requires that Every Member Is Responsible for the Group's Effectiveness and Succcess

For discussion to be successful, every group member must participate. Don't allow one or two group members to generate all of the ideas and do the majority of the talking in groups. What makes groups truly effective is when every member contributes to the overall discussion. Those individuals who say nothing during group interaction are cheating themselves and their groups. Also, those group members who are not allowed to participate in the discussion might feel so frustrated that they stop participating in the discussion. For any group to be successful, a contribution from every member is essential. The only way to achieve this success is through purposeful discussion.

Effective Discussion Presumes Cooperative Efforts and Attitudes

Effective discussion also requires cooperation between all members. It is important for all group members to strive for consensus and agreement, but this assumes a sense of cooperation by all members in the group toward achieving a common goal or solving a problem facing the group. All too often one or two group members attempt to "dominate" or control the discussion making other group members frustrated and angry. Moreover, discussion is the only tool group members have to resolve differences between each other and reach group consensus. It is also up to the leader to make sure that each group member has an opportunity to "speak up" and contribute to the group in an orderly manner.

Effective Discussion Requires Strong and Solid Leadership

Finally, the role of the leader in regulating and moderating group discussion is essential. The leader must make sure that every group member is getting "equal time" during panel interaction and that no members are dominating the conversation. As indicated earlier, the leader must also insist that the discussion be limited to the agenda items established for the group. It is no coincidence that those leaders, who lose control of the group discussion and interaction, often begin to lose their authority and the respect of group members.

Effective Discussion Leads to Either Decision-Making, Problem-Solving, or Policy Recommendation

When groups engage in discussion, their major purpose is to engage in one or more of three functions or objectives: decision-making, problem-solving, and policy recommendation. Groups use these three objectives in the attempt to reach consensus or agreement. **Decision-making** is when group members reach a decision. Some of the common ways a group can reach a decision are by consensus, compromise, majority vote, leader's discretion, or arbitration. For example, the duty of any jury in our legal system is to decide on the guilt or innocence of a defendant. In doing so, a number of decisions must be made about evidence and testimony. Furthermore, in most groups, decisions must be made about who will serve as the "leader" or moderator of a group, what roles or responsibilities will be assigned to each group member, or even something as simple as what topic or issue will be selected for a classroom panel presentation.

Problem-solving is the generation of solutions, ideas, and recommendations to solve a specific issue or problem. A jury will be asked to solve any problems that might arise if group members disagree on what topic should be selected, who should serve as group leader, or how to respond to group members who are not doing their fair share of the work. Meanwhile, **policy recommendation** is the generation of guidelines, rules, principles, or mandates by a group. The actual verdict of any jury serves as a recommendation to the court based on the law, while most groups set "policy" for their members to abide by.

TYPES OF GROUP FORMATS

Although the objective of effective group discussion is to make a decision, solve a problem, or offer a policy recommendation, there are different ways groups can be structured to reach one of these three objectives. The type of group formats we discuss in this chapter represent some of the most common group structures. Each format offers different characteristics and operate in various ways depending on the goal of the group. At the end of this chapter we provide a specific example of how a panel can be structured for group discussion (see Example 1).

Closed or Insular Group

No audience interaction or participation characterizes the **closed** or **insular group.** This type of group is comprised of the leader (moderator) and the group members engaged in a "round table" format. Examples of closed or insular groups would include a group of company executives, the CBS Board of Directors, a closed senate subcommittee, a college faculty meeting, the executive board of a local union, or a meeting of college administration. This format recognizes the need for confidentiality and also demonstrates the private nature of many group meetings. This is apparent by the absence of any "outside" audience.

Forum

The forum is a general format for public discussion and group interaction in which the full audience in attendance participates from the beginning of the presentation under the direction and guidance of a leader, moderator, or chair. There are normally no formal presentations from the panelists, but rather a format that includes a spontaneous interaction of comments and questions from an audience. The panel members then respond to the audience comments, often resulting in a spirited discussion or debate of some issue or problem. The overall purpose of the forum is to allow the audience to share information and engage in the discussion of an issue with a selected panel of experts or community leaders. A classic example of the forum today would be a "town hall" or public meeting to discuss local and community issues, as well as public hearings, community forums, and television talk shows such as *Nightline* and *Meet the Press*.

Panel

The **panel** is perhaps the most commonly used, and one of the more popular group formats, used in our society today. The panel format is characterized by interaction between the panelists, as well as audience participation. A leader-moderator, a selected number of panel members, and an audience characterize the panel structure. The leader-moderator is responsible for introducing the topic, issue, or problem. In addition, the primary function or role of the leader-moderator in the panel format is to control and regulate the group interaction. Several perspectives or viewpoints may be expressed by the panelists, including a "pro-con" format to stimulate debate and discussion of an issue or problem. The leader-moderator is also responsible for regulating audience feedback and participation because the audience is a central part of the panel format. Examples of the panel format would include scholarly/academic panels, a community or political task force, corporate presentations, and some press conferences. For a more detailed and thorough discussion of the panel format see Figure 17-3.

Colloquium

A **colloquium** is a form of group discussion in which a group of three to six panelists discuss a problem among themselves and with an audience under the leadership and direction of a moderator or chairperson. The colloquium or colloquy is often considered a "hybrid" of the panel and forum group formats. The panelists in the colloquium are usually "experts" on the topic under discussion, and their viewpoints are usually diverse and divergent. The purpose of the colloquium is to identify, develop, and attempt to generate solutions to a problem. The role of the audience in the colloquium is central since they participate in the discussion of the problem and the solutions that address the problem.

Symposium

The **symposium** is typically more detailed and structured than panel group formats. It consists of a leader (moderator), panel (group) members, and an audience. The symposium is a series of brief speeches on various aspects of a particular problem that is presented to an audience. The number of panelists in a symposium ranges from two to six persons, including a moderator or chairperson. The panelists (speakers) are generally expected to prepare their statements without being interrupted by the moderator or the audience. Therefore, the symposium usually lacks some of the spontaneity found in the panel discussion. The symposium, however, is somewhat more formal than a panel, the forum, or a colloquium. Although the primary purpose of the symposium is to present information to an audience, it often leads to a panel discussion or a combination of symposium and panel-forum discussion. A symposium may be applicable to scholarly or academic panels, a community or political task force, corporate presentations, and some press conferences.

17

Formal Investigative Group

The final type of group format is the formal investigative group. These groups are typically more structured and formal than panels, forums, and symposiums. These formal investigative groups participate in decision-making, problem-solving, and policy recommendation, while being characterized as research-oriented and less spontaneous than other types of group formats. In addition, these groups tend to be regulated by a strict agenda where group members work together to identify and research a problem, while generating possible solutions to alleviate the problem or address an issue.

Another significant difference with the formal investigative group is the role of discussion in creating solutions. Unlike panels, forums, and symposiums, the formal investigative group rarely engages in discussion or debate during the actual presentation of its findings. Instead, the majority of all group interaction, discussion, or debate takes place *before* the actual presentation. During the actual panel presentation, panelists simply review the recommendations or solutions that were agreed upon in advance of the presentation. Furthermore, the role of the audience and the level of audience participation, will vary in these more formal group presentations with some presentations allowing audience question and answer, while other presentations do not. Examples of groups incorporating the formal investigative format would include a community task force, problem-solving groups in college discussion classes, corporate policy recommendation groups, or senate subcommittees.

GROUP PROBLEM-SOLVING TECHNIQUES

Our explanation of the formal investigative group in the previous section moves us into an important function of groups—to solve problems. Frequently, the primary reason why groups are created is to address a problem and generate solutions or recommendations to alleviate the problem. These problem-solving groups (such as the formal investigative group) tend to incorporate a number of effective, time-tested techniques for solving problems and recommending policy. We will briefly discuss several techniques that are implemented by problem-solving groups.

The Standard Agenda

One of the most influential individuals in group problem-solving was John Dewey. In the early 1900s, Dewey wrote the book, *How We Think*, which explained a set of practical steps a rational person should follow in order to solve a problem. Over time, Dewey's ideas on "reflective thinking" were developed into a systematic approach for solving a problem, which is called the standard agenda. The standard agenda involves six steps, starting with understanding the charge (identifying the problem) and moving logically to generating possible solutions. We summarize these six steps in Figure 17-2.

THE STANDARD AGENGA

+ Step 1: Understanding the Charge

+ Step 2: Understanding and Phrasing the Question

+ Step 3: Fact-Finding (Evidence)

+ Step 4: Establishing Criteria and Limitations

+ Step 5: Generating Possible Solutions

+ Step 6: Preparing and Delivering the Final Report

Figure 17-2.

Brainstorming

Brainstorming is often used to generate ideas in panel discussions, and can be equally useful in generating solutions or recommendations to address a problem that needs to be resolved by a group. Brainstorming is a group technique normally employed when the group is facing a time constraint or is confronted with a rapidly approaching deadline. For the brainstorming technique to be effective, several "rules" must be observed. First, since the goal of brainstorming is to generate as many ideas (solutions) as possible in a short amount of time, "quantity" is more important than "quality." Brainstorming is an attempt to encourage an uninhibited flow of ideas by all group members. Second, all ideas, solutions, or recommendations are to be recorded since they will be discussed at the conclusion of the brainstorming session. Third, no criticism, feedback, evaluation, or judgment of ideas is permitted during the brainstorming process, no matter how bizarre or far-fetched the ideas or solutions might seem. Remember the goal is quantity, not quality, and time is of the essence. After the brainstorming session has ended, the group is free to analyze and evaluate the ideas, solutions, or proposals generated by accepting some and rejecting others.

Position Papers

Groups who are not facing any time constraints or approaching deadlines often use what are commonly referred to as **position papers**. Unlike brainstorming, position papers can be quite time consuming and involved. Phillips, Pedersen, and Wood state that, "One effective way of handling…solution-finding is to ask the group members to prepare *position papers* in which they evaluate each of the

17

possible solutions and make a case for the one they determine to be the best. Position papers permit individuals to devote themselves thoughtfully to matters that concern them, and not to deal with the details they would prefer to ignore."[2]

Position papers are often used to make sure that each solution, recommendation, or idea is carefully and thoroughly considered by the group. The process of implementing position papers works in the following manner. Let's suppose a group has generated three possible solutions or recommendations in addressing a problem. One group member would be responsible for writing a position paper for the "pro" side (in favor) of solution one. Another group member will take the "con" (against) perspective on the same solution. A third person will do the "pro" for solution two, while a fourth member will write a position paper for the "con" side of solution two. This will continue until the "pro" and "con" perspectives have been addressed for all of the proposed solutions or ideas. After the position papers have been written, they are distributed to the group members. At this point, the group will reconvene to discuss, argue, and debate the positions taken for each solution or idea. As you can see, this process takes a great deal of time and should be used when a group has ample time to devote to this complicated process.

Nominal Group Technique

Another popular technique used in problem-solving groups has been termed the **nominal group technique** and can be used in all phases of group discussion or problem solving.[3] This technique involves the generation of ideas by all group members and is used to identify problems, create solutions, and determine strategies for implementation. The nominal group technique involves four steps: *idea formation, idea documentation, idea ranking,* and *evaluation.* Idea formation is the generation of ideas and solutions by group members during a predetermined time period. These ideas are generated when each member writes down as many ideas or solutions as possible. The group members do this privately and silently with no interaction between the panelists. Idea documentation then results when the group leader asks for each group member to orally present one idea or solution. These are then written on a blackboard or flipchart for the entire group to see. The process continues until all ideas or solutions have been listed and clarified. Idea ranking is the next step as group members rank the ideas and solutions in order of preference and importance. The final step of idea discussion and evaluation allows the group members to rank-order each choice and discuss them more fully until a final ranking and order is determined. The nominal group technique is best suited for complex problems and groups with skilled and experienced leaders.[4]

EXAMPLE 1: STRUCTURING THE PANEL DISCUSSION (ISSUE SYMPOSIUM)

This format is excellent for presenting, discussing, and debating any topic, issue, or problem. Three group "format options" will also be provided to add to the flexibility and objectives of the group using the panel discussion/issue symposium.

PANEL DISCUSSION (ISSUE SYMPOSIUM) GROUP FORMAT

- Groups, teams, or panels must be selected according to a predetermined agreement or plan. These groups can be appointed, randomly selected, or completely voluntary. Groups ideally should contain between four and eight group members or panelists, including a leader-moderator.

- Each group is responsible for selecting, researching, and discussing/debating some topic, issue, or problem that is relevant to the audience or the group. In addition, the group must select an appropriate "format option" to be used ("pro-con," "individual topic area," or "role-playing/hypothetical").

- Each group must select a "leader-moderator" who will introduce the topic and its background/history, discuss the group's purpose and rationale, set the agenda and "cue" the audience, and introduce the panelists. This is accomplished with the "leader-moderator opening statement."

- Each group member (panelist) will then present a 1–2 minute prepared opening statement (panelist opening statements). The leader-moderator will then regulate and control the discussion between the panelists according to a pre-determined agenda agreed upon by the panel in advance.

- The leader-moderator is also responsible for regulating any comments or questions from the audience during the panel discussion; the leader-moderator must decide at what point the audience will be asked to join the discussion and participate.

- Both the leader-moderator and the panelists are required to support their statements and assertions with personal opinions and legitimate evidence (statistics, expert testimony, personal testimony, illustration/detailed example, and analogy).

- Each group presentation will have a time limit to be determined by all of the participants. The group should allow ample time for audience feedback and participation.

NOTE: Feel free to modify the guidelines above by adding or deleting items to suit your personal preferences. You might decide, for example, to make the group presentations less formal and more spontaneous or even adhere to another format and type of group discussion. Keep in mind that the goal of the group in this panel discussion (issue symposium) format is *not* to generate solutions or recommendations to a given problem or issue, but to explore the issues through discussion and debate. The panelists are not necessarily seeking a solution. For example, suppose a group decides to discuss the topic, "Mandatory Drug-Testing." The purpose of the panel discussion/issue symposium is to engage in a dialectical (verbal exchange of ideas during a local debate) discussion of your topic and an exchange of ideas or opinions. The panelists are under no obligation to generate any solutions or persuade the audience to accept a particular position on the issue.

Figure 17-3.

To achieve your goals during this panel discussion/issue symposium, each group should consider three possible "format options" available to them. The topic or issue chosen by the group will usually determine the format selected. Each group might select from either the pro-con, individual topic areas, or the role-playing/hypothetical format options.

Pro-Con Format

The **pro-con format** option allows for opposing viewpoints and perspectives to be aired and discussed. In a panel discussion on "legalizing marijuana," perhaps three panelists would be in favor of legalization (pro), while three would be opposed to such an idea (con). This format option usually encourages lively and spontaneous interaction between the panelists.

Individual Topic Area Format

The **individual topic area format** allows each panelist to present a different aspect of the issue or topic under consideration. For instance, in a panel presentation on the topic of "Mandatory Drug-Testing," one panel member might address the legal aspects, another the economic considerations, and yet another, the social and moral perspective. This format might not be as lively or spontaneous as the pro-con format, but panelists should still feel free to disagree with each and debate various aspects of the topic.

Role-Playing or Hypothetical Format

The third format option for the panel discussion/issue symposium is the **role-playing** or **hypothetical format**. One of your authors once watched a panel presentation on the topic of "Legalizing Sports Gambling." One panelist played the role of a "sports gambler," while other group members took the roles of a "social worker," "clergy member," and "law enforcement officer." Other examples using this format would be a hypothetical senate subcommittee on gambling and a congressional task force investigating sports gambling on the Internet. It should be noted, however, that even though these panels are "hypothetical" and role-playing is involved, the panelists must still incorporate legitimate evidence and support material throughout the presentation.

Finally, also consider that your panel can utilize more than one of these three format options during the same presentation under the panel discussion/issue symposium format. For example, it is possible to combine the **pro-con** option with **role-playing**, or the **individual topic area** option with the hypothetical,

role-playing format. The topic you select and the format option you choose are entirely up to you. In fact, it is possible to incorporate all three formats in some combination, depending on your topic and the approach your group takes in presenting the issue to an audience. What is essential in any group presentation is group discussion and cooperation, evidence, or support material, and a leader-moderator to control and regulate the panel interaction and audience feedback. We also strongly recommend that the leader-moderator remain "neutral" or objective during this type of panel format or group presentation in order to maintain balance and equality during the presentation.

The selection of groups can be achieved in several ways. Panelists might have the freedom and flexibility to select their own panels, while a more "democratic" approach might be a random selection by drawing names or different colored candy from a hat. Finally, the groups can be predetermined and assigned, which would be a more "autocratic" method of group selection. For the groups to work most effectively, we recommend between four and seven group members or panelists be selected per group, depending on the size of the class or "pool" of potential panelists.

Once the groups have been selected and formed, it is the responsibility of the leader-moderator and the panelists to conduct thorough research and gather evidence in the "fact-finding" phase of group preparation. Even though personal opinions and feelings are important, your audience will demand much more from you. Legitimate evidence in the form of statistical data, scientific findings, expert testimony, personal testimony, illustrative evidence, and comparison/analogy is expected. It is also imperative to cite your sources and document your evidence in the same way you would for an individual speech or presentation.

17

The groups might begin the presentation with a 2–3 minute **leader-moderator opening statement**, which should include a brief background or history of the issue being discussed. In addition, the leader-moderator should include a clear **purpose statement** to explain the goals and objectives of the panel, as well as an explicit **rationale**, in order to illustrate the importance and significance of the issue for the audience. Your audience is much more likely to be attentive and interested if you show them the significance of the issue and how it affects them directly. The leader-moderator should then *set the agenda and cue the audience* by explaining what the format will be for the presentation and when the audience will be invited to participate. This will greatly enhance the overall structure and organization of the presentation. Finally, the leader-moderator should conclude this opening statement by introducing each of the panelists by name and possibly the topic area they will be discussing. If the group is incorporating the "pro-con" format option, the panelists can be introduced according to which "side" of the issue they represent.

Each panelist will then have 1–2 minutes for a **panelist opening statement**. These statements should include a preview of the stance or perspective taken by the panel member on the issue. They should also combine personal opinion with research, evidence, and documentation to support the remarks and assertions made by each panelist. It is important that the panelists limit their statements to the time constraints established by the group.

Once the opening statements have been completed, the panel is free to open discussion between the panel members (panel interaction and debate). The leader-moderator might ask a series of specific questions to individual panelists or ask general questions which are to be addressed by the entire panel. Panelists should feel free to disagree with one another to provide alternative perspectives. The leader-moderator is responsible for regulating the interaction between the panelists, while making sure no single panel member "dominates" the discussion. In a "pro-con" presentation, the leader-moderator must reserve "equal time" for both sides and allot sufficient time for audience feedback and participation. In turn, the panelists should strive for spontaneous interaction with lively "give-and-take" on the issue. Both the leader-moderator and panelists are expected to engage in effective extemporaneous delivery, while avoiding "manuscript" (reading word-for-word) delivery and "staged" or "rehearsed" presentations. The same rules for effective delivery, discussed earlier in the chapters in public speaking, are applicable for any group presentation or panel discussion.

EXAMPLE 2: THE STANDARD AGENDA FOR GROUP PROBLEM-SOLVING

The **Standard Agenda** is a flexible and time-tested format for problem-solving and policy recommendation groups because it is appropriate for a variety of group contexts and situations.[5] The Standard Agenda is based on John Dewey's system of "reflective thinking." This is a process where people engage in a process of generating solutions to problems encountered in everyday life by experiencing a problem, exploring the causes of the problem, thinking about possible solutions to alleviate the problem, weighing the merits of the possible solutions, and selecting the most appropriate solutions to address the problem.[6]

The Standard Agenda consists of six steps that must be followed in order. Each step or "phase" of the Standard Agenda must be completed before the group is able to move on to the next phase. It is imperative that groups employing the Standard Agenda not succumb to the temptation of "jumping the gun" during the process of problem-solving and policy recommendation.

Step 1: Understanding the Charge

It is imperative that all group members **understand the charge** before any further discussion and interaction can take place. How often have we been in groups where somebody asks, "Does anybody understand what we're supposed to be doing?" Actually, that is an excellent question! The goal of this step or phase of the Standard Agenda is to fully understand the assignment, goals, and objectives for the group. If necessary, the group leader must serve as liaison between the group and the charging authority (boss, manager, supervisor, or chair) to clarify the assignment and the responsibilities of the group members. The group should not proceed to the next phase of the Standard Agenda until all group members know where they stand and exactly what their job is.

Step 2: Understanding and Phrasing the Question

Once the group has fully understood the assignment and group objectives, they must agree on exactly what the problem is and design a problem-statement (also called the phase two statement) reflecting the exact nature of the problem. This is called **understanding and phrasing the question**. The goal of this step in the Standard Agenda process is to generate a specifically worded statement in question form to guide the group through the problem-solving or policy recommendation process.

Here are a few hypothetical and real examples of phase two statements generated by our students over the past several years:

> *"What recommendations, if any, can we, a committee appointed by the Parent's Music Resource Center (PMRC), propose to that body, to generate a uniform code of ethics and standards that will be implemented by the Recording Industry Association of America (RIAA), and associated sales, marketing, and distribution companies?"*

> *"What recommendations, if any, can we, a task force consisting of concerned parents, generate for the purpose of evaluating and monitoring violence in the media, while investigating the effects of such violence on society, to be presented to our local elected official and media outlets in Western New York and Erie County?"*

> *"What recommendations, if any, can we, a task force appointed by the United States Surgeon General, generate and propose to the United States Congress, to combat the increasing number of new smokers in the United States today?"*

> *"What recommendations, if any, can we, a task force appointed by the governor, propose to the New York State Legislature, to alleviate the ever-growing problem of drunk driving in New York State?"*

17

"What solutions, if any, can we, a task force appointed by the Buffalo Common Council, propose to that body and the community in general, to generate better conditions in order to attract more business and people to the downtown Buffalo area?"

"What solutions, if any, can we, a group of concerned college students, generate to the college administration, to alleviate the increasing climate of racial tension on campus?"

"What solutions, if any, can we, a task force appointed by the Erie County Department of Health, generate and propose to various college and university health centers, to decrease the number of AIDS/HIV cases on campus, by increasing the college community's awareness of this disease?"

"What recommendations, if any, can we, a task force appointed by the Erie County Executive's Office, propose to that office, to improve the services and awareness provided by the various community and county agencies, to meet the growing needs of the 'sandwich generation'?"

While these phase two statements (problem statement) are primarily hypothetical, they reflect the need for a detailed question indicating exactly what the group's goals and objectives are. The statements explain who the group is, what specific problem will be addressed, and who will be receiving the final report or recommendations. More importantly, the more focused and specific the question is, the less research and fact-finding will be required. While these groups are primarily hypothetical in nature, the problem statement is an essential step in the Standard Agenda process.

Step 3: Fact-Finding (Evidence)

The next step of the Standard Agenda is **fact-finding** during which the group engages in research and gathering evidence to investigate the problem and guide possible solutions or recommendations. It is during this step that the group might decide to modify or revise the phase two statement by changing the question. This is the only opportunity available to revise or change the question. Often a group, while conducting the fact-finding phase of the Standard Agenda, will realize they have not addressed the real problem, or the problem is far more complex than originally anticipated. In some cases, the group might even discover that no problem exists at all!

Step 4: Establishing Criteria and Limitations

The fact-finding and evidence-gathering step allows the group to research the background of the topic and investigate what others previously addressing the problem have recommended. Once the evidence is gathered and the fact-finding process is completed, the group is ready to **establish criteria and limitations** to serve as guidelines for their solutions and recommendations. This is a vital step in the Standard Agenda process and one that many groups tend to "skip over" or omit. If this happens, the consequences may be disastrous. Without any criteria and limitations, any solution will be satisfactory or acceptable because there are no standards by which the group can judge or evaluate them.

Criteria are standards or yardsticks a group must use to evaluate possible solutions. They offer a critical measure to weigh the legitimacy and validity of those possible solutions generated by a group. Any solution generated by a group must meet all of the criteria before being accepted by the group. Let's look at a common example of how criteria work. If a company is hiring new employees, they must establish a list of criteria for possible job candidates to meet. These criteria might include three to four years of experience in the field, specific expertise, and an ability to operate a particular "software" program. Any job candidates not meeting *all* of these requirements (criteria) should be eliminated from the job search. Only those candidates meeting all of the criteria should be considered.

Limitations are constraints and obstacles the group must work with. They represent the realities of group work and problem-solving. Some of the more common limitations facing groups are time constraints, legal and ethical considerations, financial concerns, and jurisdictional limits. Any possible solutions must be met or achieve within the constraints of time, law, ethics, money, and group authority.

17

Step 5: Generating Possible (Alternative) Solutions and Juxtaposing Possible Solutions against the Criteria and Limitations

With the criteria and limitations in place, the group is now ready to **generate possible or alternative solutions**. The group might want to incorporate a brainstorming session to generate as many possible solutions or recommendations as possible. After all of the possible solutions have been generated, the group must now **juxtapose the possible solutions with the established criteria and limitations**. Any possible solutions not meeting all criteria, or violating any limitation, must be *rejected*. Those alternative (possible) solutions meeting all criteria and limitations are *accepted solutions* and should be presented to the charging authority.

Step 6: Preparing and Delivering the Final Report

All that remains after juxtaposing the criteria and limitations with all possible or alternative solutions is the delivery and presentation of the final report to the charging authority. It should be noted that most groups are not typically responsible for implementing the solutions or recommendations, only generating and presenting them. The presentation itself consists of the group members explaining the six steps of the Standard Agenda and how it was used to generate solutions in addressing the problem.

EXAMPLE 3: STANDARD AGENDA PRESENTATION: "THE SANDWICH GENERATION"

We conclude this chapter by providing the basic elements of a Standard Agenda presentation delivered by a group of our graduate students who are all associated with the social services profession. They examined a problem that is commonly recognized as the "sandwich generation," where parents must take care of their own children, as well as the needs of their elderly parents. They are literally being "sandwiched" between their children and their parents, a dilemma facing millions of "baby boomers" in our society today. The following is the group's phase two statement, their criteria and limitations, as well as their rejected and accepted solutions or recommendations.

Phase Two Statement

"What recommendations, if any, can we, a task force appointed by the Erie County Executive's Office, propose to that office, to improve the services and awareness provided by the various community and county agencies to meet the growing needs of the 'sandwich generation'?"

Criteria

1. Any solution (recommendation) must be legal and insure the constitutional rights of those involved.

2. Any solution must fall within the county's responsibility.

3. Any solution must be focused on the needs of the "sandwich generation."

4. Any solution must utilize resources available to Erie County.

Limitations

1. Any solution will be subject to the county's budget.

2. Any solution must be able to be implemented within five years.

3. Any solution must be limited to a recommendation and be "advisory" in nature and approved by the Erie County Legislature since we are only a task force and do not have the authority or jurisdiction to accept or implement the solutions.

Rejected Solutions (Recommendations)

1. Form a support group for members of the sandwich generation families outside of any government system.

2. Introduce legislation to guarantee that businesses receive incentives to support family care leave and keep existing support programs.

3. Form an independent agency to oversee and monitor the activities and services of the county.

4. Establish an emergency fund to ensure care-giving costs are not financially devastating to the affected families.

Accepted Solutions (Recommendations)

1. Investigate the possibility of the formation of a centralized information agency to assist the "sandwich generation" personally in the location of available services.

2. Enhance the awareness of area services through marketing and public relations campaigns.

3. Increase the awareness of health care proxies and "living wills."

4. Improve current transportation services and explore less costly alternative modes of transportation.

5. Ensure that all services are accessible in every community within the county.

6. Recommend that Erie County (government) attempt to work with the private sector to provide subsidized services.

7. Research the feasibility of a county-operated intermediate health-care facility for the elderly who require a minimal amount of care.

In discussing the solutions that were "rejected" by the group, it is important to indicate specifically which criteria and limitations were not met by each solution, thereby justifying their exclusion by the group.

17

VOCABULARY

Autocratic leadership — autocratic tendencies by a leader where communication is one-way only with little or no feedback from group members.

Brainstorming — group technique used to generate ideas normally employed when the group is facing a time constraint or a rapidly approaching deadline.

Coercive power — when a leader intentionally inflicts "pain" or "punishment" on a group member in order to achieve a desirable behavioral response. Firing, ridiculing, and disciplining are the most common examples of coercive power.

Colloquium — a form of group discussion in which a group of three to six panelists discuss a problem among themselves and with an audience under the leadership and direction of a moderator or chairperson.

Criteria — standards or "yardsticks" by which possible solutions may be judged.

Decision-making — when group members reach a decision. Some of the common ways a group can reach a decision is by consensus, compromise, majority vote, leader's discretion, or arbitration.

Democratic leadership — type of leadership that is characterized by two-way communication between the leader and the group members.

Designated leadership — a leader that has been officially appointed or elected where power is often due to position, rank, or status.

Discretionary power — held by those who recognize the opportunity to become self-directed and who possess an awareness of their freedom to choose, the power to act, and the courage to make decisions.

Discussion — purposive talk that is goal directed and regulated by a set agenda and requiring cooperative efforts and attitudes under solid leadership.

Emerging leadership — group members aspiring to control and possess power in a group who may attempt to wrestle control of the ground from the group's designated leader.

Empowerment — contemporary approach to leadership stressing the transformational aspects of leadership, rather than the transactional aspects.

Expert power — power based on a person's expertise, specialization, or technical skill.

Formal investigative group — more structured and formal than panels or forums for decision-making, problem-solving, and policy recommendation. These groups are research oriented and less spontaneous than other types of group formats.

Forum — a general format for public discussion and group interaction in which the full audience in attendance participates under the guidance of a leader-moderator.

Information power — lies in a person's possession of data, knowledge, and information that allows others to make decisions, understand issues, and perform their jobs and duties. The departmental secretary would be an example of this type of power.

Insular group (closed group) — type of group comprised of a leader and group members engaged in a "round table" format.

Laissez faire — a "hands-off" approach to leadership, often characterized by a lack of leadership or control by the group's designated leader.

Legitimate power — control or influence that is exerted by virtue of a person holding a particular position, rank, or status in the group.

Life-cycle theory of leadership — approach to leadership that stresses the role of the leader based on the maturity and responsibility of the group members.

Limitations — constraints or obstacles such as time, money, legal, jurisdictional, and ethical/moral facing groups engaged in decision-making, problem-solving, and policy recommendation.

Nominal group technique — group technique that involves the generation of ideas by all group members; used to identify problems, create solutions, and determine strategies for implementation.

Panel (issue symposium) — one of the most commonly used and popular group formats consisting of a leader-moderator, panel members, and a participating audience where several perspectives or viewpoints on an issue are discussed and debated.

Policy recommendation — the generation of guidelines, rules, principles, or mandates by a group.

Position papers — group technique for generating ideas and solutions that is far more time consuming than brainstorming; this technique requires the preparation, exchange, and evaluation of written "pros and cons" of different ideas and recommendation generated by group members.

Power — crucial variable in group communication and leadership that establishes and controls relationship between the leader and group members.

Problem-solving — the generation of solutions, ideas, and recommendations to solve a specific issue or problem.

Punishment power — see coercive power.

17

Referent power — a type of power people hold because of being respected, trusted, and liked by other group members. A person's charisma or persona adds to the appeal of those holding referent power.

Single-leader approach to leadership — stresses the importance of a "single" leader, versus multiple leaders or shared leadership.

Situational-contingency leadership — characterized by a leader able to adapt to a variety of group situations or contexts by exhibiting democratic, autocratic, and laissez faire leadership as the situation dictates.

Socio-emotional leadership — type of leader who addresses the social and psychological dimensions of group interaction and behavior.

Standard Agenda — problem-solving group technique based on Dewey's system of reflective thinking that involves the generation of criteria and limitations to judge or evaluate potential solutions.

Symposium — more detailed and structured than the panel format that includes a series of brief speeches on various aspects of a particular problem presented to an audience.

Task-oriented leadership — type of leader who is very regimented and concerned with structure, organization, and deadlines.

REFERENCES

[1] Gerald M. Phillips, Douglas J. Pedersen, and Julia T. Wood, *Group Discussion: A Practical Guide to Participation and Leadership* (Boston: Houghton Mifflin Company, 1979), 1–12.

[2] Phillips, Pedersen, and Wood, 212.

[3] A. L. Delbecq, A.H. Van de Ven, and D. H. Gustafson, *Group Techniques for Program Planning: A Guide to Nominal Groups and Delphi Processes* (Glenview, Ill.: Scott, Foresman, 1975).

[4] Larry L. Barker, Kathy J. Wahlers, and Kittie W. Watson, *Groups in Process: An Introduction to Small Group Communication*, 5th edition (Boston: Allyn and Bacon, 1995), 224–225.

[5] Phillips, Pedersen, and Wood, 122–241. Also see, J. Dan Rothwell, *In Mixed Company: Small Group Communication*, 2nd edition (New York: Holt, Rinehart and Winston, 1995), 194–198.

[6] John Dewey, *How We Think* (Boston, Heath, 1902).

INDEX

A